CAMBRIDGE STUDIE[S IN]
ANGLO-SAXON ENGLAND

9

THE OLD ENGLISH LIVES OF
ST MARGARET

CAMBRIDGE STUDIES IN
ANGLO-SAXON ENGLAND

GENERAL EDITORS

SIMON KEYNES

MICHAEL LAPIDGE

ASSISTANT EDITOR

ANDY ORCHARD

Editors' preface

Cambridge Studies in Anglo-Saxon England is a series of scholarly texts and monographs intended to advance our knowledge of all aspects of the field of Anglo-Saxon studies. The scope of the series, like that of *Anglo-Saxon England*, its periodical counterpart, embraces original scholarship in various disciplines: literary, historical, archaeological, philological, art historical, palaeographical, architectural, liturgical and numismatic. It is the intention of the editors to encourage the publication of original scholarship which advances our understanding of the field through interdisciplinary approaches.

Volumes published

THE OLD ENGLISH
LIVES OF
ST MARGARET

MARY CLAYTON
University College, Dublin

and

HUGH MAGENNIS
The Queen's University of Belfast

CAMBRIDGE
UNIVERSITY PRESS

CAMBRIDGE UNIVERSITY PRESS
Cambridge, New York, Melbourne, Madrid, Cape Town, Singapore, São Paulo

Cambridge University Press
The Edinburgh Building, Cambridge CB2 2RU, UK

Published in the United States of America by Cambridge University Press, New York

www.cambridge.org
Information on this title: www.cambridge.org/9780521433822

First published 1994
This digitally printed first paperback version 2006

A catalogue record for this publication is available from the British Library

Library of Congress Cataloguing in Publication data
The Old English lives of St. Margaret / edited by
Mary Clayton and Hugh Magennis.
p.   cm. (Cambridge Studies in Anglo-Saxon England: 9)
Includes bibliographical references (p.   ).
ISBN 0 521 43382 7 (hc)
1. Margaret of Antioch, Saints – Legends.
2. Christian women saints – Turkey – Antioch Legends.
3. Christian literature, English (Old)
I. Clayton, Mary.   II. Magennis, Hugh.
III. Title: Old English lives of Saint Margaret.   IV. Series.
PR1749.M28043   1994
270'.092–dc20   93–33754 CIP

ISBN-13 978-0-521-43382-2 hardback
ISBN-10 0-521-43382-7 hardback

ISBN-13 978-0-521-03267-4 paperback
ISBN-10 0-521-03267-9 paperback

For Éamonn Ó Carragáin and in memory of
John Braidwood, with gratitude

Contents

Plates

Acknowledgements

This book began when each of us wrote to Gordon Whatley, within the space of a month, enquiring whether he knew of anyone working on the Margaret texts. He proposed a joint edition, which has resulted in a very happy collaboration. Our thanks to him. University College, Dublin, Queen's University, Belfast, and Ken Churchill and the British Council provided funds for travel and microfilms, for which we are most grateful, and University College, Dublin also made a grant to aid the publication of this book. Jimmy Cross made unpublished material available to us, for which we thank him. We would also like to thank Maureen Alden, Mary Brennan, Yolande de Pontfarcy, Jodi-Anne George, Helmut Gneuss, Ivan Herbison, Peter Jackson, Robert Miller and Brian Scott for their help. Michael Lapidge's generosity with editorial comments and suggestions has been invaluable throughout.

Permission to reproduce photographs has been granted by the British Library and Corpus Christi College, Cambridge.

Abbreviations (including sigla used in referring to versions of the legend of St Margaret)

A	London, BL, Cotton Tiberius A. iii, 73v–77v: text as written by the original scribe
AB	*Analecta Bollandiana*
As	Assmann, ed., *Angelsächsische Homilien und Heiligenleben*, pp. 208–20
ASPR	The Anglo-Saxon Poetic Records, ed. G. P. Krapp and E. V. K. Dobbie, 6 vols. (New York, 1931–53) (All references to Old English poems are to this edition)
ASE	*Anglo-Saxon England*
ASS	*Acta Sanctorum*
Aug	Karlsruhe, Badische Landesbibliothek, Augiensis perg. 32, 55v–59v
B	London, BL, Cotton Tiberius A. iii, 73v–77v: scribal interventions of first reviser
BHG	*Bibliotheca Hagiographica Graeca*, ed. Halkin
BHL	*Bibliotheca Hagiographica Latina*, ed. Bollandists
Bibl. mun.	Bibliothèque municipale
BL	British Library
BN	Bibliothèque Nationale (Paris)
BT	Bosworth and Toller, *An Anglo-Saxon Dictionary*
C	London, BL, Cotton Tiberius A. iii, 73v–77v: scribal interventions of second reviser
Campbell	Campbell, *Old English Grammar*
Cas	Benedictines of Monte Cassino, ed., *Bibliotheca Casinensis* II, Florilegium, 3–7 (references to this are to the text printed below, Appendix 3, pp. 224–34)
CCCC	Cambridge, Corpus Christi College 303, pp. 99–107

CCCM   Corpus Christianorum, Continuatio Mediaevalis
Comp.   London, BL, Cotton Tiberius A. iii, 73v–77v: composite
         text
DOE   *The Dictionary of Old English*
EETS   Early English Text Society
  os   original series
  ss   supplementary series
H   Montpellier, Bibliothèque de l'Université (École de Méde-
         cine), H 55, 118r–122v
HBS   Henry Bradshaw Society Publications
lWS   late West Saxon
M   Mombritius, ed., *Sanctuarium* II, 190–6
ME   Middle English
MED   *Middle English Dictionary*
MGH   Monumenta Germaniae Historica
Mp   Montpellier, Bibliothèque de l'Université (École de Méde-
         cine), H 55, 222rv
N   Paris, BN, lat. 17002, 7r–11r
O   Saint-Omer, Bibl. mun., 202, 13r–20r
OE   Old English
OES   Mitchell, *Old English Syntax*
Os   Vienna, Österreichische Nationalbibliothek, 649, 228v–229r
P   Paris, BN, lat. 5574, 18r–32r
Pip   Piper, ed., *Nachträge zur älteren deutschen Litteratur*,
         pp. 334–46
PL   Patrologia Latina, ed. J. P. Migne, 221 vols. (Paris,
         1844–64)
PMLA   *Publications of the Modern Language Association of America*
RB   *Revue Bénédictine*
Rm   Reims, Bibl. mun., 1395 (K. 784), 79v–89r
T   Turin, Biblioteca Nazionale, D. V. 3, 220r–229r
Tib   London, BL, Cotton Tiberius A. iii, 73v–77v
Us   Usener, ed., 'Acta S. Marinae et S. Christophori', pp. 15–46
Vr   Verona, Biblioteca Capitolare, 95, 162v–173v
W   Vienna, Österreichische Nationalbibliothek, 377, 255r–260v
WS   West Saxon

Introduction

1

The legend of St Margaret of Antioch

Although Margaret of Antioch, virgin and martyr, came to be one of the most widely celebrated of saints in the medieval period, nothing certain is known about the origin and development of her legend.[1] In the eastern church the name of the saint appears not as Margaret but as Marina. Some early Latin accounts preserve the Greek name Marina, but from the ninth century onwards this was being systematically changed in the West to Margarita or Margareta. According to the legend itself, the martyrdom of Marina/Margaret took place at Antioch (in Pisidia), but there are no records of her in accounts of persecution at Antioch, nor is there evidence for an early cult. Her martyrdom is traditionally associated with the persecution under Diocletian and Maximian (AD 305–13), though the mainstream versions of the story show no interest in placing it in a specific historical context.[2] The lack of any evidence for early devotion to Marina/Margaret, or even for her existence, coupled with the sensationalism of aspects of the story itself, led eventually to the Vatican's suppression of the cult of St Margaret in 1969.

As shown below, literary evidence for the veneration of St Marina/Margaret dates from only the end of the eighth century and later. From this

---

[1] See *ASS*, Iul. V, 30E–31B; Tammi, *Due versioni*, pp. 9–20; Sauget, 'Marina (Margherita)', cols. 1150–2.

[2] The Rebdorf version, however, printed in *ASS*, begins, 'Annorum ab Incarnatione Domini salvatoris fere ducentorum nonaginta circulus volvebatur, quando Dioclitianus, Dalmatae scribae filius, dominatu crudelissimo Romani imperii retinebat habenas . . .' (*ASS*, Iul. V, 34D). Tammi notes the opinion of C. Baronius (*Martyrologium*, 4th ed. (Rome, 1630), p. 352), that the martyrdom should be associated with the persecution of Julian the Apostate (361–3), but Tammi himself, like most scholars, favours the earlier setting (*Due versioni*, pp. 16–17).

period on, however, the saint features increasingly in martyrologies and legendaries. Margaret becomes especially popular in the West from the twelfth century,[3] from which time she comes to be regarded as the patron saint of childbirth, a notion which, unsurprisingly, does not appear in our early medieval texts. Margaret's position in later medieval popular piety is indicated by her being included as one of the 'Fourteen Holy Helpers'. She is also one of the saints whose voices Joan of Arc is supposed to have heard. From the earliest period unease was felt about the more extravagant features of the legend,[4] but these, particularly the saint's struggle in her prison cell with a dragon-demon, also contributed to the popularity of the legend: the presence of the dragon-demon is a definitive feature of iconographic representations of St Margaret.[5]

The following is a brief outline of the legend of Marina/Margaret, as it appears in the earliest and most influential of the Greek and Latin versions. Marina/Margaret was the daughter of the chief pagan priest at Antioch, whose name was Aedesius (in the Greek tradition),[6] or Theodosius (in most Latin versions and their derivatives).[7] She was filled with the Holy Spirit from an early age and was brought up by a fostermother in a city fifteen stades from Antioch. After the death of her mother she was loved all the more by her fostermother, but she was hated by her pagan father. At the age of fifteen Marina/Margaret was looking after the sheep of her foster-mother one day when the prefect Olibrius rode by on his mission of persecuting Christians. He saw the girl and immediately desired her. He wished to have her as his wife if she were free-born or as his concubine if a

---

[3] See Mack, *Seinte Marherete*, pp. x–xii.

[4] The tenth-century Greek hagiographer Metaphrastes, as transmitted in the Renaissance Latin version of Surius, was highly sceptical of the sensational and supernatural details of the story, regarding them as malicious interpolations (Surius, *Vitae Sanctorum* III, 248). Among western writers, Jacobus a Voragine was notably scornful of the episode of Margaret being swallowed by a dragon: 'istud autem, quod dicitur de draconis devoratione et crepatione, apocryphum et frivolum reputatur' (*Legenda Aurea*, ed. Graesse, p. 402). As noted below (pp. 54–5), the *Old English Martyrology* version is among those which show reticence in its treatment of the legend, omitting all mention of the episode with the dragon. The Rebdorf writer 'has striven to correct' (*corrigere studui*) the passion of St Margaret (*ASS*, Iul. V, 34B) and presents a restrained account.

[5] See Celletti, 'Marina (Margherita): Iconografia'.

[6] Also in the Rebdorf version: see *ASS*, Iul. V, 34F.

[7] The Turin version, discussed below (pp. 9–13), has 'Themistius'.

slave. On discovering that she was a Christian, angrily he had her thrown into prison while he determined how to destroy her chastity.

The following day Marina/Margaret was put on trial before Olibrius. She refused to repudiate her faith and was scourged with canes. Her torture moved the bystanders to pity but she still refused to give in, fearlessly denouncing her persecutor. After further torture she remained as resolute as ever, and so was consigned to prison for a second night.

It was at this point that the saint had her celebrated struggles with demons. She prayed that she might see the enemy who contended against her. Immediately a demon appeared in the form of a terrifying dragon and swallowed her up. She made the sign of the cross, however, which caused the dragon to burst apart, allowing her to escape unharmed. Then she saw another demon, in the form of a black man. Unperturbed, and fortified by the miraculous appearance of the cross of Christ and of a heavenly dove, she engaged in a long interrogation of this demon, finally dismissing him into the earth.

The next day Marina/Margaret was again brought before Olibrius and again refused to give in to him. She was tortured with burning torches and by being bound and immersed in a large vessel of water. But as she prayed in this vessel an earthquake took place and a heavenly dove appeared, and the saint, her fetters loosed, emerged triumphantly from the water. A multitude of people was converted to Christianity through this miracle and they were martyred for their faith.

It was then time for the saint's own execution. Before her death her executioner (whose name is given as Malchus in a number of versions of the legend) allowed her time to pray. She prayed that those who venerate her memory in particular ways might be freed from their sins and that no physically impaired child be born in their house. Immediately after this prayer the heavenly dove again appeared and made a speech solemnly granting the saint's request.

After a final prayer Marina/Margaret was ready for her execution. At first the executioner refused to kill her but she insisted that he must, and she was beheaded. The executioner fell at her side. After the saint's death many ill and physically impaired people were healed by touching her body. Her head (or, in variant accounts, her body, or soul) was borne heavenwards by chanting angels, while devils were tormented by her glorification.

This narrative appears in the influential Greek *passio* designated by the

Bollandists *Passio a Theotimo*,[8] which purports to be the composition of an eyewitness to the saint's martyrdom, a Christian writer called Theotimus. The *Passio a Theotimo* is the oldest of the considerable number of extant Greek versions of the legend.[9] It exists in three distinct recensions,[10] the first of which, *BHG* no. 1165, is also of key significance to the study of western versions of the legend. Manuscript evidence for this Greek version is from the later ninth century and after. A text of *BHG* no. 1165 was printed by Hermann Usener in 1886 from a manuscript of the end of the ninth century.[11]

It has been suggested that *BHG* no. 1165 dates from the first half of the ninth century and this version has been associated particularly with the name of Methodius.[12] Even if this ascription is correct, it is clear that a highly developed older Greek tradition of the *Passio a Theotimo* lies behind the existing Greek texts and that the 'Methodius' version itself represents a subdivision of this tradition. It is from this older Greek tradition that the major Latin versions of the legend, discussed below, derive. Although the Greek text edited by Usener does not reflect exactly the direct source of any of the Latin versions (the earliest of which survives in a copy of the late eighth century), this text can be shown, by means of comparative study, to be similar to the older Greek tradition in many ways, and so it provides considerable assistance in tracing the literary development of the legend.

The date of the composition of the original *Passio a Theotimo* remains unknown. Whatever the specific origin of the legend, however, the story of St Margaret clearly follows the classic form of the passion of the virgin martyr. It is composed of familiar narrative elements, portraying threats to the saint's chastity, heroic defiance before a hostile judge and assured perseverance in the face of torture, and it ends, typically, with the saint's execution by a single clean sword-blow. In its interlude of verbal contest with demons the legend particularly resembles the passion of St Juliana.

---

[8] *BHG* II, 84–5.

[9] As well as the three recensions of the *Passio a Theotimo*, Tammi lists seven other Greek versions (*Due versioni*, pp. 31–44).

[10] *BHG* nos. 1165–7c.

[11] Paris, BN, gr. 1470; ed. Usener, 'Acta S. Marinae et S. Christophori', pp. 15–46. There is an Italian translation of Usener's text in Tammi, *Due versioni*, pp. 33–42.

[12] See Usener, 'Acta S. Marinae et S. Christophori', pp. 4–5; Tammi, *Due versioni*, p. 32.

2

The Latin versions of the legend

The transmission of the legend of St Margaret in the West can be traced back at least as far as the late eighth century, the date of the earliest extant Latin manuscript containing a version of her *passio*. Among the Latin versions there exist several which derive from the Greek *Passio a Theotimo* discussed in the previous chapter. The Latin versions deriving from this Greek source are classified in the *Bibliotheca Hagiographica Latina* as subdivisions of 'Version 1' of the *passio*.[1] The most widespread and influential member of this group is that listed as *BHL* no. 5303, 'Version 1 (a)'. As well as existing in a large number of manuscripts of widely differing date and provenance, *BHL* no. 5303 is also the source of a substantial number of vernacular adaptations and paraphrases, including at least one of those composed in Old English (the CCCC version). Variation between the texts identified as belonging to Version 1 is such as to suggest that *BHL* no. 5303 does not represent the original form of the translation from the Greek, but has been somewhat revised and adapted from an existing Latin version (evidence for this appears in other Latin texts and in vernacular derivatives); it also seems likely that not all variants classified under Version 1 go back to the same translation of the Greek.

BHL NO. 5303: THE MOMBRITIUS VERSION

The earliest known manuscripts of *BHL* no. 5303 date from the ninth century. They are Karlsruhe, Badische Landesbibliothek, Augiensis perg. 32 (Aug), which was written by the scribe Reginbert of Reichenau before

---

[1] *BHL* II, 787; Suppl., p. 210.

846;[2] Saint-Omer, Bibl. mun., 202 (O);[3] a second Saint-Omer manuscript, Bibl. mun., 257, a fragmentary copy, containing less than half of
the text;[4] Reims, Bibl. mun., 1395 (K. 784), a manuscript which also has
a copy of a different version of the legend under the name Marina;[5] and
Vienna, Österreichische Nationalbibliothek, 649, an incomplete text.[6]
Two tenth-century manuscripts are also of special note: Paris, BN, lat.
5574 (P), a manuscript of Anglo-Saxon origin;[7] and Paris, BN, lat. 17002
(N),[8] in which the closing part of the narrative is much abbreviated. There
is a copy of this *passio* in London, BL, Cotton Nero E. i, which has been
assumed to be from the eleventh century,[9] but the Margaret text in this
manuscript is a later addition.[10] There are printed editions of *BHL*
no. 5303 in Mombritius's *Sanctuarium* (M) and in the works of a number of
nineteenth- and twentieth-century scholars, Assmann (As), Piper (Pip),
Gerould, Francis and Mack.[11] Mack compares a number of later manu-

---

[2] 55v–59v. See Holder, *Die Reichenauer Handschriften*, I, 118 and 648–9.

[3] 13r–20r. The date and location are given by Cross, 'St Marina', based on discussion with
Bernhard Bischoff. See also Bollandists, 'Catalogus codicum hagiographicorum latinorum bibliothecae publicae Audomaropolitanae', p. 244. On this manuscript, which
contains some Old English words in eleventh-century hands, see below, p. 192.

[4] 12v–14v, 165r–166v. See Bollandists, 'Catalogus codicum hagiographicorum latinorum bibliothecae publicae Audomaropolitanae', p. 246. Cross, 'St Marina', speaks of a
different phraseology in this version, but the differences are no greater than between
other copies of *BHL* no. 5303.

[5] See Loriquet, *Catalogue Général* XXXIX.2, 541. The Margaret text is heavily abbreviated, especially in speeches. On the Marina version, see below, pp. 9–10, n. 17.

[6] 228v–229v. See Academia Caesarea Vindobonensis, *Tabulae codicum manu scriptorum* I,
112.

[7] 18r–32r. See Avril and Stirnemann, *Manuscrits enluminés*, p. 11; Bollandists, *Catalogus
codicum hagiographicorum latinorum* II, 482–3. On this manuscript, see below,
pp. 95–6 and 191–2.

[8] 7r–11r. See Bollandists, *Catalogus codicum hagiographicorum latinorum* III, 364–76. This
text is printed by Francis, in her edition *Wace: la vie de sainte Marguerite* (parallel with
French text).

[9] Mack, *Seinte Marherete*, p. xxv.

[10] On this manuscript, see P. H. Zettel, 'Ælfric's Hagiographic Sources and the Latin
Legendary Preserved in BL MS Cotton Nero E. i + CCCC MS 9 and Other Manuscripts'
(unpubl. DPhil dissertation, Oxford Univ., 1979) and 'Saints' Lives in Old English:
Latin Manuscripts and Vernacular Accounts: Ælfric', *Peritia* 1 (1982), 17–37.

[11] *Sanctuarium*, ed. Mombritius II, 190–6; *Angelsächsische Homilien und Heiligenleben*, ed.
Assmann, pp. 208–20 (an edition of the eleventh-century manuscript, London, BL,
Harley 5372, fols. 1–34); *Nachträge zur älteren deutschen Litteratur*, ed. Piper, pp. 334–46

scripts of *BHL* no. 5303, and other later manuscripts are listed by Joly.[12] Version 1 (a) is often referred to as the 'Mombritius version' and it will be convenient to use this title in the present study. This version is discussed further in ch. 3.

THE TURIN VERSION

Among manuscripts catalogued as containing copies of *BHL* no. 5303 is a number which in fact preserves texts of a different Latin version, as yet unedited. J. E. Cross[13] has demonstrated the separateness from the Mombritius version of the version found in the following manuscripts: Turin, Biblioteca Nazionale, D. V. 3, 'saec. VIII ex., written in north-east France, probably at Corbie or some neighbouring centre' (T);[14] Montpellier, Bibliothèque de l'Université (École de Médecine) H 55, 'saec. IX in., probably Metz' (this manuscript contains two witnesses, one (Mp) almost complete but deficient at the beginning, omitting some 200 words found in the other manuscripts listed here, the other (H) a fragment of only one leaf);[15] Verona, Biblioteca Capitolare, 95, 'in the school of Archdeacon Pacificus, died 844 A.D.' (Vr);[16] Reims, Bibl. mun., 1395 (K. 784), 'saec. IX med., Reims' (Rm);[17] Vienna, Österreichische Nationalbiblio-

---

(an edition of the fourteenth-century manuscript, Muri-Gries 4, 45v–77r); Gerould, 'A New Text of the *Passio S. Margaritae*', pp. 527–36 (an edition of a fourteenth-century manuscript in the possession of F. J. Mather); *Wace: la vie de sainte Marguerite*, ed. Francis (BN 17002: see above, n. 8); *Seinte Marherete*, ed. Mack, pp. 127–42 (an edition of BL, Harley 2801, 63r–65r, dated *c.* 1200).

[12] Joly, *La vie de sainte Marguerite*, p. 14, with quotations, pp. 131–41.

[13] Cross, 'St Marina'; on early Latin texts of the *passio*, see also Siegmund, *Die Überlieferung*, p. 240.

[14] 220r–229r. The dating and location are by Lowe, *Codices Latini Antiquiores* IV, no. 446.

[15] 118r–122v; 222rv. On this manuscript, see Moretus, 'Catalogus codicum hagiographicorum latinorum bibliothecae scholae medicinae in universitate Montepessulanensi', pp. 251–4. The date and location are given by Cross, 'St Marina', based on discussion with Bernhard Bischoff.

[16] 162v–173v. The ascription is by Cross, 'St Marina'. See also G. Turrini, *Indice dei codici Capitolari di Verona* (Verona, 1965), p. 18. The script is discussed by T. Venturini, *Ricerche paleografiche intorno all'arcidiacono Pacifico di Verona* (Verona, 1929), pp. 111–13.

[17] 79v–89r. See Loriquet, *Catalogue Général* XXXIX.2, 541. This manuscript was noted above as also containing a copy of *BHL* no. 5303 (see p. 8). The Marina text is distinguished by the presence of a major lacuna, omitting much of the speech of

thek, 377, 'saec. XI' (W).[18] Because of the place of preservation of its oldest manuscript this newly-identified version may be referred to as the 'Turin version'.

There is no evidence for knowledge of this Turin version in Anglo-Saxon England, but it is relevant to discuss it briefly in the context of the wider picture of the reception and transmission of Margaret material in the early medieval West. Cross plausibly suggests that this version represents an independent Latin translation of a Greek original similar to that lying behind the Mombritius version.[19] The similarity of the opening of the Turin version to that of *BHL* no. 5303 had deceived library cataloguers into assuming that they were dealing with a variant of the same text. The Turin version begins, 'Post resurrectionem inlustrem domini nostri Iesu Christi et saluatoris et gloriosam ascensionem eius in caelis ad patrem, postquam acceperunt beati apostoli singuli coronas suas et adsumpti sunt de hoc saeculo, et alia magna multitudo sanctorum certaret per uirtutem crucis et uincere malignum et coronari . . .'[20]

The Turin version, which preserves the Greek name Marina for the saint (though revisers have carefully corrected this to Margarita in Vr and Mp), closely follows the course of the narrative as reflected in the Mombritius version, and there is sometimes striking agreement even in the choice of

confession by the black demon (corresponding to *BHL* no. 5303, chs. 16–17). In the other copies of the Turin version, this speech is more expansive than in the Mombritius version.

[18] 255r–260v. See Academia Caesarea Vindobonensis, *Tabulae codicum manu scriptorum* I, 58; Levison, 'Conspectus codicum hagiographicorum', pp. 697–8.

[19] Cross, 'St Marina'.

[20] Vr, 162v: quotations from this version are here, as throughout (unless it is specified otherwise), taken from Vr. Vr is of a later date than T but presents a less corrupt text: 'After the illustrious Resurrection of Our Lord and Saviour Jesus Christ and his glorious Ascension to the Father in heaven, after the blessed apostles each received their crowns and were taken up out of this world, and many another great multitude of saints battled through the power of the cross both to defeat the wicked one and to be crowned. . . .'

Cf. *BHL* no. 5303, as printed by Mombritius (with omissions supplied here from As): 'Post resurrectionem Domini nostri Iesu Christi et gloriosae tempus ascensionis eius in caelum ad Patrem omnipotentem, in illius nomine multi martyres passi sunt, et apostoli coronati sunt, et innumerabiles sancti facti sunt in nomine Domini nostri Iesu Christi, et [uicerunt] hunc mundum [et] tyrannos et carnifices superauerunt' (M, p. 190, lines 16–19). On the beginning of P, see below, p. 220, nn. 1–3.

words.[21] Such close verbal correspondence is unusual, however, and even when the content of the two versions is very similar, as in the opening lines, quoted above, the Turin version for the most part maintains a distinctive phraseology.

The course of the narrative in the Turin version indeed might be described as running parallel to, rather than exactly coinciding with, that of the Mombritius version. Speeches and prayers show considerable differences in content and internal organization, and there are some speeches and prayers in the Turin version which do not appear in the Mombritius version at all: the exchange between the saint and the heavenly dove, for example, prior to her inquisition of the black demon in the prison cell, is rhapsodically developed at greater length in the Turin version.[22] Generally, the Turin version cultivates an ecstatic and heightened tone, particularly in the prayers of St Marina and in the heavenly responses to these prayers: in one speech, the details of which are not reflected in the Mombritius version, the dove exclaims, 'Haue Margarita quae draconem adlisisti. Haue Margarita quae molas eius contriuisti. Haue Margarita unguenta suauitatis per orationes referens. Parata est tibi corona gloriae; apertus est tibi paradysus. Tu eris cum patribus requiescens; tu quem occidisti per fidem adligabis usque in finem.'[23]

There are many local details in the Turin version unparalleled in Mombritius.[24] Among the parts of the Turin version which show the most

---

[21] For example, after the opening, just quoted, Vr continues, 'adhuc enim obtinebat insania hominum' (162v), closely paralleling M, 'Adhuc tamen obtinebat insaniam hominum' (p. 190, lines 19–20), but immediately thereafter the two versions begin to diverge greatly.

[22] Vr. 169r.

[23] Vr, 169r: 'Hail, Margaret, who have smashed the dragon. Hail, Margaret, who have ground him down. Hail, Margaret, restoring through prayers the ointments of sweetness. A crown of glory is prepared for you; paradise is open for you. You will be in repose with the patriarchs; you will bind for ever him whom you have killed through your faith.'

[24] An interesting example of this is the comparison, in the Turin version, of Marina to the Old Testament figure Rachel, as she tends her fostermother's sheep: 'Et ipsa cum pascentibus puellis inmitabatur nouam Rachel antequam matrem Ioseph' (Vr, 163v). This reflects the Greek, ἐξωμοιοῦτο τῇ μητρὶ τοῦ μακαρίου Ἰωσήφ (Us, 133r, line 9). The comparison is found in the Latin 'Paris' and 'Rebdorf' versions discussed below (for 'Paris', see Orywall, *Die alt- und mittelfranzösischen Prosafassungen der Margaretenlegende*, p. 182,

notable differences from Mombritius is the interview between Marina and the black demon. The course and content of the demon's speeches demonstrate independence from all Latin analogues. This version carries the interest in demonology even further than Mombritius, providing information not paralleled in the latter. It relates that Satan took the first-born daughter of Jupiter and then became most fully the devil, living at the bottom of the abyss, producing eggs and bringing forth devils: 'Accepit autem diabolus filiam Iovis primogenitam et factus est plenissime diabolus; hic habitat in radicibus abyssi et ova paret et generat daemones.'[25] It also reports that, according to the book of Dionisus and Jamnes and Mambres, demons arose from Egypt and Ethiopia: 'quia de Aegypto et de Aethiopia [Vr *dethiopia*] orti sumus, sicut Dionisi [T *demonis*; Mp has *Dionisius*, with different grammatical structure] liber interpretat et Iamnen et Mambrae.'[26] All of this demonological information has been inherited from the Greek and is reflected in Usener's text.[27]

The most striking feature of the treatment of narrative in the Turin version, however, comes in the closing part of the legend, where Marina's last words are given, her execution is reported and the *passio* is concluded. This passage corresponds to *BHL* no. 5303, chs. 19–24.[28] In *BHL* no. 5303 it amounts to some 844 words, bringing the account of the saint to a triumphant conclusion. The equivalent part of the Turin version comes to only about 280 words. The latter version omits entirely the saint's final prayer of intercession on behalf of those who venerate her and treats the execution itself very cursorily. The debate between Marina and the executioner does not appear and there is no mention of post-mortem miracles. Overall, the Turin version consists of some 3500 words, whereas Mombritius has just over 4000. Had the closing stages of the Turin version been treated with a discursiveness comparable to what we find in Mombritius, both texts would have been roughly the same length. This kind of radically abbreviated treatment of the end of the *passio* occurs also in the 'Rebdorf' version of the legend (as mentioned below) and in at least one variant of the *BHL* no. 5303 tradition, Paris, BN, lat. 17002 (both of

lines 8–9; for 'Rebdorf' see *ASS*, Iul. V, 34F–35A), but does not appear in the Mombritius or in the closely related Casinensis version.

[25] Vr, 170v. [26] Vr, 170v–171r. [27] Us, 138r, lines 1–15.

[28] The *BHL* no. 5303 chapter-divisions are those of As, subsequently adopted by Gerould.

these latter with entirely different texts from that of the Turin version). As in these, the ending in the Turin version is remarkably abrupt and factual after the triumphal assertiveness of the narrative itself.[29]

BHL NO. 5304: THE *CASINENSIS* VERSION

A separate strand of Version 1, classified by the Bollandists as 'Version 1 (b)', *BHL* no. 5304, is represented by the *Passio Beate Marine* printed in *Bibliotheca Casinensis* from an eleventh-century Monte Cassino manuscript.[30] The 'Casinensis version' has not been thought of as belonging to the main stream of the transmission of the Margaret legend in the early Middle Ages, existing as it does in only one copy. However, this version provides essential evidence about the development of Version 1, since it and the Mombritius version are so close in phraseology that it is apparent that they go back to a common Latin original. This Latin original would have been somewhat longer than its extant derivatives: Mombritius excludes material which Casinensis has inherited from the Greek, and vice versa. It will be convenient to refer to this common original, which is also of key importance to the study of Anglo-Saxon versions of the legend, as the 'pre-Mombritius Version'.

Departures from *BHL* no. 5303 readings in the Casinensis version consist largely of omissions, some of them quite substantial: most notably, Casinensis has nothing corresponding to chs. 14 and 15 of *BHL* no. 5303 (material which must have been in the original Latin translation): there is no triumphant appearance of the heavenly dove after Marina's victory over

---

[29] Vr ends as follows: 'Et postquam orauit, amputatum est caput eius, et ecce angeli, omnibus uidentibus, tulerunt animam [on the reading *animam* see below, n. 32] eius in caelo. Ego uero inutilis seruus Christi Theotimus collegi corpus eius et deposui in optimo et oportuno loco. Ego enim eram qui et ministrabam ei in carcere. Ego considerabam per fenestram et excipiebam omne [MS omnem] certamen quod [MS qui] habuit cum daemonibus et omnes orationes eius. Ideo et cum multa astutia scripsi et transmisi omnibus ubicumque qui [om. MS] Christiani sunt omnia in ueritate. Certauit beata Margarita .xiii. die Iulii. Celebrantes ergo eius commemorationem, et pro me peccatore orate ad Dominum Iesum Christum. Ipsi enim decet gloria et potestas nunc et semper et in saecula saeculorum. Amen' (173r–v).

[30] Ed. Benedictines of Monte Cassino, *Bibliotheca Casinensis* II ('Florilegium Casinense'), 3–7. The manuscript, Monte Cassino 52, is described in *Bibliotheca Casinensis* II, 57–75. The text of this version is printed below, pp. 224–34 (Appendix 3).

the dragon which appears to her in her prison cell, and the first part of the black demon's confession to her is omitted. Similarly, there is nothing corresponding to ch. 20, which in *BHL* no. 5303 includes a further appearance of the heavenly dove and contains the divine promise granting the saint's final prayer. There are also many minor omissions in the Casinensis version. The 'editor' of this version seems deliberately to have toned down some of the more extravagant features of the *passio*.

What makes Casinensis of particular interest with regard to the study of the transmission of the Margaret legend in the early Middle Ages is not, however, the absence in it of material which appears in the Mombritius version but rather the appearance in it of material which has no equivalent in Mombritius. There are instances of such material throughout the text but they tend to occur particularly towards the end. Some of this material may be the result of independent additions made by the Casinensis compiler but some of it can be shown to go back to our 'pre-Mombritius version', the original on which both the Casinensis and Mombritius versions are based. The view that distinctive features of Casinensis are inherited from an earlier version is borne out by the fact that a number of significant readings corresponding to those in Casinensis, which are absent in Mombritius, are found in the Greek version of the legend edited by Usener, and some are also reflected in the Latin Turin version.

Casinensis is among the versions of the legend which speak of angels carrying Marina's head to heaven after her death: 'Et uenerunt angeli et tulerunt capud martyris beate Marine.'[31] Most texts of *BHL* no. 5303 speak of the saint's *soul* or *body*[32] being taken to heaven but the Casinensis reading agrees with that of Usener: κατῆλθον δώδεκα ἄγγελοι ἐπὶ τὸ λείψανον καὶ λαβόντες τὴν κεφαλὴν τῆς μάρτυρος ἀπήγαγον πρὸς τὸν κύριον.[33] The number of angels is not specified in the Latin (interestingly, it is

---

[31] Cas, p. 233: 'And angels came and bore the head of the blessed martyr Marina.'

[32] Our edited text of *BHL* no. 5303, given in Appendix 2, is taken from O at this point, P being deficient: 'Tunc descendentes angeli cum uirtutibus tollentes corpus beatae Margaritae in gremio suo ascenderunt super nubem' (ch. 23; M, p. 195, lines 46–7, has *animam*).

The Turin version has *caput* at the corresponding point, though Vr (as quoted above in n. 29) is aberrant in having *animam*.

[33] Us, 140v, lines 38–141r, line 2: 'Twelve angels came down to the remains, and taking the head of the martyr they bore it off to the Lord.'

14

specified in the Old English Cotton Tiberius version),[34] but apart from this the Casinensis account is close to that of the Greek.

One other part of the narrative, showing significant agreements between Casinensis and Usener, might also be mentioned. In the scene of Marina's torture with burning torches there is a longer passage of prayer by Marina in Casinensis than in *BHL* no. 5303.[35] During this sequence Marina exclaims, 'Probasti, Domine, cor meum et uisitasti nocte, et non est inuenta in me iniquitas. Transeo per ignem et aquam, et deducis me in refrigerium.'[36] The corresponding passage in *BHL* no. 5303 has a supplication rather than a statement in the beginning of this – 'Vre renes meos, Domine, et cor meum, ut in me non sit iniquitas'[37] – and the remainder is missing altogether. Usener, however, is closely similar to Casinensis: περὶ σοῦ γὰρ ἤτασάω με, καὶ οὐχ εὑρέθη ἐν ἐμοὶ ἀνομία . . . καὶ νῦν, κύριε, διῆλθον διὰ πυρὸς καὶ ὕδατος, καὶ ἐξήωεγκάς με εἰς τὴν ἀνάπαυσίν σου.[38] The Turin reading at this point is also closely similar to that of Casinensis.[39]

In this same part of the narrative the exchange between Marina and the persecutor Olibrius is not quite as brief in Casinensis as in Mombritius. Among the extra material in this sequence in Casinensis is the sentence which is added to Olibrius's short speech 'Consente michi et sacrifica diis.'[40] After this imperative, Casinensis continues, in a detail unparalleled in *BHL* no. 5303, 'Non enim potest uincere precepta imperatorum et conuentum omnium deorum.'[41] Once again Usener provides a direct equivalent to the Casinensis reading: οὐ δύνασαι κόρη ὑπάρχουσα ἀφανίσαι τὸν θεσμὸν τῶν

---

[34] Beginning of ch. 23.   [35] Cas, p. 231; cf. P, ch. 17.

[36] Cas, p. 231: 'You have proved my heart, Lord, and visited it by night, and iniquity has not been found in me [Ps. XVI. 3]. I pass through fire and water and you bring me out into a refreshment [Ps. LXV. 12].'

[37] P, ch. 17: 'Burn up my loins, Lord, and my heart, so that there may not be wickedness in me.'

[38] Us, 138v, lines 24–7: 'For you they examined me, and no transgression was found in me . . . And now, Lord, I went through fire and water and you bore me out to your repose.' Us lacks the quotation of Ps. XVI. 3 (as identified above, n. 36), but has that of Ps. LXV. 12.

[39] 'Vristi renes meos, Domine, et non est inuenta in me iniquitas [Ps. XVI. 3]. Transeo per ignem et aquam, eo quod deduces me in refrigerium [Ps. LXV. 12]' (Vr, 171v).

[40] P, ch. 17; Cas, p. 231: 'Give in to me and sacrifice to the gods.'

[41] Cas, p. 231: 'It is not possible to defeat the precepts of the emperors and the assembly of all the gods.'

βασιλέων καὶ τὰς τῶν θεῶν ἡμῶν συναγωγάς.[42] And again the Greek reading is reflected in the Turin version.[43]

Such correspondences between Casinensis and Usener show that the former cannot simply be a variant deriving from *BHL* no. 5303. Casinensis preserves readings from the Greek otherwise rarely found in the Latin tradition and completely lacking in *BHL* no. 5303.

BHL NO. 5305: THE PARIS VERSION

Different again from the Mombritius version of the legend of St Margaret is *BHL* no. 5305, 'Version 1 (c)', according to the classification of the Bollandists. Substantial extracts from the tenth-century copy of this in Paris, BN, lat. 17005, are printed by Ingelore Orywall in her edition of medieval French prose versions.[44] Although this version follows in the main the storyline of *BHL* no. 5303, it is entirely different in its phraseology and is written in a florid style unlike that of other members of Version 1. Elizabeth Francis points out that the demon and dragon episodes are treated in the manner of 'Version 4' (the 'Rebdorf' version discussed below) and in the manner of the Greek version attributed by Surius to Metaphrastes. She notes that 'certain passages indicate clearly affiliation to some other version which must have been used by Vincent de Beauvais (*Speculum historiale*) and by Jacobus a Voragine (*Legenda aurea*), since the same passages reappear in those two versions.'[45] A notable agreement with Vincent and Jacobus concerns Olibrius's response to Margaret's threefold statement about herself when she is first questioned by

---

[42] Us, 138v, lines 29–30: 'You cannot, as a maiden, lead astray the law of the emperors and the assemblies of our gods.'

[43] 'Consente mihi, et sacrifica. Non enim potest muliercula uincere praecepta imperatorum et conuentum omnium deorum' (Vr, 171v).

[44] *Die alt- und mittelfranzösischen Prosafassungen der Margaretenlegende*, ed. Orywall, pp. 182–7.

[45] Francis, 'A Hitherto Unprinted Version of the *Passio Sanctae Margaritae*', p. 88. The standard edition of the *Legenda aurea* of Jacobus a Voragine is by Graesse. This version is particularly discussed by Orywall, *Die alt- und mittelfranzösischen Prosafassungen der Margaretenlegende*, pp. 80–9. Orywall usefully gives Jacobus's Margaret text (pp. 178–81). For Vincent of Beauvais, see *Speculi Maiores*, ed. Benedictines of Douai, IV, Book XII, chs. 27–8 (pp. 514–15). This version is also printed and discussed by Orywall (pp. 66–8 and 176–7).

him: he approves of two of her answers but not the third (that she is a Christian). In this version also, unlike the Mombritius and Casinensis versions, the devil appears to Margaret in her prison cell without the prompting of a prayer from the saint that she might see her enemy (in this Vincent agrees, but not Jacobus); and the dragon does not swallow the saint (again Vincent agrees, but not Jacobus). Orywall takes *BHL* no. 5305 as 'very probably' having served as a source for these Latin epitomes.[46]

There are copies of this version in Paris, BN, lat. 11758, 16734 and 17005, but no copies in English libraries are known. This Paris version clearly does not have the close similarity to the Mombritius version that Casinensis has. It stands somewhat apart from these other two, de-emphasizing, as Orywall points out,[47] the popular elements in the legend and developing the philosophical aspect of the confrontation between Margaret and Olibrius.

VERNACULAR DERIVATIVES AND THEIR SOURCES

The two extant late Old English versions of the legend edited here have been generally agreed to follow Latin texts of the Mombritius type, but the existence of features in both of these vernacular versions unparalleled in any of the above variants indicates further layers of complication in the Latin textual tradition.[48] Indeed in the case of the Old English version in Cotton Tiberius A. iii, it will be shown below that the hitherto accepted identification of the source as a copy of *BHL* no. 5303 is unsatisfactory.

---

[46] Orywall, *Die alt- und mittelfranzösischen Prosafassungen der Margaretenlegende*, p. 35.

[47] *Ibid.*, pp. 34–5.

[48] The surviving *incipit* and *explicit* of the OE Cotton Otho B. x version, as transcribed by Wanley, provide tantalizing but inconclusive evidence of this version's relationship to the Latin tradition. There is no parallel to the *explicit*, which may therefore be the original composition of the OE writer. The *incipit* begins by quoting the Latin opening, 'Post Christi passionem et resurrectionem et ascensionem . . .', but curiously the OE leaves out the reference to the Passion, 'Æfter æriste ures drihtenes hælendes cristes and his wuldorfæstan upastigenesse on heofonas . . .' The OE writer appears to translate a version different from that which is quoted, omitting *passionem et* and translating *gloriosam*, even though the latter adjective is lacking in the Latin quotation. The OE text closely reflects Cas and As, but this is not so of the Latin quotation. On the Cotton Otho version, see below, pp. 94–5.

The epitome of the Margaret legend in the *Old English Martyrology*[49] (where the saint is called Marina) is also in the 'Version 1' tradition, but again its source could not have been identical to any of the known variants of the Latin. J. E. Cross has pointed to some significant particular agreements between the account of the saint in the *Martyrology* and that in the Cotton Tiberius version.[50]

Other vernacular versions of the legend are later than the Old English texts, but these too can furnish evidence concerning the transmission of Version 1, and particularly of *BHL* no. 5303, the Mombritius version: it was variants of *BHL* no. 5303 which in the main provided the sources used by later vernacular writers. As well as the version in verse by Wace,[51] there are two prose versions in Old French based on texts of *BHL* no. 5303.[52] The Middle English versions, *Seinte Marherete*,[53] *Meidan Maregrete*[54] and *Seinte Margarete þat Holi Maide*[55] are also relevant to discussion of the transmission of the Mombritius version. Medieval vernacular versions of the legend of St Margaret are also found in Provençal, Italian, Spanish and German.[56]

BHL NO. 5306: THE CALIGULA VERSION

Having described the main Latin texts and vernacular derivatives associated with the Bollandists' Version 1, we may now go on to mention briefly the two other major Latin versions of the legend of St Margaret which are known. The first of these is the version *BHL* no. 5306, 'Version 2', edited by Francis from the twelfth-century manuscript London, BL, Cotton Caligula A. viii.[57] Francis collates a number of other manuscripts of this 'Caligula version',[58] of which the earliest, Paris, BN, lat. 5565, dates from

---

[49] Ed. Kotzor, *Das altenglische Martyrologium* II, 141–4. See below, pp. 51–6.

[50] Cross, 'St Marina'.

[51] Ed. Francis, *Wace: la vie de sainte Marguerite*; also ed. Joly, *La vie de sainte Marguerite*.

[52] Ed. Orywall, *Die alt- und mittelfranzösischen Prosafassungen der Margaretenlegende*.

[53] Ed. Mack, *Seinte Marherete þe Meiden ant Martyr*.

[54] Ed. Horstmann, *Altenglische Legenden. Neue Folge*, pp. 489–98; also ed. Cockayne, *Seinte Marherete þe Meiden ant Martyr*, pp. 34–43.

[55] Ed. Cockayne, *Seinte Marherete þe Meiden ant Martyr*, pp. 24–33.

[56] On these vernacular versions, see Tammi, *Due versioni*, pp. 20–8.

[57] Francis, 'A Hitherto Unprinted Version of the *Passio Sanctae Margaritae*', pp. 97–104.

[58] Listed by Francis, *ibid.*, p. 88.

the eleventh century. She does not mention the copy of this version in Hereford, Cathedral Library, P. 2. V (a twelfth-century manuscript). Francis notes that this version is closely related to the Mombritius version but insists that it is nevertheless quite independent: 'The points of similarity between the two accounts seem to be due to their descent from a common Greek original.'[59] This version was a source for certain later vernacular renderings[60] but had no influence upon the Anglo-Saxon writers. It is, in comparison with the Mombritius and Casinensis versions, a restrained and sober account narrated in a brief, factual manner and showing a careful modification of the more extravagant parts of the legend.

BHL NO. 5308: THE REBDORF VERSION

BHL no. 5308, 'Version 4', according to the classification of the Bolland-ists, is edited in *Acta Sanctorum* from a manuscript in the Augustinian monastery of Rebdorf in Bavaria.[61] The date of this version is not known, though a passage in the prologue appears to suggest that it was written well after the time of Gregory the Great (d. 604): the prologue speaks of the *moderni* following in hagiographical writing the example of Gregory and Ambrose.[62] The Rebdorf version was not widely known or of major literary influence in the early Middle Ages. It does, however, merit consideration as a highly thoughtful and accomplished piece of hagiographical writing, and it provides a number of useful comparisons and contrasts with the Mombritius and Casinensis versions.

The prologue of the Rebdorf version announces a critical attitude on the part of its writer to aspects of the story of St Margaret. The writer voices unease concerning certain Latin saints' lives which are 'depravata per imperitiam translatorum'[63] and praises the high standards set by Ambrose and Gregory.[64] The present version is the result of a careful attempt to

---

[59] *Ibid.*, p. 87.   [60] See *ibid.*
[61] Ed. Bollandists, *ASS*, Iul. V, 33–9. There is also a copy of this version in the twelfth-century manuscript, London, BL, Arundel 169.
[62] 'Horum [Ambrosii et Gregorii] autem validissimam auctoritatem, qui coelestis aedificii jure possent vocare columnae, moderni etiam non improbabili tenore secuti sunt, cupientes videlicet herili gregi si non patulis phialis, augustis saltem cyathis propinare' (34A).
[63] 33F: 'distorted through the ignorance of the translators'.   [64] *Ibid.*, 34A.

'correct' the legend of St Margaret as it has been received: 'non propriis sed divinis viribus innixus corrigere studui.'[65]

The prologue does not specify how in particular this version modifies inherited material but two features of *BHL* no. 5308 are immediately noticeable in comparison with most other versions. Firstly, the whole dragon-demon episode appears in a very much truncated form. Only some 300 words in a text of over 4000 are devoted to this scene: the corresponding scene in Mombritius covers more than a quarter of the narrative and even in the more restrained Caligula version it takes up about a sixth of the total. The other major point of contrast between Rebdorf and most of the versions so far discussed is the complete absence in it of any references to Margaret's prayer of intercession for those who venerate her.[66] Thus the two elements which probably contributed most to the popularity of the Margaret legend in the Middle Ages are, respectively, de-emphasized and completely ignored.

Instead of these popular elements the Rebdorf writer shows a preoccupation with the historical facts of the story not evident in other versions. The account of Margaret begins with an introductory passage giving the historical setting of her martyrdom. It tells of the accession of Diocletian to the empire (even giving the approximate date, *c.* 290) and of his joint rule with Maximian. It then goes on to deal with the cruel persecution of the Christians carried on by these two rulers and mentions that this persecution continued into the first years of the reign of Constantine.[67] Moving on to the immediate subject of the *passio*, the writer reports the name of Margaret's father, Aedisius,[68] and – by means of a flashback just before her persecution begins – gives a succinct account of Margaret's childhood.[69] In the course of the story itself a sense of authenticity is lent to the narrative by the constant use of direct discourse, as if the actual speeches of Margaret's trial were being reported verbatim.

Despite this apparent concern with placing the story in a firm historical setting, however, and with providing a sense of authenticity in its narration, the writer's real interest is not in historical accuracy but in the

---

[65] *Ibid.*, 34B: 'I have striven to correct, supported not by my own but by divine power.'

[66] The prayer is also omitted in the summary of the legend in the *Martyrologium* of Hrabanus Maurus and in the virtually identical summary in the *Martyrologium* of Notkerus Balbulus (on these see below, pp. 22–3).

[67] *ASS*, Iul. V, 34C–D.   [68] *Ibid.*, 34E.   [69] *Ibid.*, 34E–F.

archetypal world of hagiography. The 'historical' aspect of the story has little depth and when the central conflict gets under way all factual references are excluded. Indeed, the impression of a firm historical setting may be seen as itself representing a conventional aspect of hagiography.

Theodor Wolpers has traced the progress that Margaret makes in the course of the Rebdorf narrative from fear to confidence and joy.[70] Related to this theme too is that of the saint's humility, highlighted all the more by the writer's preoccupation with her noble birth.[71] Her customary reference to herself as the *famula* 'servant' of Christ, though conventional, is itself a sign of this humility. Humility is the very first quality mentioned in connection with Margaret at the beginning of the *passio* and it is significantly stressed as the narrative proceeds.[72]

In the Rebdorf version a dignified and elevated style is combined with brevity in the treatment of narrative. This version is roughly of the same overall length as Mombritius (the Caligula version is only about half as long) but it approaches the story differently, toning down its sensationalism: in Rebdorf, for example, the dragon does not swallow Margaret. This version also gives particular emphasis to the element of formal debate in the exchanges between Margaret and Olibrius. In these there is much cultivation of rhetorical figures.

MARTYROLOGIES AND EPITOMES

The range of extant Latin versions of the legend of St Margaret is evidence that this saint was of considerable interest to monastic audiences from the Carolingian period onwards. Another indication of this interest is her appearance in martyrologies and epitomes. We have already mentioned the

---

[70] Wolpers, *Die englische Heiligenlegende des Mittelalters*, pp. 103–4.

[71] When questioned by Olibrius about her background, Margaret replies, 'Mea quidem progenies omnibus in hac urbe notissima est, nec adeo de infimo et ignobili genere sum, ut mea possit latere origo' (35F).

[72] Note the opening account of Margaret's virtues: 'Inter cetera enim virtutum magnalia, quae illi divina gratia contulerat, adeo se Virgo Domini sanctae humilitati subdiderat, ut de nobilitatis genere nullam haberet jactantiam' (34F). Note also the comparison with the Old Testament figure of humility, Rachel (as mentioned above, n. 24): 'Pascebat autem eas [oviculas] cum omni humilitate, et mansuetudine: sicut illa quondam Rachel, mater patriarchae Joseph, puella humilis et decora, patris sui oves humiliter custodiebat' (34F–35A).

summaries of the Margaret legend in the *Old English Martyrology* and in the later epitomes, the *Speculum historiale* and *Legenda aurea*, all of which base their accounts on 'Version 1' sources. In the *Old English Martyrology* Marina appears under the date 7 July. The *Martyrologium* of Hrabanus Maurus, composed between 840 and 854, has an entry for Margaret under 13 July and a very similar one for Marina under 18 June. The Marina entry is as follows:

Eodem die [18 Iun.] in Antiochia celebratur passio Marinae uirginis, quae per Olibrium praefectum multa tormenta passa est pro nomine Christi, uincula, carceres, flagella, eculeum. Quam et diabulus in draconis specie similiter et in Aethiopis temptauit et subuertere uoluit, sed per signum sanctae crucis effugatus et superatus est. Nouissime uero per praedictum praefectum decollata cum sacro martyrio uitam finiuit.[73]

To this may be compared Hrabanus's account of St Margaret:

In Antiochia passio Margaretae uirginis, quam Olibrius consul stuprare uolens et a fide Christi auertere, multis tormentis eam affixit, hoc est in eculeo suspensam ungulis aceruissimis iussit carnes eius lacerare. Postea in carcerem tenebrosum eam misit, ubi diabuli seductiones, qui in specie draconis et Aethiopis illi apparuit, superauit, et nihil illi eius fraus nocere potuit. Nouissime uero gladio percutoris decollata est et ad uitam migrauit aeternam.[74]

The almost contemporary poetical *Martyrologium* of Wandalbert, monk of Prüm, has a brief reference to St Margaret, along with St Vitus, whose feast-day falls on the same day as that given for St Margaret (15 June):

[73] *Rabani Mauri Martyrologium*, ed. McCulloh, p. 59, lines 202–8: 'On the same day at Antioch is celebrated the passion of the virgin Marina, who through the prefect Olibrius suffered many torments for the name of Christ, fetters, imprisonments, scourgings and the rack. The devil tested her in the form of a dragon and similarly of an Ethiopian, and wished to destroy her, but through the sign of the holy cross he was put to flight and defeated. Finally, she was beheaded by means of the aforementioned prefect and ended her life with holy martyrdom.'

[74] *Ibid.*, pp. 67–8, lines 120–6: 'At Antioch [is celebrated] the passion of the virgin Margaret, whom the consul Olibrius wishing to ravish and to turn from the faith of Christ afflicted with many torments: namely, he ordered her to be hung on the rack and her flesh to be lacerated with very sharp hooks. Afterwards he sent her into a dark prison, where she overcame the seductions of the devil, who appeared to her in the form of a dragon and of an Ethiopian, and his deception was unable to harm her at all. Finally, she was beheaded by the sword of the persecutor and passed into eternal life.'

Septeno deno Vitus cum uirgine clara
Margarita, martyrii splendore nitescit.[75]

Margaret also appears, under the date 13 July (III Id. Iul.), in the
Martyrologium of Notker Balbulus, monk of Sankt Gallen (d. 912).[76] The
Notker Balbulus entry closely follows Hrabanus Maurus's account of St
Margaret.

---

[75] Ed. E. Dümmler, *Poetae Latini Aevi Carolini*, MGH, Poetae II (Berlin, 1884),
578–602: 'On the seventeenth [day before the Kalends of July] Vitus shines along with
the illustrious Margaret in the splendour of martyrdom' (p. 587).

[76] 'In Antiochia passio Margarethae virginis, quam Olibrius consul a Christi fide seducere
et constuprare cupiens, non consentientem sibi plurimis tormentis afflixit: hoc est, in
equuleo suspensam ungulis acerbissimis lacerari, ac postea in carcerem tenebrosum
conjici praecepit, ubi multimodas diaboli seductiones, quas ei in specie draconis et
Aethiopis ingerere nisus est, in nomine Domini Jesu exsuperans, novissime decollata,
ad requiem migravit aeternam' (PL 131, col. 1119).

3

The treatment of the legend in the Mombritius and pre-Mombritius tradition

The version of the legend of St Margaret designated in the previous chapter the 'pre-Mombritius' version is by far the most productive and influential of the Latin versions. The variant *BHL* no. 5303, the Mombritius version, is the most widely found of all Latin versions, and representatives of the Mombritius and pre-Mombritius tradition lie behind nearly all vernacular adaptations. In particular, variants of this tradition served as sources for all three extant Anglo-Saxon versions of the legend (the two edited here and the *Old English Martyrology* account of St Marina), and it is also virtually certain that a text from this group provided the source of a fourth Anglo-Saxon version, the non-extant Cotton Otho B. x version.[1] The distinctive qualities of the Old English versions and the major departures from known texts of the Mombritius and pre-Mombritius tradition apparent in them will be discussed in ch. 4. It is appropriate, however, before turning to the Old English adaptations themselves, to give an account of the treatment of the legend in the Latin tradition lying behind the Old English.

The pre-Mombritius version, as represented both in the Mombritius version (*BHL* no. 5303) and in the somewhat more restrained Casinensis (*BHL* no. 5304), presents a powerful example of celebratory hagiography. The extant texts display a style which takes its inspiration from the language and imagery of the Bible, particularly the psalms, and of the liturgy. Many of the features of this version commented on in the following pages are derived from the Greek original on which the Latin is based, as can be seen by comparing the Latin to the Greek version edited by Usener.

---

[1] On this version, see above, p. 17, n. 48.

24

The stylistic verve of the Latin is readily apparent, however, and reveals the pre-Mombritius version as a considerable work of literature in its own right. This *passio* reads as a definitive product of monastic civilization, celebrating the receiving of Margaret into the community of the saints venerated by the church, and itself hymnally expressing that veneration. The writing, particularly in the incantatory *BHL* no. 5303 version, displays an insistence on self-conscious rhetorical patterning but bases this especially on the verbal structures of the sacred writings which provided the foundation of monastic life. There is no pronounced cultivation of exotic or unusual vocabulary.

The indebtedness to the liturgy reflected in *BHL* no. 5303 has been studied by Theodor Wolpers[2] and can be seen particularly in the direct discourse of Margaret's speeches, with their combination of the poetry of the psalms and the careful balancing of phrase and clause of the collectary. Margaret's prayer to the Lord, for example, beginning 'Deus, qui iudicium sapientiae decreuisti',[3] commences with a petition using what students of the liturgy refer to as 'relative predicate' structure (a relative predicate is an ascription of praise to the Almighty, arranged in the form of a relative clause):[4] Margaret's prayer takes the form, 'Deus, qui . . ., quem . . ., quem . . ., + PETITION'. Between the series of relative clauses and the petition 'Respice in me . . .' a short litany-like sequence is inserted, qualifying the vocative 'Deus' with which the sentence had begun: 'tu es desperatorum spes; tu es pater orfanorum et iudex uerus; tu es lumen de lumine.'[5] The speech contains a number of allusions to particular psalms, as well as generally being influenced by the language of the psalter: some of the phrases in the litany-like sequence just quoted are psalm reminiscences,[6] and immediately after the opening sentence of the speech come the pleas 'Respice in me et miserere mei'[7] and 'Ne tu me derelinquas,

---

[2] Wolpers, *Die englische Heiligenlegende des Mittelalters*, pp. 170–7.

[3] P, ch. 11; Cas, p. 228: 'God, who have determined the judgement of wisdom'.

[4] See T. Klauser, *A Short History of the Western Liturgy: An Account and Some Reflections*, trans. J. Halliburton, 2nd English ed. (from 5th German ed.) (Oxford, 1979), p. 38.

[5] P, ch. 11; Cas. p. 228: 'you are the hope of those who are desperate; you are the father of orphans and the true judge; you are light from light.'

[6] Ps. CXLI. 6; LXVII. 6. Reminiscences of particular psalms are identified in the Commentary on the Latin text.

[7] Ps. CXVIII. 132: 'Look upon me and have pity on me.'

Domine Deus meus.'[8] Like most of Margaret's prayers, this one ends with a *Benedictus* formula, acknowledging the blessedness of the Lord.

In contrast to the Rebdorf version of the legend of St Margaret, we notice in the Mombritius and pre-Mombritius tradition a lack of specific narrative detail. The setting is Antioch[9] but no specific date or persecution are referred to. There is a curious precision in the statement that the 'certain town' where Margaret is brought up is fifteen stades from Antioch,[10] but the name of the town is not given, nor are we told how in particular Margaret happens to have been brought up there. Little is said about the relationship between Margaret and her pagan father Theodosius. We know only that she is raised and loved by her Christian fostermother (unnamed) and that she is not loved by her father, presumably because of her Christianity. This last point emerges only incidentally, however, when the *passio* develops a rhetorical contrast between the love shown to her by her earthly and her heavenly father: 'Odiosa erat a patre suo, dilecta namque a Domino Iesu Christo.'[11] Similarly, even the important fact that the fostermother is a Christian emerges only incidentally: she loves Margaret because of the girl's devotion to Christ.[12]

Even the gruesome tortures which Margaret undergoes are related with extreme brevity, the emphasis being on the superhuman spirit of the saint and on the impression made upon the onlookers at the time, who act as emotive representatives of the *passio* audience. Olibrius has to hide his face in his cloak at one point, overcome by the sight of so much blood flowing from Margaret.[13] The presentation is highly stylized and the saint's individuality is absorbed into type. In her ecstatic imperviousness to suffering and in her superiority of mind over her persecutors, Margaret is universalized into the perfected saint, powerful and distinctively removed from ordinary life.

The one part of the narrative which displays graphic attention to

---

[8] Ps. XXXVII. 22: 'Do not abandon me, Lord my God.'

[9] P, chs. 3 and 5; Cas, p. 225.

[10] P, ch. 3; Cas, p. 225.

[11] P, ch. 3: 'She was hateful to her father, for she was beloved by the Lord Jesus Christ.' In Cas (p. 225) *patre suo* is corrupted to *sua matre*. The correctness of the former reading is confirmed by Us, 132v, lines 30–31: ὁ μέντοι πατὴρ αὐτῆς ἐβδελύττετο αὐτήν, 'Her father hated her.'

[12] P, ch. 3; Cas, p. 225.   [13] P, ch. 10; Cas, p. 228.

physical descriptive detail is that dealing with the dragon which attacks Margaret in her prison cell. As explained below, this episode stands out from the rest of the narrative in its immediacy and in its power to disturb. Here, if only momentarily, Margaret loses the serene composure which her ritual exchanges with Olibrius fail to threaten, and we move outside the saint's otherwise unbroken progress of triumph. Her victory over the dragon and over the companion black demon are all the more impressive, however, and they establish another aspect of Margaret's heroism.

In general, despite this interruption, the emphasis is on celebration rather than on documentary narration. This version in no sense tries to establish the authenticity of a cult but is a work in honour of a woman who has achieved acknowledged sainthood: the epithets constantly used of Margaret are *beata*, *beatissima* and *sancta*. The narrative style itself contributes to the glorification of Margaret, enhancing unobtrusively the audience's overall sense of participation in the honouring of a great saint. For in syntax and in vocabulary the narrative echoes the style of the Vulgate, recalling in particular that of the gospels (just as the speeches of Margaret recall the psalms). This is reflected in the paratactic style of the narration and in the cultivation of phrases familiar from the Vulgate.[14] Such undemonstrative phrases are not so much allusions to particular passages as reflexes of a style moulded by familiarity with the bible. There are *explicit* references to the gospels as well, of course, but the general sense of biblical association which is built into the narrative is a constant element in the treatment of the story.[15]

The narrative style, like that of the gospels, is unadorned by descriptive particularity, but, unlike in the gospels, superimposed upon it is a level of heightened emotive commentary, seen in the use of epithets expressing value-judgement and attitude: the gods worshipped by Olibrius, for

---

[14] The narrative begins (ch. 5) with reminiscences of phrases familiar from the gospels: cf. *factum est autem in diebus illis* (Luke II. 1), *cum transiret* (Matt. IX. 9), *de ciuitate Nazareth . . . in ciuitatem David* (Luke II. 4), *pasce oues* (John XXI. 17).

[15] Specific gospel allusions are identified in the Commentary on the Latin text. On biblical reminiscence in monastic culture, see Leclercq, *The Love of Learning and the Desire for God*, pp. 79–83. Compare the comments of Benedicta Ward on Anselm's assimilation of biblical language in his *Prayers and Meditations*: these compositions 'are made up from the remembered language of the bible: Anselm had so assimilated divine truth through reading, that the scriptures had become his spontaneous prayer' (*The Prayers and Meditations of Saint Anselm*, p. 46).

example, are typically described as deaf and mute: 'deos suos surdos et mutos'.[16] In this emotive aspect the narrative is more restrained than that of many other saints' lives, and much more restrained than the speeches of Margaret, but this use of affective colouring is an essential component of the approach to narrative reflected in the Latin.

The basic pattern of the story is the familiar one of the young Christian virgin opposed by the raging heathen figure of Roman authority, who also wishes to overcome the chastity of the saint. The contrast is between seemingly irresistible and obdurate physical power and authority on the one hand and the spiritual strength of the apparently weak female on the other. Even the black demon is dismayed that he has been defeated by a girl – had she been a young man it would not have been so bad! He laments, 'uel si iuuenis me uinceret, non curassem. Ecce a tenera puella superatus sum.'[17]

Through her heroism Margaret takes her place among the great martyrs who have defeated this world: 'uicerunt hunc mundum.'[18] In defeating the world she also defeats the devil: Olibrius is the devil's son,[19] and of course in the prison interlude Margaret also defeats the devil in an even more direct way. On the appearance of the dragon she prays that she may overcome his strength, 'uincere fortitudinem eius',[20] and later the black demon acknowledges the completeness of her victory over him and the dragon: 'Cum ipso signo uicisti me, et per ipsum Ruffonem occidisti.'[21] At the beginning of the text the narrator is concerned to find out how Margaret defeated this world, 'uicit hunc mundum.'[22] In a statement which appears to be unique to *BHL* no. 5303, Margaret herself declares in her final scene that in dying she has defeated the world: 'Ecce iam uici mundum.'[23]

---

[16] P, ch. 6; Cas, p. 226.
[17] M, p. 193, lines 51–2: 'Even if a young man defeated me, I would not have worried. Behold, I am overcome by a tender girl.' P omits the *iuuenis* reference (15); Cas has none of the material treated in *BHL* no. 5303, ch. 15.
[18] P, ch. 1; Cas, p. 225.
[19] M, p. 191, line 51 (at the beginning of ch. 10, P omits the phrase *patris tui*: see Commentary on Latin text, n. 47); Cas, p. 227.
[20] P, ch. 12; Cas, p. 229.
[21] M, p. 193, lines 38–9; omitted in Cas: 'With that sign you have defeated me, and through it you have killed Rufo.' In P, ch. 16, the detail *uicisti me* is lacking.
[22] P, ch. 2; Cas, p. 225.   [23] P, ch. 22; not in Cas or Us.

This theme of overcoming the world and of defeating the devil is thus one which runs through the texts of the Mombritius and pre-Mombritius tradition and which is picked up by the use of refrain-like, recurrent phrases. The use of such themes, identifying the saint as a *miles Christi*[24] and gaining a more and more triumphant resonance as the narrative progresses, is a characteristic feature of the celebratory style of this *passio*. But the theme of overcoming the world also exemplifies the immersion in the words of the Bible reflected in this version. The ultimate source of the theme lies in Christ's statement before his Passion, 'Ego uici mundum.'[25] In attributing these famous words to Margaret as she goes to her death, the *BHL* no. 5303 adaptor presents a striking instance of *imitatio Christi* and one which powerfully conveys the sublimity of Margaret's triumph.

The opening sentences of the *passio* already show some of the rhetorical features which are found throughout the narrative:

Post resurrectionem Domini nostri Iesu Christi et gloriosae tempus ascensionis eius in caelum ad Patrem omnipotentem, in illius nomine multi martyres passi sunt, et apostoli coronati sunt, et innumerabiles sancti facti sunt in nomine Domini nostri Iesu Christi, et [uicerunt] hunc mundum [et] tyrannos et carnifices superauerunt. Adhuc tamen obtinebat insaniam hominum diaboli rabies, et idola surda et muta et caeca manu hominum facta adorabant, qui nec illis proderant nec sibi.[26]

In the first sentence the initial prepositional phrase splits neatly into two parts, one focusing on the Resurrection, the other on the Ascension of Christ, the latter linking too with the theme of the omnipotence of God the Father.[27]

---

[24] On this theme, see Hill, 'The Soldier of Christ'.   [25] John XVI. 33.

[26] M, p. 190, lines 16–21; Cas, pp. 224–5 (the passage is cited from M, with omissions supplied from As, as P has several irregularities in the opening sentences): 'After the Resurrection of Our Lord Jesus Christ and the time of his glorious Ascension into heaven to the omnipotent Father, in his name many martyrs suffered, and apostles were crowned, and innumerable people were sanctified in the name of Our Lord Jesus Christ, and they defeated this world and conquered tyrants and tormentors. As yet, however, the raging of the devil maintained the insanity of men, and they worshipped deaf, dumb and blind idols, fashioned by human hand, which were of benefit neither to them nor to themselves.'

[27] The reading 'Post passionem et resurrectionem . . .', found in P and a number of other witnesses to the Mombritius and pre-Mombritius tradition, has the effect of imparting to the introductory words of the *passio* an expansive triplet structure, in harmony with

29

In this sentence the ideas of divine power and invincibility are
established as the context of the heroic struggles of the martyrs. After the
prepositional phrase comes a brief cumulative triplet composed of noun/
adjective subjects, with verbs in the perfect tense passive: 'multi martyres
passi sunt, et apostoli coronati sunt, et innumerabiles sancti facti sunt.'
The use of such triplets, of individual word or of phrase, is a constant
feature of the style. A couple of lines later we hear of the deaf, dumb and
blind idols, 'idola surda et muta et caeca', a virtually formulaic triplet
which recurs several times. Doublets are also widely used, as is illustrated
here in the linked verbal phrases, 'uicerunt hunc mundum' and 'tyrannos et
carnifices superauerunt.' These phrases express, at the beginning of the
passio, the central hagiographical concern of the victory of the saints.

This opening sequence also shows a preoccupation with the *name* of the
Lord – 'in illius nomine' and 'in nomine Domini' – thus announcing a
major theme of the *passio*, which receives particularly insistent expression
in the speeches of Margaret. In treating the relationship of the saint to
Christ the *passio* makes use of the ideas of the virgin martyr as 'bride of
Christ'[28] and 'handmaiden of the Lord',[29] but these motifs are not
developed. Instead there is a constant dwelling on and attachment to the
name of Christ. Time and again the saint calls upon this name: 'invoco
nomen Christi'.[30] This repeated invocation recalls the 'In nomine . . .'
formulas of the liturgy and vividly exemplifies the indebtedness of the
passio to the language of the psalms, for it is in the psalms above all that the
name of the Lord is invoked. The psalms exalt the name of the Lord[31] and
call upon it in prayer.[32] The greatness of the name of the Lord[33] is seen as a
source of wonder and inspiration in the psalms, and this is strongly taken
up in our *passio*. The name in this incantatory usage contains in itself the
person of the Lord.

The emotive and colourful aspects of the style come out in the closing
sentence of the short introductory passage. Here the fury of the devil is

the overall pattern of this opening sentence. On the P reading, see Commentary on
Latin text, n. 1.
[28] P, ch. 14; material omitted in Cas.
[29] P, chs. 14 and 15; material omitted in Cas.
[30] P, ch. 6; Cas, p. 226: 'I call upon the name of Christ.'
[31] See Ps. XXXIII. 4; LXV. 4.
[32] See Ps. LXIX. 19; CIV. 1.   [33] Ps. LXXV. 2.

linked with the madness of humankind – 'obtinebat insaniam hominum diaboli rabies'[34] – and the uselessness of the deaf, mute and blind idols of the heathens is contemptuously pointed out. The *insania* is all the greater in the context of the power of God, as seen in his own actions and in those of his saints, which this prologue as a whole has celebrated. The idols, in contrast, are the useless creations of the hands of men.[35]

The language of the Mombritius and pre-Mombritius versions is at its most heightened in the speeches, and particularly the prayers, of Margaret. The main stylistic features of the prayers can be illustrated by an examination of the first of them, which is offered up when the saint has been apprehended by the soldiers of Olibrius.[36] The formal and measured expression of this speech is typical of what we find in all of Margaret's prayers. The prayers adopt a public and proclamatory mode which is apparent even when Margaret is on her own. This first speech is a tissue of psalm and other biblical quotations and recollections, from the repeated 'Miserere mei'[37] with which it begins, through the next sentence, 'Ne perdas cum impiis animam meam et cum uiris sanguinum uitam meam',[38] to the closing petition, 'Ne derelinquas me in manus impiorum.'[39] The structure of sentence within the prayer is marked by the use of double petitions linked by *et*. In *BHL* no. 5303 the short sentence 'Fac me laetari semper in te, Domine Iesu Christe, et te semper collaudare',[40] presents a double petition, but also employs chiasmus and alliteration of the dominant elements, the infinitives *laetari* and *collaudare*, and the parallelism is brought out further through the repetition of *semper* and *te*. In the petition 'Non proiciatur margareta mea in lutum'[41] Margaret combines the psalmist's image of being cast in the mire[42] with a striking and mannered pun on her own name. And she ends the speech with a series of emotive comparisons of herself to trapped animals, again drawing strongly on

---

[34] M, p. 190, line 20: 'The raging of the devil maintained the insanity of men.'
[35] This is a further allusion to an Old Testament idea: see Ps. CXV. 14; Is. XXXI. 7; XXXVII. 19.
[36] P, ch. 5; Cas, p. 226.   [37] 'Have mercy on me.' Cf. Ps. IV. 2; VI. 3; IX. 14.
[38] 'Do not destroy my soul with the wicked nor my life with men of blood': Ps. XXV. 9.
[39] 'Do not abandon me into the hands of the wicked': Ps. XXXVII. 22; cf. XXXVI. 33.
[40] M, p. 190, lines 50–1 (reworded in P, ch. 5; and Cas, p. 226, abbreviates): 'Make me to rejoice always in you, Lord Jesus Christ, and always to praise you greatly.'
[41] P, ch. 5; Cas, p. 226: 'Let not my pearl be cast forth into the mud.'
[42] As in Ps. LXVIII. 15.

biblical images. Margaret sees herself as a sheep surrounded by wolves,[43] a sparrow caught by a fowler,[44] a fish on a hook[45] and a doe in a snare.[46]

Despite its insistence on emotive elements the prayer has a composure and maturity of expression which immediately puts the heroine on a higher plane than that of the ordinary mortal. It is not the prayer of a frightened fifteen-year-old but already the assured and timeless utterance of the perfected saint speaking in the public language of God's church. Neither in this first response to the orders of Olibrius nor in her subsequent exchanges with him is there any sense of the personal feelings which Margaret might have in the face of tortures and threats. The human aspect of the heroine is not explored. Her first statement to Olibrius, in response to his question, 'Es libera an ancilla?',[47] is a defiance: 'Libera sum et Christiana',[48] and in the oppositional relationship to her persecutor she remains strong and resolute.

Margaret's composure is again emphasized at the beginning of her second day of confrontation with Olibrius in the self-conscious wordplay of her retort to his offer of marriage to her: 'Ego tradam corpus meum Domino meo Iesu Christo ut cum iustis uirginibus coronam accipiam. Christus semetipsum tradidit ⟨in⟩ mortem pro nobis, et ego pro ipso mori non dubito.'[49] Here the elements *tradere* and *mors* and the *pro* phrases combine in a series of carefully balanced oppositions. In a later confrontation with Olibrius Margaret calls him a dog, a dragon (Casinensis) or lion (Mombri-

---

[43] Cf. Matt. X. 16 and Luke X. 3.

[44] Cf. Ps. CI. 8. This comparison is omitted in Cas, but is reflected in Usener (133r, lines 28–9) and the Turin version (Vr, 164r).

[45] Cf. Eccles. IX. 12. Cas and some copies of *BHL* 5303 omit this comparison. Usener and the Turin version have a fish image, but without the mention of the hook: ὥσπερ ἰχθὺς ἐν μέσῳ δικτύων τῶν ἁλιευόντων (Us, 133r, lines 29–30), 'like a fish in the nets of fishermen'; 'Ecce sum inter piscatores uelut piscis' (Vr, 164r), 'Behold, I am like a fish among fishermen.'

[46] Cf. Ecclus. XI. 32. On the manuscript variation between *caprea* 'doe' and *capra* 'she-goat', see Commentary on Latin text, n. 21 (p. 220). *Caprea* also occurs in the Turin version (Vr, 164r).

[47] P, ch. 6; Cas, p. 226: 'Are you free or a slave?'

[48] *Ibid.*: 'I am free and a Christian.'

[49] P, ch. 7; Cas, p. 227: 'I will commit my body to my Lord Jesus Christ, so that I may receive the heavenly crown with the just virgins. Christ committed himself to death for us, and I do not hesitate to die for him.'

32

tius), and a unicorn,[50] and appears to express heroism to the point of foolhardiness, but again of course she is drawing upon the language of the psalms, seeing herself in particular as the follower of God of Ps. XXI, surrounded by hostility and danger.[51] As in her other speeches, there is a sense that Margaret is impregnable in that she is outside the experience.

In her second prayer[52] Margaret again expresses herself by means of reference to the psalms. Her opening declaration is 'In te speraui, Domine',[53] and there is a constant flow of allusions to the psalms as the speech proceeds.[54] Among other such allusions, this prayer emphasizes the notion of the name of the Lord – 'propter nomen tuum, Domine, quia nomen tuum benedictum est'[55] – which, as noted above, is a constant focus for Margaret. In the second part of this prayer Margaret voices her fear in the face of persecution, but the self-conscious and stylized presentation of this fear militates against any feeling of the real vulnerability of the saint and suggests her remoteness from personal emotion. The sense is rather of public and controlled emotion: 'Sed mitte rorem de caelo ut mitigentur plagae meae, et dolor meus requiescat, et tristitia mea uertetur in gaudium.'[56]

Although detailed description of the tortures inflicted on Margaret is avoided, the *passio* conveys a sense of the enormity of these tortures both through affective comments like 'sanguis eius tamquam aquae de fonte purissimo decurrebat',[57] and by emphasizing the reactions of others. At one point a representative of the crowd emotively contemplates Margaret's

---

[50] P, ch. 10; Cas, p. 228. It is impossible to tell whether in the second of these comparisons *draco* or *leo* was the original reading in the pre-Mombritius version, as the analogues have neither. The words 'dragon' and 'lion' occur together in the Old Testament (Ps. XC. 13; Ecclus. XXV. 23). The present variation may be the result of scribal reminiscence of this collocation.

[51] Cf. especially Ps. XXI. 17–22.   [52] P, ch. 8; Cas, p. 227.

[53] 'In you I have trusted, Lord': Ps. VII. 2; XXX. 2; XXXVII. 16.

[54] See Commentary on Latin text, Appendix 2, below, nn. 32–42. Note also such phrases as *propter nomen tuum* and *in saecula saeculorum*, too familiar to be regarded as allusions to particular psalms.

[55] P, ch. 8; Cas, p. 227: 'on account of your name, Lord, because your name is blessed'.

[56] P, ch. 8: 'But send dew from heaven, so that my wounds may be soothed, my sorrow may find repose and my sadness may be turned to joy.' Cas has the different wording, 'Mitte mihi angelum sanctum tuum ut dolor et plage iste veniat mihi, Domine, in gaudium' (p. 227).

[57] P, ch. 9; Cas, p. 227: 'her blood flowed like water from the purest spring.'

suffering: 'O Margareta, uere dolemus te, quia uidimus te nudam lacerari et corpus tuum macerari. O Margareta, qualem decorem perdidisti propter incredulitatem tuam!'[58] After this rhetorically developed apostrophe the speaker, appalled at what is happening to the saint, tries to tempt her to surrender. However, this only earns Margaret's implacable contempt for the crowd, expressed in terms which pick up and extend the 'O' pattern of the previous speaker's address: 'O mali consiliarii! O pessimi omnes!'[59] Margaret continues her reply by developing a soul-body contrast, 'Si corpus meum est exterminatum, anima autem mea cum iustis uirginibus requiescit',[60] of a kind to which she will return later.[61]

The episode of the dragon and the black demon is one which caused considerable concern to some medieval commentators. Jacobus a Voragine declared that this part of the legend is thought to be 'apocryphum et friuolum',[62] and it is interesting that the episode is not mentioned at all in the account of St Marina in the *Old English Martyrology*. As Jocelyn Price points out, the Rebdorf version is careful to make it clear that the devil appeared to Margaret in prison 'in draconis specie', i.e. as an illusion.[63] A similar unease may be detected in the Casinensis variant of our *passio*, in which the detail of the dragon swallowing the saint is omitted and the discussion of demonology is much abbreviated. The version from which Casinensis derives, however, appears to have treated this episode with fascination and enthusiasm. In *BHL* no. 5303 the episode covers more than a quarter of the text and it contains the most graphic writing in the whole narrative. Nonetheless, the *passio* shows a concern about the authenticity of the episode by interrupting the narrative to insist, developing a detail going back to the Greek original,[64] on the presence of Theotimus as an eyewitness. He observes the whole thing through the

[58] *Ibid.*: 'O Margaret, truly we pity you, because we see you tortured naked and your body weakened. O Margaret, what beauty you have destroyed because of your lack of belief!'

[59] *Ibid.*: 'O evil counsellors! O most wicked all of you!'

[60] *Ibid.*: 'If my body is destroyed, my soul will repose with the just virgins.'

[61] See P, ch. 10; Cas, p. 228.

[62] *Legenda Aurea*, ed. Graesse, p. 401: 'apocryphal and worthless'.

[63] Price, 'The Virgin and the Dragon', p. 337: 'in the form of a dragon'.

[64] See Usener, 135v, lines 19–20, where it says that Theotimus gave Marina bread and water through the window of her cell, though it does not mention that he wrote down her prayers.

window of Margaret's cell.[65] Many copies of *BHL* no. 5303, however, including P and M, are corrupt at this point and lack the proper name.

In the vivid and detailed description of the figure of the dragon we move away from the well-signposted world of the *passio* into a world of demonology derived from passages in the lives of the desert fathers and, as Frances Mack has explained, from apocryphal books containing Eastern demon-lore.[66] The description also strongly recalls that of Leviathan in Job.[67] Parallels with the debate between Margaret and the black demon are known in other hagiographical narratives. In an Anglo-Saxon context one thinks at once of *Juliana* and *Andreas*;[68] Pelagia is visited by the devil in the *Old English Martyrology*;[69] Ælfric reports that devils came frequently to St Martin but he always knew them and (like Margaret) dispelled them with the sign of the cross.[70]

This part of the narrative has a sense of immediacy and shock about it, to the extent that Margaret's composure suddenly evaporates. Events have become genuinely threatening and for the first time Margaret does not know what to think or how to react: 'Sancta autem Margareta facta est ut herba pallida et formido mortis cecidit in eam et confringebantur omnia ossa eius.'[71] Margaret had asked in the first place that she might see her enemy and speak to him face to face: she prays, 'Precipe ut uideam inimicum meum qui mecum pugnat, ut iudicium adferam contra eum et loquar cum eo facie ad faciem.'[72] But when the dragon suddenly appears in response to this request Margaret is completely disconcerted and does not realize that the dragon is the devil. The narrative is organized in such a way that it is not made clear to the reader to begin with what this terrible figure

---

[65] P, ch. 12; Cas, p. 229.   [66] *Seinte Marherete*, ed. Mack, pp. xxvi–xxix.

[67] Job XLI. 4–23.

[68] *Juliana*, lines 242–558; *Andreas*, lines 1311–87.

[69] *Das altenglische Martyrologium*, ed. Kotzor II, 234–5.

[70] *Ælfric's Lives of Saints*, ed. Skeat II, 264. In stressing the influence of apocryphal literature on the debate between Margaret and the demon, Mack mentions as a particular source the *Testament of Solomon* (*Seinte Marherete*, pp. xxvii–xxviii).

[71] P, ch. 12; cf. Cas, p. 229: 'The blessed Margaret became as pale as grass and the fear of death came upon her, and all her bones were shattered.'

[72] P, ch. 11; Cas, p. 229: 'Command that I may see my enemy who fights me, so that I may bring forth justice against him and speak to him face to face.' In the 'Paris' version (*BHL* no. 5305) the devil (immediately identified as such) appears completely

is. In the Rebdorf version of the legend the first thing the reader is told about the apparition is that it is the devil, but the Mombritius and pre-Mombritius tradition agrees with the Greek version edited by Usener in presenting the dragon without first specifically identifying it as the devil.[73]

The grotesque and appalling image of Margaret being swallowed by the dragon, again described with graphic attention to detail,[74] is omitted in Casinensis but present in all manuscripts of the Mombritius version and in the Turin version. This is immediately followed by the saint's victory through making the sign of the cross. Her subsequent ecstatic hymn of victory and praise is much abbreviated in P[75] but in most copies of *BHL* no. 5303[76] is among the most insistently exultant of all her utterances. A cumulative series of images of her victory, each beginning with the verb *uidi* forms the basis of a 'canticum'[77] which has its climax in a rhapsodic litany to the Almighty.[78] In this speech Margaret, who was a moment ago vulnerable and frightened, is suddenly able to express full knowledge concerning the demon, even to the extent (at least in *BHL* no. 5303) of knowing its name 'Rufo'.[79]

The transition from fearful girl back to perfected saint is abrupt and instantaneous, the devil suddenly destroyed by the sign of the cross. Margaret refers to herself after this (in sections omitted in Casinensis) as 'ancilla'[80] and 'domestica'[81] of Christ (also 'sponsa'[82]) and the black demon calls her 'famula . . . Christi',[83] but there is little sense of the humility and submissiveness suggested by these images in other contexts. As the black devil perceives with full clarity in his speech of confession and submission (at nearly thirty lines this speech, containing an extended account of

---

unexpectedly, without any prayer from Margaret; see Orywall, *Die alt- und mittel-französischen Prosafassungen der Margaretenlegende*, p. 184.

[73] ἐξῆλθεν ἐκ τῆς γωνίας δράκων μέγας καὶ φοβερὸς σφόδρα (Us, 135r, lines 23–4): 'A great and terrible dragon came out from the corner.' So also the Turin version: 'Ecce de angulo carceris exiuit draco magnus et inmanis' (Vr, 167r): 'Behold, there came out from the corner of the prison a great and horrible dragon.'

[74] P, ch. 13.   [75] *Ibid.*

[76] See M, p. 192, line 54–p. 193, line 10; As, lines 207–24; cf. Cas, pp. 229–30.

[77] M, p. 193, line 16.

[78] M, p. 193, lines 7–10; omitted in Cas, but reflected in the Turin version (Vr, 168r).

[79] M, p. 192, line 57.   [80] P, ch. 14: 'handmaid'.

[81] M, p. 193, line 21 (omitted in P): 'domestic servant'.

[82] P, ch. 14: 'bride'.   [83] P, ch. 15: 'servant/attendant of Christ'.

demonology, is by far the longest in the whole text),[84] Margaret is a glorious heroine who imitates Christ in binding the devil: 'cum signaculo crucis Christi ipsum Rufonem occidisti et me alligasti'.[85]

Indeed, apart from her sudden loss of equanimity when the dragon first appears, Margaret is very much in control throughout the *passio*, whether rebuking the crowd, instructing the executioner how to carry out his task, or expressing contempt for Olibrius. Her natural form of expression, even more than Olibrius's, seems to be the imperative mood. This is particularly brought out in the *BHL* no. 5303 variant. In this variant the insistently personal emphasis of the *uidi* speech[86] and the assumption of personal victory and of confident comparison with Christ in her declaration 'Ecce iam uici mundum'[87] and in her earlier speech to the devil, 'Vade ex [M *post*] me, Satanas',[88] reflect the dominance of Margaret's personality and her sanctified status. Even her prayers to the Almighty have a striking forcefulness and directness about them (the dove appears in response to these prayers, not as an unexpected messenger of mercy). Before her death she is declared *beata* by the black demon,[89] the voice from heaven[90] and the heavenly dove which lights upon her.[91] As well as the theme of imitation of Christ there is a series of comparisons with the Blessed Virgin, also elevating the standing of the saint: Margaret is the *ancilla* of the Lord;[92] she puts her foot upon the neck of the devil;[93] the dove praises her in the words 'Beata es inter mulieres';[94] and in some copies of *BHL* no. 5303 she is even granted a bodily assumption into heaven.[95]

In the closing part the story takes on something of the ecstatic nature of a

---

[84] P, ch. 15.

[85] P, ch. 15: 'With the sign of the cross of Christ you have slain Rufo himself and have bound me.'

[86] M, p. 192, line 54–p. 193, line 10.

[87] P, ch. 22: 'Behold, I have defeated the world' (John XVI. 33).

[88] P, ch. 16: Matt. XVI. 23; Mark VIII. 33.   [89] P, ch. 15.   [90] P, ch. 18.

[91] P, chs. 15 and 20 (four times).   [92] P, ch. 14: cf. Luke I. 38.

[93] P, ch. 14; cf. Gen. III. 15.

[94] P, ch. 20: 'Blessed are you among women': cf. Luke I. 28, 42. Other texts of *BHL* no. 5303, including M (p. 195, line 18) have instead 'Beata est namque uenter mulieris' ('Blessed is the womb of woman'): cf. Luke XI. 27. There is nothing corresponding to either phrase in Usener or in the Turin version, and all of ch. 20 is omitted in Cas.

[95] P, ch. 23. On variation at this point between *body*, *soul* and *head*, see above p. 14.

heavenly procession. The impact of this is somewhat reduced in Casinensis by the severe abbreviation which is apparent in this version at this stage. The major abbreviation here consists of the omission of all of the material in *BHL* no. 5303, ch. 20, but there is also significant abbreviation elsewhere in the closing stages of Casinensis. In *BHL* no. 5303 the divine blessing upon Margaret is manifested in the presence of the dove and in the solemn words accepting her into the heavenly kingdom before her execution has even begun: 'Veni, Margareta, in regnum caelorum et in requiem Christi.'[96] Margaret herself speaks out beyond the crowd to address the *passio* audience.[97] She refers to herself here as *peccatrix*,[98] but only in a conditional clause (which follows closely a reading in Usener's Greek[99]), and it is clear that she is already transcendent and beatified.

The ultimate sign of Margaret's glorification and of her power and control before her death is her remarkable last prayer.[100] Her own place in heaven is now assured and so she prays here not for herself but instead for those who venerate her. What is particularly striking here is the specific, itemizing nature of the prayer and its overtones of legal language. This formal petition has an insistent and reiterative quality, the second part forming a repetition and variation of the first. The terms of Margaret's prayer are re-emphasized when they are taken up in the heavenly response which solemnly grants her request – 'Per memetipsum iuro . . .'[101] – and they are confirmed yet again in Margaret's subsequent address to the crowd and to the audience of the *passio*.[102]

Margaret's authority at this stage of the narrative is also brought out in her final speech to the unwilling executioner (also lacking in Casinensis): with Christ-like assurance she tells him that if he does not carry out his

---

[96] P, ch. 18: 'Come, Margaret, into the kingdom of the heavens and into the repose of Christ.' See also P, ch. 15: 'Beata es Margareta. Te expectant portae paradisi' ('Blessed are you, Margaret. The gates of heaven await you').

[97] 'Patres et matres et sorores et fratres, omnes uos adiuro per nomen magnum regis omnium saeculorum, memoriam meam facite' (O, ch. 21; P is deficient here): 'Fathers and mothers and sisters and brothers, I adjure you through the great name of the king of all ages, make recollection of me.'

[98] O, ch. 21: 'sinner'.

[99] εἰ δὲ καὶ ἐλαχίστη εἰμί (Us, 139v, line 11): 'even if I am the worst'.

[100] P, ch. 19.   [101] P, ch. 20: 'By my very self I swear.'

[102] O, ch. 21 (quoted above, n. 97).

office he will not have his place with her in paradise.[103] Upon her death, by one clean sword blow, the efficacy of her famous prayer is immediately demonstrated in the healing of the sick and handicapped who touch her body.[104] The head[105] itself is assumed into heaven by an angelic choir singing the *Sanctus*. The liturgical, devotional aspect of the *passio* is thus stressed again in this final action.

In its hymnal celebration of the passion of St Margaret the Mombritius and pre-Mombritius version of the legend portrays an extension of the glory of the heavenly kingdom into the world. This is especially evident in *BHL* no. 5303 but it is reflected too in Casinensis. As Margaret goes to her death she is more and more transfigured from an earthly state to a heavenly and the narrative ends with praise for her extending from heaven to earth. The whole treatment given to the legend in this tradition centres on this aspect of the extension of heavenly glory into the world. Indeed the *passio*, with its increasingly ecstatic tone, is itself a reflection of this extension. The text envelops itself in the language of the liturgy and of the Bible and strives after a sublimity of expression which achieves its final completeness in the Hosannas sung by the angelic choir as Margaret is received into heaven. Through the medium of this *passio* the audience (the insistently public style of the piece makes one think in terms of a communal audience rather than an individual reader) participates in the heavenly glorification of Margaret's heroism.

In its celebration of the extension through Margaret of heavenly glory into the world there is less interest than in other saints' lives, and indeed than in other versions of the Margaret legend, in the idea of confrontation with the powers of the world. From the beginning Margaret is on a higher level than her adversaries and her progress is one of triumph rather than of testing. Only in the scene with the dragon, in which her opponent is supernatural, does she briefly lose her composure, and even this encounter redounds to her greater glory. Olibrius remains a subsidiary figure, necessary to Margaret's surging advance to glory, but pale and insubstantial in comparison with the heroine. There is no serious debate between the two, and Margaret, in overcoming the world, is quite unperturbed by Olibrius's physical threats.

---

[103] O, ch. 22. In some texts of *BHL* no. 5303 Malchus's prayer that his killing of Margaret be not counted against him is transferred to Margaret. These include N, as well as London, BL, Add. 34633 and BL, Harley 2801.

[104] O, ch. 23.   [105] On this detail, see above, p. 14.

The humanity of the heroine is firmly de-emphasized. As noted above, Margaret appears to stand outside the experience of her own martyrdom, speaking always with composure and from a communal rather than a personal point of view and uniting in her utterances the planes of heaven and earth. She orchestrates the audience's praise for God and leads the prayer which the text as a whole represents. Human responses to her suffering, like those of the crowd or the executioner, are rebuked and transcended. The audience is constantly prevented from sympathizing with Margaret at a human level and can only admire. She herself scarcely recognizes her own humanity, subordinating the individual to the public persona.

This *passio* gives its audience a picture of splendour and glory beyond worldly experience. It presents a triumphal celebration in which the divine order of heaven is seamlessly united with that of earth. The *passio* itself becomes a figure of this divine order, giving exultant confirmation of spiritual truth and imitating in its language the splendour of heavenly praise. Margaret, as perfected saint, exemplifies pre-eminently the embracing of the heavenly world. God's community rejoices at Margaret's translation to this heavenly world and participates in universal praise of the saint and of the God who has brought her to glory. Even the defeated devils have to acknowledge the divine power manifested in Margaret's victory: 'Vnus Deus fortis magnus beatae Margaritae.'[106]

---

[106] O, ch. 22; Cas, p. 233: 'There is one powerful God, the great God of the blessed Margaret.'

4

The legend of St Margaret in Anglo-Saxon England

Literary evidence for interest in St Margaret in the Anglo-Saxon world begins in the mid- to late ninth century with the *Old English Martyrology* (in which, however, the saint is still called Marina). A copy of the Latin Mombritius version, *BHL* no. 5303, appears in a tenth-century English manuscript (Paris, BN, lat. 5574).[1] In the early eleventh century an Old English life of St Margaret was included in the large collection of saints' lives in London, BL, Cotton Otho B. x.[2] The text of this version was destroyed in the Cotton fire, however, and is known only from the *incipit* and *explicit* transcribed by Wanley.[3] From the middle of the eleventh century dates the Old English life of St Margaret preserved in Cotton Tiberius A. iii. The text in this manuscript was being closely revised and altered in the second half of the century.[4] Another copy of *BHL* no. 5303, written originally in north-eastern France in the ninth century (Saint-Omer, Bibl. mun., 202), was in England in the second half of the eleventh century.[5] The final Old English version appears in an early twelfth-century manuscript, Cambridge, Corpus Christi College 303. This manuscript also contains hagiographical texts by Ælfric, but in addition it has lives of St Giles and St Nicholas, saints whose cults appear to have been introduced

---

[1] The text is edited below, pp. 191–223 (Appendix 2).
[2] Cotton Otho B. x. contained lives mostly by Ælfric. The non-Ælfrician ones are the lives of SS Euphrosyne, Christopher, Mary of Egypt, the Seven Sleepers and Margaret.
[3] See below, pp. 94–5.
[4] See below, pp. 85–92.
[5] In the Latin text edited below (Appendix 2), Saint-Omer 202 is used to supply a major deficiency in the base manuscript: see below, p. 192.

into England by the Normans.[6] The present chapter concentrates particularly on the extant Old English versions of the legend.

THE TIBERIUS VERSION AND ITS LATIN SOURCE

The original Anglo-Saxon author[7] of the Cotton Tiberius A. iii version of
the legend of St Margaret followed a no-longer extant Latin variant of the
Mombritius and pre-Mombritius tradition discussed above in chs. 2 and 3.
Close examination of the Old English and relevant analogues shows that
this variant was not a copy of the Mombritius version (*BHL* no. 5303). It
either belonged to the Casinensis strand of the Latin transmission (*BHL* no.
5304) or, more likely, was a form of the common original from which both
the Mombritius and Casinensis versions derive. The Casinensis version
itself, the only extant witness to the *BHL* no. 5304 recension, cannot be
taken as an exact representation of the source of the Old English, since it
omits a significant amount of material taken over into the Old English and
displays scribal corruptions not reflected in the Old English. Casinensis,
however, presents a whole series of distinctive features clearly reflected in
our vernacular version. There is no corresponding pattern of agreement
between the Old English and distinctive readings in the Mombritius
version.[8]

In an earlier chapter we have touched on a striking agreement between
the Tiberius and Casinensis versions as against the Mombritius version. In
Tiberius, after the execution of the saint her head is borne to the heavens by
a troop of angels: 'Ða coman twelf englas and genaman hire heafod on hira

---

[6] See Schipper, 'The Normans and the Old English Lives of Saint Giles and Saint
Nicholas', p. 97.

[7] Ways in which the translation of the original Old English author of this version is
significantly modified by later revisers are discussed below, pp. 87–8.

[8] The inclusion of the reference to the Passion in the first sentence of Tib presents the only
unaccountable departure from Cas. It is not known when the reference to the Passion was
first added to the Latin *passio* text, but this reference appears not to have been present in
the pre-Mombritius tradition, at least as reflected in Cas. The Tib reading may indicate
the influence of the 'standard' *incipit*, even though the translation is based on a
'non-standard' Latin text. As mentioned above (p. 17, n. 48), the Old English Cotton
Otho version presents a curious inversion of this problem: it does not have the reference to
the Passion in its translation, but the Old English translation is preceded by a quotation
of the *incipit* of the Latin, which *does* have the reference to the Passion.

fædmum.'⁹ As mentioned earlier,¹⁰ texts of *BHL* no. 5303 are divided as to whether it is Margaret's body or her soul which is borne aloft. None of them mentions her head. Casinensis agrees with the Old English, however, the only difference being that it does not give the number of angels: 'Et uenerunt angeli et tulerunt capud martyris . . .'¹¹ The Old English evidently followed a Casinensis-type reading, but one which still preserved the number 'twelve', a detail going back to the original Greek.¹² The reference to the head (but not to the number of angels) is also present in the *Old English Martyrology* version: 'Ond ða ne wæs hire heafad no on eorðan gemeted, ac is wen þæt englas mid him hit læddan to Godes neorxna-wonge.'¹³ The *Martyrology* statement is more tentative – 'is wen þæt' – but it must derive from a source which agreed with that of the Tiberius version in having this detail, which goes back ultimately to the Greek tradition.¹⁴

Among distinctive agreements between Tiberius and Casinensis, the following decisive examples should be noted:

(i) In its account of the arrest of Margaret, Tiberius relates that Olibrius saw the saint sitting 'be þam wege'.¹⁵ This corresponds to Casinensis 'iuxta uiam'.¹⁶ Texts of *BHL* no. 5303 have 'in propinquo'¹⁷ or omit reference to the saint's situation.¹⁸

(ii) The clause, in Margaret's first prayer, 'Ac gesend me to minra swiþran healfe and to þære winstran sibbe englas',¹⁹ reflects three distinctive features in Casinensis: the mention of right and left, 'a dextera et sinistra'; the reference to angels in the plural, 'angelos'; and

---

⁹ Tib, ch. 23: 'Then twelve angels came and took her head in their embrace.'
¹⁰ See above, p. 14.
¹¹ Cas, p. 233: 'And angels came and carried the head of the martyr.'
¹² Cf. Us, 140v, line 38–141r, line 2.
¹³ *Das altenglische Martyrologium* I, 144, lines 11–14 (text also given below, pp. 52–3): 'And then her head was not met with on earth, but it is believed that angels brought it with them to God's paradise' (trans. Herzfeld, *An Old English Martyrology*, p. 117).
¹⁴ This detail is also reflected in the Turin version. Vr (as quoted above, p. 13, n. 29) is unique among texts of this version in having *animam* instead of *caput*.
¹⁵ Tib, ch. 5: 'by the road'.   ¹⁶ Cas, p. 225: 'by the road'.
¹⁷ As, line 45: 'nearby'.
¹⁸ P, ch. 5; M, p. 190, line 43.
¹⁹ Tib, ch. 5: 'But send to my right side and to my left angels of peace.'

the reference to these angels as angels of peace, 'angelos pacis'.[20] *BHL* no. 5303 has merely 'Sed transmitte mihi angelum tuum gubernatorem.'[21]

(iii) The reference to Olibrius in one of Margaret's speeches as an insatiable dragon[22] is taken from the Latin reading reflected in Casinensis, 'insatiabilis draco',[23] not from the 'insatiabilis leo' of *BHL* no. 5303.[24]

(iv) The Tiberius phrase 'ætforan þin gesihþe' a few lines later[25] has no equivalent in *BHL* no. 5303[26] but corresponds to Casinensis 'in tuo conspectu'.[27]

(v) The Old English agrees with Casinensis in having a final speech by the angels, in addition to their singing of the *Sanctus*.[28] As the saint's head is carried to the heavens the angels cry out, 'Eadig eart þu . . .'[29] This passage is paralleled in the Casinensis version, which reads, 'Beata es tu, et locum almifici inuenisti. Ecce, requiesce cum iustis uirginibus, et letantur iusti de magno triunpho martirii tui, etiam et corpus tuum ueniet ad Deum.'[30] The Old English is hardly an exact translation of this highly corrupt passage, but clear similarities can be observed between the speeches, and there is nothing corresponding in other versions.

These and other agreements demonstrate the importance of Casinensis to the study of the source of Tiberius. There is also, however, a number of distinctive features of Tiberius which are *not* found in Casinensis. But these do not militate against the argument in favour of the Old English writer's employment of a Casinensis-like source. For one thing, these features are not found in *BHL* no. 5303 either, but more importantly they occur mostly in parts of the Old English corresponding to passages excised in the

---

[20] 'Sed transmitte mihi a dextra et sinistra angelos gubernatores, angelos pacis' (Cas, p. 226).

[21] P, ch. 5 has *sanctum doctorem* instead of *gubernatorem* (supplied here from M): 'But send me your angel as a guide.'

[22] Tib, ch. 10.   [23] Cas, p. 228.   [24] P, ch. 10 (M 'irrationabilis leo').

[25] Tib, ch. 10: 'before your sight'.   [26] Cf. P, ch. 10.

[27] Cas, p. 228: 'in your sight'.

[28] Tib, ch. 23.   [29] Tib, *ibid.*: 'Blessed are you'.

[30] Cas, pp. 233–4: 'Blessed are you, and you have found the place of the beneficent one. Behold, repose with the just virgins, and the just are joyful concerning the great triumph of your martyrdom, and also your body will come to God.'

Casinensis copy of the Latin. They would have been present in the fuller version of the Latin from which Casinensis itself derives.

Casinensis has nothing, for example, of the material in chs. 14 and 15 of the Tiberius version. It is notable that in the scene between Margaret and the black demon, with which these chapters deal, Margaret's physical assault on the demon is more violent in the Old English than in any of the Latin versions of this scene. Not only does she grab him by the hair and throw him to the ground – 'Seo halga Margareta gegrap þane deofol þa be þæm locce and hine on eorþan awearp'[31] – but she also strikes out his right eye in the Old English and breaks his bones: 'his swyþran ege ut astang and ealle his ban heo tobrysde.'[32] Although texts of *BHL* no. 5303 do not have this detail they do have a reference by the demon later in the scene to the fact that Margaret has put out his eye and broken his strength: 'Tu autem oculum meum eiecisti, uirtutem meum confregisti.'[33] This later reference is also present in the Old English (but absent in Casinensis, since ch. 15 is excluded from the latter version).[34] Evidently, the Old English version preserves a fuller account of Margaret's assault on the demon, which has disappeared from texts of the Latin, though a relic of it remains in the later reference by the demon.

As in *BHL* no. 5303, a heavenly dove appears to Margaret immediately after this in Tiberius and addresses her in the presence of the demon. In the Old English, but not in the Latin, the dove tells Margaret that she will be given her heavenly reward with Abraham and Isaac and Jacob: 'forþon hit biþ þe geseald mid Abraham and mid Isaac and Iacob.'[35] This statement goes back to the source of the Old English for though it does not appear in known texts of the Mombritius and pre-Mombritius tradition there is an equivalent passage in the Greek version edited by Usener: οὕτως ἀναπαύσῃ εἰς τοὺς κόλπους Ἀβραὰμ καὶ Ἰσαὰκ καὶ Ἰακώβ.[36] This reference to the patriarchs is also reflected in the Latin Turin version.[37]

---

[31] Tib, ch. 14; cf. *BHL* no. 5303, 'Tunc sancta Margareta uirgo conprehendit daemonem per capillos, delisit eum in terram' (P, ch. 10).

[32] Tib, *ibid.*: 'and she put out his right eye and shattered all his bones.'

[33] P, ch. 15: 'You, however, have put out my eye and broken my strength.'

[34] Cf. 'Ac þu min ege utastunge and ealle mine ban tobrisdest' (Tib, ch. 15).

[35] Tib, ch. 15: 'for this reason it will be granted to you with Abraham and with Isaac and Jacob.'

[36] Us, 136r, lines 37–8: 'thus you may repose in the bosom of Abraham and Isaac and Jacob.' Cf. Luke XIII.28.

[37] 'Tu eris cum patribus requiescens' (Vr, 169r).

45

Also in ch. 15 (and therefore omitted in Casinensis, since the latter has nothing corresponding to the material in chs. 14 and 15), the speech of the dove prompts Margaret in the Old English to utter a fervent prayer in praise of Christ. The prayer is referred to in *BHL* no. 5303 – 'Tunc gratias agens Deo'[38] – but Margaret's actual words are not given. In the Old English the prayer is as follows: 'Wuldor þe sy, Crist, þu þe ane dest mænig wuldor. Ic þe wuldrige and herige, forþon þu eart halig and micel on eallum þingum, þu þe gemedomast gecyþan þinre þeowen þæt þu eart ane hiht ealra gelifiendra on þe.'[39] The fervent tone of this speech is entirely consistent with that of Margaret's other prayers both in the Old English and in the Latin. The prayer does not read like an addition by the translator but gives the impression of deriving directly from the lost Latin source. Once more this impression is borne out by comparison of the Greek version edited by Usener. The Greek has a passage closely corresponding to the Old English,[40] except that, as in other speeches, the Old English presents the prayer in a much abbreviated form. The Old English preserves the imagery seen in the Greek, including that of Margaret as the δούλη ('servant') – *þeowen* – of the Lord.[41] Among Latin versions of the legend only the Turin version has a comparable passage (though it has nothing corresponding to the *þeowen* of Tiberius).[42]

Most Latin analogues also lack the second speech made by the heavenly dove in this passage. In the Old English, the dove addresses Margaret again: 'Margareta, axie þone þe þu hæfst under þinum fotum be his dædum and he cyþ þe ealle his weorc, and mid þy þe þu hine hæfst oferswiþd, þu cymst to me.'[43] Thus in the Old English, Margaret's further questioning of the demon is not her own idea, as it appears to be in most forms of the Latin (contributing to the startling sense of power and assurance associated with Margaret particularly in *BHL* no. 5303). Instead, in interrogating the

---

[38] P, ch. 15: 'Then giving thanks to God'.

[39] Tib, ch. 15: 'Glory be to you, Christ, who alone bring about many a glorious thing. I glorify and praise you because you are holy and great in all things, you who condescend to reveal to your servant that you are the one hope of all who believe in you.'

[40] Us, 136v, lines 2–9.   [41] Us, 136v, line 3.

[42] The corresponding speech in the Turin version begins, 'Gloria tibi, Domine Iesu Christe, quia manifestasti mihi teipsum, qui apparuisti mihi in certamine meo' (Vr, 169r).

[43] Tib, ch. 15: 'Margaret, ask him whom you have under your feet about his deeds and he will reveal to you all his works, and when you have defeated him you will come to me.'

demon, the saint is carrying out the behest of the Lord. This speech of the dove has been faithfully taken by the Old English writer from the Latin source. Although it does not occur in known variants of the Mombritius and pre-Mombritius traditions, the speech is present, in a form close to that of the Old English, in Usener's Greek version[44] and in the Latin Turin version.[45]

It is clear, then, that the 'standard' text in *BHL* no. 5303 diverges from that followed by the Old English translator in these sections. Casinensis is deficient here and so presents only negative evidence about source, but it is evident that the Old English translator could not have been following *BHL* no. 5303 at this point. *BHL* no. 5303 omits two whole speeches in this sequence and part of a third, all of which survive in the Old English Tiberius version. In the same scene we have observed that the Old English also preserves the account of the putting out of the demon's eye and the breaking of his bones, which is represented in the Mombritius version only by the relic of the demon's later speech.[46]

The overall effect of the treatment in the Old English of Margaret's encounter with the demon is to reduce its prominence in the narrative as a whole. The demon has one fewer speech in the Old English than in *BHL* no. 5303 (four as against five) and his speeches are much shorter than in the latter version. Less than half the number of words are allocated to the speeches of the demon in the Old English as compared to *BHL* no. 5303. The extent to which the prominence of this encounter is reduced in the Old English is to a degree masked by the fact that the translator was working in the first place from a version of the Latin which gave a fuller account of part of the scene than is found in the known texts of the Latin. But even with the inclusion of the material omitted in *BHL* no. 5303 the Old English allows Margaret's conflict with the demon a less central place than it has in the 'standard' *BHL* no. 5303 text, while Margaret herself appears less powerful and triumphal in the Old English.

The account in the Tiberius version of Margaret's immersion in the vessel of water on the second day of her torture has two small details unparalleled in most analogues. The vessel is described as made of lead – 'leaden'[47] – and it is also said that the water is hot – 'and dyde hit ælen

---

[44] Us, 137r, lines 2–6.   [45] Vr, 169v.
[46] P, ch. 15 (quoted above, p. 45, and n. 33).
[47] Tib, ch. 18.

swyþe hat.'[48] There is evidence that at least one of these details derives from the particular source of the Old English: no known versions of the legend specify that the vessel was made of lead, but the detail that the water was boiling is mentioned in the Old English CCCC 303 version,[49] in the Old French version 'B'[50] and in the Middle English *Seinte Margarete þat Holi Maide.*[51] It is notable that other versions of the legend insist that the water was cold: *BHL* no. 5305 indeed develops an elaborate contrast between the heat of Margaret's previous torture and the cold of the water in which she is immersed;[52] Vincent of Beauvais also speaks of 'aqua frigida'.[53]

A third discrepancy with existing copies of the Mombritius and pre-Mombritius version in this passage certainly does go back to the source. According to the Old English, fifteen thousand men plus an unnamed number of women and children were converted to Christianity after Margaret's miraculous emergence from the vessel of water.[54] The corresponding figure in *BHL* no. 5303 is 'five thousand',[55] while *BHL* no. 5304, the Casinensis version, has 'eighty-five'.[56] Clearly, scribal corruption has taken place in the transmission of the figure. The error has occurred, however, in the transmission of the Latin rather than the Old English, for the Old English figure is confirmed by the Greek version edited by Usener[57] and also by Surius.[58]

Another significant discrepancy between the Old English and most Latin versions comes in the speech which the heavenly dove makes in response to Margaret's famous prayer of intercession on behalf of those who venerate her. This occurs in ch. 20 of the *passio*, one of the sections omitted

---

[48] Tib, *ibid.*: 'and ordered [the water] to be made very hot'.

[49] Cf. 'þone weallende cetel' (CCCC, ch. 18).

[50] Cf. 'un grant vaissel plain de aigue boillant' (*Die alt- und mittelfranzösischen Prosafassungen der Margaretenlegende*, ed. Orywall, p. 132, lines 319–20).

[51] Cf. 'He let hete water oð seoþinge, ant þo hit boillede faste' (*Seinte Marherete þe Meiden ant Martyr in Old English*, ed. Cockayne, p. 31, line 247).

[52] 'Ut scilicet a nimio calore transeat ad nimium frigus et commutacio tormentorum pena sit grauior' (*Die alt- und mittelfranzösischen Prosafassungen der Margaretenlegende*, ed. Orywall, p. 186, lines 136–8).

[53] *Speculi Maiores*, ed. Benedictines of Douai, IV, Book XIII, ch. 28 (p. 515, col. i): 'cold water'.

[54] Tib, ch. 18.

[55] P, ch. 18 (with some variation among the manuscript readings).

[56] Cas, p. 232.   [57] Us, 139r, line 28.   [58] Surius, *Vitae sanctorum*, p. 250.

entirely by Casinensis. In the Old English the speech of the dove, granting Margaret's supplication, is easily the longest in the whole text: only Margaret's prayer, which it answers, comes anywhere near in length. In *BHL* no. 5303 Margaret's prayer is longer than the response by the dove, and one of the speeches by the black demon[59] is much longer than either. In the Old English the speech of the dove begins with the biblical allusion, 'eadig wæs se innoþ se þe þe gebær.'[60] At the corresponding point most copies of *BHL* no. 5303 have a different biblical allusion, 'Beata es inter mulieres.'[61] The 'standard' text in *BHL* no. 5303 compares Margaret directly with the Virgin Mary, whereas in the Old English the comparison is (indirectly) with Christ. The only Latin text which offers a direct parallel is the variant of *BHL* no. 5303 printed in Mombritius's *Sanctuarium*, which at this point has the distinctive reading, 'Beatus est namque uenter mulieris.'[62] The Greek analogue, which is organized differently here, is of no help on this occasion.[63] Evidently, however, the source of the Old English differed from the normal text of *BHL* no. 5303 at this point, following instead the unusual (but probably authentic) *Sanctuarium* reading.

Other aspects too of this speech in the Tiberius version are not reflected in the known copies of the Latin. In the Old English God appoints three hundred angels to receive the prayers of those who call upon the Lord in the name of Margaret: 'God gesættet on þinum cyrcan þreo hund engla to þon þæt hi onfoþ ælc þæra manna bena þe to Drihten clypaþ on þinum naman.'[64] The reading is partly confirmed by Usener's Greek: θήσω ανα έκκλησίαν εκάστην άγγέλους, οΐ τινες διακονήσουσιν αὐτοῖς, οἵ . . .[65] The number three hundred does not appear in the Greek but a variant noted by Usener has έκατὸν ('hundred') instead of έκάστην ('each (church)').

The Old English then goes on to say, anticipating the later narrative, that angels will come and take Margaret's head to heaven and that her body will remain honoured among men, so that anyone touching it will be

---

[59] P, ch. 15.
[60] Tib, ch. 20: 'Blessed was the womb that bore you' (cf. Luke XI.27).
[61] P, ch. 20: 'Blessed are you among women' (cf. Luke I.28 and 42).
[62] M, p. 195, line 17: 'For blessed is the womb of woman.'
[63] Cf. Us, 140v, lines 5–26.
[64] Tib, ch. 20: 'God will set in your church three hundred angels so that they will receive all of the prayers of those who call upon the Lord in your name.'
[65] Us, 140v, lines 6–7: 'I shall appoint to each church angels who will minister to those who . . .'

healed from whatever infirmity he has: 'Nu get ic cyþe þe þæt englas cumaþ
ongean þe and neamaþ þin heafod and lædaþ hit on neorxnawonge; and þin
lichama biþ wurþful mid mannum, þæt swa hwa swa hrineþ þine reliquias,
of þære tide fram swa hwylcre untrumnesse swa he hæfþ he biþ gehæld.'[66]
This is not exactly paralleled in the Greek but there is a reference in the
corresponding speech there to the angels taking away the saint's head after
her martyrdom: προστάξω τοῖς ἀγγέλοις μου ἀποκρύψαι αὐτήν.[67]

The closing part of this speech of the dove in the Old English contains
elements which occur in no other known version. In the Old English the
dove declares (in a somewhat clumsily expressed statement, excised by a
later corrector) that no one in heaven has met more with the mother of the
Creator of all things except three women: 'nænig on neorxnawonge mare
gemetod mid meder ealra Gescippendes nimþe þreo fæmnan.'[68] The end of
the speech identifies the two other holy women as Thecla and Susanna,
thereby reinforcing the references to these women in the prologue of the
Old English.[69] The speech concludes with an invitation to Margaret, a
lamb of God, to come to her Lord: 'Cum nu, Godes lamb, ic þin anbide.'[70]
None of this appears in the Latin or Greek versions (as noted above, the
whole of ch. 20 is omitted in Casinensis).

We have already noticed the agreement of the Old English with the
Greek in declaring that twelve angels bore the head of the saint to heaven.
The Old English also says at this point that a thousand angels came down
and blessed Margaret's body: 'þider coman þa þusend engla ofer þære halgan
Margaretan lichaman and gebletsodon hine.'[71] Casinensis is abbreviated at
this point but has 'et omnes angeli congratulabantur ei'.[72] The figure of a
thousand angels is also mentioned in the Middle English *Meidan Maregrete*.[73] The Greek mentions this host of angels without giving a number:

[66] Tib, ch. 20: 'I further reveal to you now that angels will come to you and take your head
and bear it to paradise; and your body will be honoured among men, so that whoever
touches your relics will be healed from that moment on of whatever infirmity he has.'
[67] Us, 140v, lines 16–17: 'I shall command my angels to conceal it.'
[68] Tib, ch. 20: on this textually problematic passage, see below Commentary on Tib,
pp. 146–7, n. 59.
[69] Tib, chs. 1 and 2.   [70] Tib, ch. 20: 'Come now, lamb of God, I await you.'
[71] Tib, ch. 22: 'Then a thousand angels came over the body of the blessed Margaret and
blessed it.'
[72] Cas, p. 233: 'and all the angels rejoiced together at it.'
[73] *Altenglische Legenden. Neue Folge*, ed. Horstmann, p. 497, line 298 (also ed. Cockayne,
Seinte Marharete þe Meidan ant Martyr in Old English, p. 43, line 76).

the Lord flies from the heavens in the midst of his company of holy angels –
ἐλθὼν ὁ κύριος ἀπὸ τοῦ οὐρανοῦ ἱπτάμενος μετὰ τῶν ἁγίων ἀγγέλων αὐτοῦ
κύκλῳ.[74] It is notable that the number a thousand, like other 'non-
standard' *BHL* no. 5303 features in the present passage, is excised in the
revised form of the Tiberius text.[75]

TIBERIUS AND THE *OLD ENGLISH MARTYROLOGY*

The frequent close correspondence between the Tiberius version and
Usener's Greek is among the most notable features to have emerged from
our analysis of the Old English so far. There is also, however, an important
series of distinctive agreements, which we have not as yet stressed in our
discussion, between Tiberius and the summary of the legend which appears
in the *Old English Martyrology*. These agreements can be seen to provide
further evidence concerning the source of our Old English text.

Only one entry in the *Old English Martyrology* is longer than that for St
Marina. The entry for the Ascension has fifty-three lines (in Kotzor's
edition) to Marina's fifty, but hers is the longest account of a saint. Only St
Christopher, with forty-five lines, is comparable, and most accounts of
saints are very much shorter indeed. But although it is expansive by the
standards of the *Martyrology*, the account of St Marina is a truncated one
compared to those of the other versions of her legend discussed in this
study. This makes it difficult for us to make definitive statements about its
source. The correspondence between the *Martyrology* and Tiberius versions,
however, indicate that the sources used for the two vernacular works must
have been in some respects very similar.

It will facilitate comparison to quote in full the St Marina entry from the
Martyrology:[76]

---

[74] Us, 140v, lines 36–8: 'The Lord, coming from heaven, flying with his holy angels in a
circle.'
[75] On this see below Commentary on Tib, n. 57.
[76] *Das altenglishe Martyrologium*, ed. Kotzor II, 141–4: 'On the same day is the
commemoration of the noble virgin St Marina. She was born in the town of Antioch,
and her father was high-priest of the pagans. In her childhood she was soon entrusted to
a Christian woman for her education, and from her she learned to believe in God with
chastity. Then it happened that when she was fifteen years old, she fed her
foster-mother's sheep and watched them together with other girls of the same age.
When the prefect Olybrius passed on his way to the town of Antioch, he saw the girl

On ðone ilcan dæg bið þære miclan fæmnan gemynd Sancta Marinan; seo wæs acenned on Antiochia ðære ceastre, ond hire fæder wæs hæþenra monna heahfæder. Ond heo wæs sona on hire cild [p. 142] hade befæsted Cristenum wife to fedanne, ond æt þære heo geleornode þæt heo on clænnesse God gelefde. Ða gelomp þæt heo wæs fiftene geara, ða læswede heo hire festermodor sceapum ond heold mid oþrum mægdenum hire efnealdum. Þa ferde ðær Olibrius se gerefa to Antiochia ceastre; ða geseah he Marinan þæt mægden. Þa het he his þegnas hi geniman ond him togelæ-dan, ond cwæð to hire: 'Ic þe onfo me to wife, ond þe bið ðonne well ofer eall oþer wif.' Ða cwæð Marina: 'Ic þe þonne selle minne lichoman to deaðe, þæt ic on heofonum reste hæbbe mid þæm halgum fæmnum.' Ða het se gerefa hi swingan þæt þæt blod fleow of hire þæm merwan lichoman swa wæter of æspringe, ond het mid monige wite hi þreagan from Cristes geleafan; ond he mid nænge ðara ne mihte hire geþoht [p. 143] oncierran. Ða bead he þæt hi mon lædde to þære beheafdunga. Ða gebæd heo hi to Drihtne ond cwæð: 'Drihten, ic þe bidde þæt swa hwelc mon swa cierecean getimbre on minum naman, oþþe swa hwelc mon swa condella onbærne on cirecean of his gestreonum on minum noman, syn þæs monnes synna adilgade. Ond gif hwilc mon sie on ondrystlecum wisum, ond he sy mines naman gemyndig – Drihten, gefriða þu hine from þæm brogan. Ond gif hwilc mon his synne geondette on minum naman – Drihten, forgif þu him þa. Ond on swa hwelcre

Marina. Then he ordered his soldiers to seize her and lead her before him and said to her: "I shall take thee for my wife, and thou wilt fare better than all the other women." Marina answered: "Then I shall deliver up to you my body to kill it, that I may have rest in heaven with the holy women." The prefect ordered her to be flogged that the blood flowed from her tender body like water from a fountain, and commanded that by many tortures she be forced to renounce the belief in Christ; but by none of these tortures was he able to make her change her mind. When he ordered her to be led to her execution, she prayed to God and said: "O Lord, I beseech thee, which man soever build a church in honour of my name, or which man soever light a candle in church from his earnings in my name, may the sins of this man be blotted out; and if any man be in dreadful straits and he remember my name, O Lord, protect him from his terror; and if any man confess his sins in my name, O Lord, forgive him them; and wherever my martyrdom be described and it be celebrated, from this place remove thou, O Lord, blindness, lameness, dumbness and devil-sickness, but there may come to this place happiness, peace and true love." Then a voice from heaven answered her: "Thy prayers are heard in God's presence, and wherever thy martyrdom is described, no evil will ever appear, but there will be joy and bliss; and which man soever prays to God with tears and with his whole heart in thy name, he will be freed from his sins." Then St Marina was beheaded for Christ's sake, and the executioner [at once] killed himself with the same sword. And then her head was not met with on earth, but it is believed that angels brought it with them to God's paradise. Otherwise the body is buried in the town of Antioch' (trans. Herzfeld, *An Old English Martyrology*, pp. 115–17).

stowe swa min þrowung awriten sy, ond man þa mærsige – afyr þu, Drihten, from þære stowe blindnesse, ond helto, ond dumbnesse [p. 144] ond deofolseocnesse; ah cume on þa stowe blis ond sib ond soðlufu.' Þa ondswarode [hyre] stefn of heofonum: 'Þine bene syndon gehered beforan Godes gesihðe, ond swa hwær swa þin þrowung bið awriten, þonne ne bið þær næfre yfel acenned, ah þær bið gefea ond blis. Ond swa hwelc mon swa of ealre heortan mid tearum him to Gode gebideð on ðinum noman, he bið fram his synnum gefreod.' Þa wæs Sancta Marina for Criste beheafdad; ond se cwellere sona hine selfne ofslog mid ðy ilcan sweorde. Ond ða ne wæs hire heafad no on eorðan gemeted, ac is wen þæt englas mid him hit læddan to Godes neorxnawonge; se lichoma elles is geseted on Antiochia ceastre.

J. E. Cross[77] has shown that the account of St Marina in the *Martyrology* follows a variant of the Latin broadly similar to *BHL* no. 5303, the Mombritius version. By means of a meticulous analysis of the Old English text, Cross has been able to identify distinctive features of the particular source used by the Anglo-Saxon writer. The variant of the Latin cannot have been a 'standard' text of *BHL* no. 5303 but must have contained features unparalleled in most Latin texts. We have already noted one such feature: the *Old English Martyrology* agrees with Tiberius and Casinensis but disagrees with copies of *BHL* no. 5303 in speaking of the saint's head, rather than her body or her soul, being borne to heaven by angels.[78]

Three further interesting correspondences between Tiberius and the *Martyrology* are noted by Cross.[79] They occur in the sequence in which Margaret utters her prayer of intercession on behalf of those who venerate her and receives the reply of the heavenly voice. This is one of the few parts of the legend which the *Old English Martyrology* gives in enough detail to allow significant comparison:

(i) In Margaret's prayer of intercession she asks in Tiberius that where the book of her passion is kept there may be peace and love and the spirit of righteousness: 'sib and lufu and soþfæstnesse gast':[80] there is no equivalent to this at the corresponding point of *BHL* no. 5303[81] or in the slightly abbreviated version of the speech in *BHL* no. 5304.[82] The phrase 'pax caritatis et spiritus ueritatis' occurs in the divine reply to Margaret's prayer in texts of *BHL* no. 5303,[83] where Tiberius has 'sib

---

[77] Cross, 'St Marina'.   [78] See above, p. 43.   [79] Cross, 'St Marina'.
[80] Tib, ch. 19.
[81] Cf. P, ch. 19.   [82] Cf. Cas, p. 232.
[83] M, p. 195, lines 23–4: 'The peace of love and the spirit of truth.'

and lufu and soþfæstnesse and blis and gefean', [84] but there is no similar list in Margaret's own speech. In the *Old English Martyrology*, however, the phrase 'blis ond sib ond soðlufu'[85] occurs at the corresponding part of Marina's speech (in the divine reply the *Martyrology* has 'gefea ond blis'[86]).

(ii)   At the beginning of the speech by the heavenly voice Margaret is assured in Tiberius, 'swa hwæt swa þu bæde, eall hit biþ gehered ætforan Godes gesyhþe'.[87] The reference to the saint's prayers being heard in the sight of God is not paralleled in manuscripts of *BHL* no. 5303,[88] but there is a closely similar phrase in the *Martyrology*: 'Þine bene syndon gehered beforan Godes gesihðe.'[89] Casinensis provides us with no information here since it omits ch. 20 entirely.

(iii)   In this same speech God grants in Tiberius that he who calls upon Margaret 'of ealra heortan'[90] will be cleansed of his sins. The same phrase 'of ealre heortan' appears in the *Old English Martyrology*[91] but there is no equivalent in known copies of *BHL* no. 5303,[92] and of course this whole passage is lacking in Casinensis.

The *Martyrology* version does not proceed evenly in the amount of detail it allows to different parts of the narrative. It concentrates particularly on Marina's prayer of intercession on behalf of those who venerate her and on the divine reply she receives having made this prayer. This sequence takes up almost half of the text. It is significant that most of the distinctive features isolated by Cross come from this least condensed part of the account. In contrast to the concentration on Marina's prayer is the complete omission in the *Martyrology* of the episode of the dragon and the black demon, the episode which provides the most famous scene in the legend as a whole. Other hagiographical writers express disquiet con-

---

[84]   Tib, ch. 20.
[85]   *Das altenglische Martyrologium*, ed. Kotzor I, 144, lines 1–2: 'happiness, peace and true love'.
[86]   *Das altenglische Martyrologium*, ed. Kotzor I, 144, line 6: 'joy and bliss'.
[87]   Tib, ch. 20: 'whatever you have asked for shall all be heard in the sight of God.'
[88]   Cf. P, ch. 20.
[89]   *Das altenglische Martyrologium*, ed. Kotzor I, 144, lines 3–4: 'Thy prayers are heard in God's presence.'
[90]   Tib, ch. 20: 'wholeheartedly'.
[91]   *Das altenglische Martyrologium*, ed. Kotzor I, 144, line 7.
[92]   Cf. P, ch. 20.

cerning this sensational episode but the *Martyrology* is surely unique among medieval versions of the legend in omitting it altogether. The Anglo-Saxon writer is evidently interested in tailoring the account to suit particular devotional needs, which do not include a cultivation of sensational elements. All reference is excluded to the heavenly dove which in the analogues periodically appears to provide divine approval for the saint. Even the account of the receiving of Marina's head into heaven, with which the narrative ends, is related in a tentative manner: 'is wen þæt englas mid him hit læddan to Godes neorxnawonge.'[93]

Cross also points out one striking agreement between the *Martyrology* version and the copy of *BHL* no. 5303 preserved in the ninth-century Karlsruhe manuscript, Augiensis perg. 32.[94] The *Martyrology* relates that immediately after beheading her Marina's executioner killed himself with the same sword as he used to put the saint to death: 'se cwellere sona hine selfne ofslog mid ðy ilcan sweorde.'[95] Among known copies of *BHL* no. 5303 this detail is found only in the Augiensis manuscript: 'Ipse uero cum gladio in quo percutiebat beatam uirginem semetipsum perfodiens cecidit ad dexteram partem beatae Margaretae.'[96] Other manuscripts of *BHL* no. 5303 have the executioner falling by the right side of Margaret[97] but do not mention that he killed himself with his sword. According to the Middle English *Seinte Margarete Pat Holi Maide*, the executioner fell by the right side of Margaret and died with her: 'In hir riht half he ful adoun ant deide wiþ hir also.'[98]

Among known witnesses to the Mombritius and pre-Mombritius tradition this detail of the executioner killing himself with his own sword

---

[93] *Das altenglische Martyrologium*, ed. Kotzor I, 144, lines 12–14: 'it is believed that angels brought it with them to God's paradise.'

[94] Cross, 'St Marina'.

[95] *Das altenglische Martyrologium*, ed. Kotzor I, 144, lines 6–7: 'the executioner at once killed himself with the same sword.'

[96] Aug, 59v, col. i: 'He, however, piercing himself with the sword with which he struck the blessed virgin fell at the right side of the blessed Margaret.'

[97] Cf. P, ch. 22.

[98] *Seinte Margarete þat Holi Maide*, ed. Cockayne, *Seinte Marherete þe Meiden ant Martyr*, p. 33: 'On her right side he fell down and died with her also' (line 312). Note also the 'Caligula' version: 'Qui confestim ad dexteram partem beate Margarete corruit, et expirauit' (ed. Francis, 'A Hitherto Unprinted Version of the *Passio Sanctae Margaritae*', p. 103, lines 30–1).

occurs in only one other text (apart from Augiensis), the Old English Tiberius version: 'and hine sylfne mid his swurde ofastang and gefeol to þære eadegan fæmnan swyþran healfe.'[99] One other important analogue, however, which includes the detail of the executioner killing himself with his own sword, should be mentioned, the Greek version of the legend edited by Usener. This has the following account of the death of the executioner: οὕτως πάλιν εἰς ἑαυτὸν τὸ ξίφος ἀπηνέγκατο καὶ ἔπεσεν ἐξ ἀριστερῶν αὐτῆς.[100] Apart from having 'left' instead of 'right', this could hardly be closer to the Tiberius reading and clearly the *Martyrology* writer also must have worked from a similar Latin reading at this point. The Usener parallel shows that the Augiensis reading is not an aberrant innovation within the tradition of *BHL* no. 5303 but has been inherited from an earlier form of the *passio*. The highly abbreviated treatment of the execution in Casinensis renders this version unhelpful for comparison at this point.

The agreements between the two Old English texts, Tiberius and the *Martyrology*, suggest that their vernacular writers, working at different periods in Anglo-Saxon England, were using sources with similar distinctive readings. It appears then that there was a distinctive variant or textual tradition of the pre-Mombritius *passio* used in England over a long period. This tradition, with its significant contrasts with the 'standard' text of *BHL* no. 5303, is of particular interest in that it preserves elements in the *passio* going back to the Greek but represented rarely or not at all in known western texts. As we have seen, considerable light is thrown on the form of this non-extant textual tradition by the Casinensis version, but unfortunately the latter is deficient at key stages of the legend.

THE TREATMENT OF THE LEGEND IN THE TIBERIUS VERSION

Having established the nature of the source used by the Tiberius translator, we can see that this Old English version represents a reasonably faithful translation of its original. The generally evident closeness of the Old English writer's dependence on the source is such as to suggest that even

---

[99] Tib, ch. 22: 'and he pierced himself with his sword and fell on the right side of the holy maiden.'

[100] Us, 140v, lines 35–6: 'and so he brought the sword back against himself, and fell on her left side.'

when we come across apparently idiosyncratic readings in the Old English these are likely to derive from the source rather than being independent additions by the translator. The Old English writer is clearly uninterested in transforming the original in any ambitious way. This writer sets out to transmit the essential narrative and the spirit of the original, remaining faithful to the source-text, though abbreviating and simplifying aspects of it, particularly in direct discourse.

The translation technique evident in the Tiberius version may be illustrated by an examination of aspects of the treatment of the opening part of the Old English text. The very opening sentence in Tiberius, for example, faithfully follows the Latin seen in *BHL* no. 5303 and *BHL* no. 5304: the Old English begins, 'Æfter þære ðrowunge and þære æriste and þære wuldorfæstan upastignesse ures Drihtnes, Hælendes Cristes, to Godfæder Ealmihtigum, þa wæron swiþe manniga martyres þrowiende . . .'[101] This corresponds closely to the Latin: 'Post [passionem et] resurrectionem Domini nostri Iesu Christi et gloriosam ascensionem eius in caelum ad Patrem omnipotentem, in illius nomine multi martyres passi sunt . . .'[102]

In this sentence the Old English has only minor departures from the quoted Latin text[103] and these reflect a tendency towards abbreviation and simplification of the Latin which is apparent throughout the Tiberius version and indeed characteristic of much Old English hagiography generally.[104]

---

[101] Tib, ch. 1: 'After the Passion and the Resurrection and the glorious Ascension of Our Lord, the Saviour Christ, to God the Father Almighty, there were very many martyrs suffering . . .'

[102] The Latin text is quoted from Cas here and in the following footnotes, as this best represents the pre-Mombritius tradition reflected in Tib. Cas, p. 224 (with *passionem et* supplied from P): 'After the Passion and Resurrection of Our Lord Jesus Christ and his glorious Ascension into heaven to God the Father omnipotent, in his name many martyrs suffered . . .'

[103] The Old English lacks equivalents to the phrases *in caelum* and *in illius nomine*. The last clause in the Latin quotation develops into a measured triplet: 'multi martyres passi sunt et apostoli coronati sunt et innumerabiles sanctificati sunt', but the Old English does not broaden the picture in this way, having no reference to the apostles or the innumerable saints.

[104] On Ælfric's approach, see especially D. Bethurum, 'The Form of Ælfric's *Lives of Saints*', *Studies in Philology* 29 (1932), 515–33. On non-Ælfrician lives, see H.

The beginning of the narrative proper illustrates the same tendency on the part of the Old English writer. The opening words, 'Se eadiga Margareta wæs Ðeodosius dohter; se wæs þære hæþenre hehfæder. Deofolgeld he wurþode',[105] closely mirror the corresponding passage in the pre-Mombritius version: 'Erat Theodosii filia, qui erat gentilium patriarcha et idolis seruiebat.'[106] As this exposition proceeds, however, the Old English reduces the amount of information given about Margaret and her background. The precise distance from Antioch of the town where Margaret is brought up is not given;[107] there is no reference to Margaret's beauty[108] or to her fostermother's love for her Christianity.[109]

The Old English has one detail in this passage which does not appear in known texts of the Latin. It declares that Margaret was filled with the Holy Ghost and renewed through baptism: 'þurh fulwiht heo wæs geedniwod.'[110] The Latin has the reference to the Holy Ghost[111] but not to baptism. The reference to baptism could be the Old English writer's independent addition, fleshing out for the vernacular audience the presentation of Margaret's Christianity in the midst of paganism. On the other hand, as mentioned above, this passage as a whole seems to lean towards abbreviation rather than expansion in the Old English. It is likely therefore that the Old English writer has taken the reference to baptism from the source, a form of the pre-Mombritius tradition containing this detail not found in other texts of the *passio*. It is notable that the reference to baptism does appear in the epitome of Vincent of Beauvais: 'Adulta se sponte baptizari fecit.'[112]

The opening part of the narrative is briefer than the Latin texts in its treatment of Olibrius and his persecution of the Christians.[113] The theme

---

Magennis, 'Contrasting Features in the non-Ælfrician Lives in the Old English *Lives of Saints*', *Anglia* 104 (1986), 316–48.

[105] Tib, ch. 3: 'The blessed Margaret was the daughter of Theodosius; he was the patriarch of the heathens. He worshipped idols.'

[106] Cas, p. 225: 'she was the daughter of Theodosius, who was patriarch of the pagans and served idols' (cf. P, ch. 3).

[107] Cf. Cas, p. 225 (P, ch. 3).   [108] Cf. Cas, p. 225 (P, ch. 3).   [109] *Ibid.*

[110] Tib, ch. 3: 'she was renewed through baptism.'   [111] P, ch. 3.

[112] *Speculi Maiores*, ed. Benedictines of Douai, IV, Book XIII, ch. 27 (p. 514, col. ii): 'When grown up she willingly had herself baptized.'

[113] In contrast to the Latin, the initial references to Olibrius in the Old English do not mention the persecution and concentrate only on his desire for Margaret. Even in the

of persecution is implicit in the Old English, of course, and had been indicated earlier in the initial description of Margaret, where it was stated that Margaret knew about this persecution: 'Heo gehyrde martyra geflitu, forþon þe mænig blod wæs agoten on þam tidum on eorþan for ures Dryhtnes naman, Hælendes Cristes.'[114] This translates the Latin source[115] virtually verbatim. Olibrius himself soon becomes the familiar raging persecutor in the Old English: only a few lines later we hear of his anger on learning that Margaret is a Christian: 'Se gerefa wæs þa swiþe yrre.'[116] However, the Tiberius version's briefer treatment of his arrival in Antioch, of Margaret's fear when she hears that he has sent for her[117] and of the first interview between the two reduce the impact made by Olibrius at the beginning of the narrative.

As in other Old English prose saints' lives, abbreviation and simplification in the Tiberius Margaret text are apparent in passages of exposition and narrative, such as those mentioned above, but are particularly pronounced where direct discourse is concerned. Speeches are characteristically abbreviated by the simple omission of material which appears in copies of the Latin. There is no attempt at summarizing. Instead, the Old English writer appears where it seems appropriate to skip over phrases and sentences in the source. This abridgement is carried out smoothly enough for the most part but there are also places, both in narrative and in discourse, where transitions are abrupt and awkward. Some of these unsatisfactory transitions – although this cannot by any means account for them all – may be due to corruptions in the Latin source manuscript, which the translator is content to carry over into the Old English, or to scribal deficiencies in the one manuscript of the Old English text.[118]

first question and response between Margaret and Olibrius there is no mention in the Old English of Christianity. When asked by Olibrius whether she is free or a slave Margaret replies simply that she is free, 'Ic eom frig' (Tib, ch. 6), whereas in the Latin her first reply incorporates a defiant statement of her faith: 'Libera sum. Ego credo, prefecte, et Christiana sum' (Cas, p. 226; P, ch. 6), 'I am free. I believe, prefect, and am a Christian.'

[114] Tib, ch. 4: 'She heard of the struggles of martyrs, for much blood was shed in those times on earth in the name of Our Lord, the Saviour Christ.'

[115] Cf. Cas, p. 225 (P, ch. 4).

[116] Tib, ch. 6: 'The prefect was then very angry.' Cf. Cas, p. 226 (P, ch. 6).

[117] Tib, ch. 6. Cf. Cas, p. 226 (P, ch. 6).

[118] Tib, for example, leaves out the name Margaret in the saint's reply to Olibrius's demand that she tell him her name: 'in Dryhten ic eom geciged' (Tib, ch. 6), 'in the

An example of the characteristic abbreviation found in direct discourse in the Tiberius version can be seen in Margaret's first prayer, which she offers up on being summoned before Olibrius.[119] This begins in the Latin with a developed sequence of urgent supplications, expressed mostly as a series of doublets and densely incorporating psalm allusions. It begins, 'Miserere mei, Domine, miserere mei, et ne perdas cum impiis animam meam, nec cum uiris sanguinum uitam meam. Fac me semper te, Christe, conlaudare'.[120] The Old English gives a shortened version of this, remaining true to the basic sense but sacrificing the cumulative rhetorical power and the richness of association of the Latin: 'Gemildsa me, Dryhten, and ne læt þu mine sawle mid arleasum, ac gedo me blissian and þe symble herian.'[121] After this the Latin has a series of images of pollution and contamination of purity, mentioning soul and body and culminating in the arresting image of a pearl being thrown into the mud: 'Non eiciatur margarita mea in luto.'[122] The Old English maintains the soul–body reference but reduces the imagery of pollution to a single word, *besmitan*.[123]

The prayer ends in the Old English as in the Latin, with a series of comparisons of Margaret to trapped or caught animals. There is some variation in this list among Latin manuscripts representing the Mombritius and pre-Mombritius tradition, though none of them has an exact equivalent for the Old English 'swa swa nytenu onmiddan feolde'.[124] The source, if any, of the Old English phrase is not known.

The Old English translator of the Tiberius version handles the inherited

---

Lord I am called'. Later Margaret is addressed by the crowd in the Latin (Cas, p. 227; P, ch. 9); in the Old English, however, she is addressed specifically by *women* bystanders (*fæmnan*, Tib, ch. 9), even though when she responds to the speech of the bystanders she addresses both men and women: 'gangaþ ge wif to eowrum husum and ge weras to eowrum weorcum' (Tib, ch. 9), 'Go to your houses, women, and to your work, men!'

[119] Tib, ch. 5.

[120] Cas, p. 226: 'Have mercy upon me, Lord, have mercy upon me, and do not destroy my soul with the wicked nor my life with men of blood. Make me always praise you, Christ' (cf. P, ch. 5).

[121] Tib, ch. 5: 'Have mercy upon me, Lord, and do not abandon my soul among the wicked, but make me rejoice and praise you always.'

[122] Cas, p. 226: 'Let not my pearl be cast in the mire' (P, ch. 5).

[123] Tib, ch. 5: 'defile'.

[124] Tib, ch. 5: 'like cattle in the midst of a field'.

material modestly and mostly competently. The Latin version represented by *BHL* nos. 5303 and 5304 is a work of considerable rhetorical sophistication, liturgical in expression and steeped in the language of the Bible, particularly of the psalms. Its rhapsodic tone is carried over into the Old English, but compared to the Latin, with the heightened and breathless quality of its language, the Old English is relatively restrained. Narrative is not submerged by incantation, as threatens to happen in the Latin. Margaret herself does not appear so remote and all-powerful, though she is the perfected saint throughout. There is a noticeable elevation of tone in the speeches in the Old English but the narrative is concise and plain and is expressed in a natural-sounding language, avoiding the temptation towards Latinism to which other vernacular hagiographers can succumb. [125]

The Old English translator does not attempt to mirror the rhetorical flights of the Latin version and produces a work which inevitably lacks the depth of association of its source. This writer does, however, succeed in conveying to the vernacular audience a compelling sense of the power of the Margaret legend and of its inspirational significance for the Christian community. The Tiberius version is thus of considerable interest in its own right, as well as being important for the light which it sheds on the development of the Latin tradition.

THE CCCC VERSION

The Old English version of the legend of St Margaret preserved in Cambridge, Corpus Christi College 303 (CCCC) is entirely independent from that in London, British Library, Cotton Tiberius A. iii. Indeed, although both Old English versions are based on variants of Latin Mombritius and pre-Mombritius tradition, it is clear that their respective sources represent different elements of the Latin textual tradition. Few of the features which we have seen in the Tiberius version as indicating the distinctiveness of its exact source are reflected in CCCC.

---

[125] Non-finite participial constructions, for example, are generally avoided in the Old English: 'aspiciens in caelum dicebat' (Cas, p. 228) becomes 'besæh up to heofonum and cwæð' (Tib, ch. 10); 'locum preparatum' (P, ch. 20) becomes 'to þære stowe þe þe is gegearwod' (P, ch. 20). It should also be pointed out, however, that the Latin *passio* itself is not written in a syntactically complicated style.

Generally, CCCC is closer to the 'standard' text in *BHL* no. 5303 than is Tiberius, but it too shows a number of radical departures from the normal text. This again points to the complexity of the history of the transmission of this Latin *passio*. The discrepancies between CCCC and regular texts of *BHL* no. 5303, unlike those between Tiberius and *BHL* no. 5303, are never supported by Usener's Greek and many of them receive no corroboration from other Latin or vernacular versions (though there are exceptions to this). As a result, it is impossible to be certain whether some of the peculiarities of CCCC derive from an unknown variant of *BHL* no. 5303 or are the contribution of the Old English writer.

The present discussion concentrates on some of the more significant and representative features of CCCC, as a fuller outline of the distinctive elements of this version is presented in the Commentary. A number of contrasts with the normal *BHL* no. 5303 version appear to be simply the result of misunderstandings of the text or of scribal variation in the Latin tradition. At the beginning of ch. 10, for example, Olibrius exclaims to Margaret, 'Ðu wyrcest þines fæðeres weorc, þæt is se deofol self';[126] the corresponding speech in the Latin is spoken by Margaret and is introduced by the phrase 'Et dixit praefecto':[127] here the grammatical case of the word *praefecto* lies at the root of the discrepancy. Later in ch. 10 Margaret oddly tells Olibrius that if she submits her body to him he will suffer the torment of hell: 'þonne scealt þu inne þæt wallende pic into hellewite';[128] in the Latin she says more logically that if she has mercy on her body her soul will go to hell, like Olibrius's: 'si ego carni mee misereor, anima mea in interitum uadit, sicut et tua':[129] the original sense has become lost in the Old English translation. In the following chapter, the Old English states that Margaret went into prison and sat praying for seven hours – 'seofon tide þæs dæges'[130] – whereas according to the Latin she went into prison at the seventh hour.[131] The Old English also fails to make sense of the reference to Jamnes and Mambres which appears in the Latin,[132]

---

[126] CCCC, ch. 10: 'You do the work of your father, that is the devil himself.'
[127] P, ch. 10: 'And she said to the prefect.'
[128] CCCC, ch. 10: 'then must you go into the torment of hell in that boiling pit.'
[129] P, ch. 10: 'If I have pity on my flesh, my soul will go to its destruction, like yours.'
[130] CCCC, ch. 11: 'seven hours of the day'.   [131] P, ch. 11.
[132] P, ch. 16.

taking these names to refer to lands rather than people. [133] Also, in the Latin, the executioner Malchus prays that he be not judged for the sin of putting Margaret to death: 'Domine, ne statuas mihi in peccatum';[134] in the Old English, on the other hand, he asks Margaret to forgive him and to pray for him, [135] and it is Margaret, not Malchus himself, who prays for his forgiveness: 'Drihten leof, forgif þu him ealle þa synne, þe he gefremeð hæfð.'[136] This change, ensuring that Margaret remains firmly in the foreground throughout the climactic scene of her execution, is paralleled in some variants of the tradition of *BHL* no. 5303. [137]

At the end of Margaret's debate with the black demon the Latin narrates that Margaret dismissed him and that the earth swallowed him: 'Et statim degluttiuit eum terra';[138] in the Old English this last detail is transferred to the direct speech of Margaret: 'sea eorðe þe forswelge.'[139] This change may have been introduced deliberately by the Old English writer in order to increase the authority of Margaret at the end of the scene, but it may also derive (like the transfer to Margaret of Malchus's prayer for forgiveness, mentioned above) from a Latin variant of *BHL* no. 5303.

In turning to larger-scale distinctive features of CCCC, it is notable that one striking peculiarity receives corroboration not from the Mombritius tradition at all but from an entirely different Latin version. The Old English describes how Olibrius consults with his advisers as to how to proceed against Margaret after her arrest: 'And he þanan to his gereorde eode and amang þam þe he æt, he to his þegnum spræc and þus cwæð: "On hwilca wisa ræde ge me hu ic muge þis mæden bismærian?"'[140] There is no corresponding reading among known variants of *BHL* no. 5303, although unexpected confirmation of the authority of this passage is provided by an analogous sequence in the Latin Rebdorf version: 'ad se conuocans

---

[133] CCCC, ch. 16: 'and him twa land agæf: an is Gamne and oðer is Mambre.'
[134] P, ch. 22: 'Lord, do not count this against me as a sin.'
[135] CCCC, ch. 22: 'Ic þe bidde, leofa eadige fæmne, þæt þu gebidde for me and forgif þu me þas wite.'
[136] CCCC, ch. 22: 'Dear Lord, forgive him all the sins that he has committed.'
[137] See Pip, p. 346, i; N (ed. E. Francis, *Wace: la vie de sainte Marguerite*, line 488); Harley 2801 (ed. F. Mack, *Seinte Marherete*, p. 141, line 20).
[138] P, ch. 16: 'And at once the earth swallowed him up.'
[139] CCCC, ch. 16: 'may the earth swallow you up.'
[140] CCCC, ch. 7: 'And thence he went to his meal and while he ate he spoke to his attendants and said, "In what way do you advise me how I may defile this girl?"'

uniuersae urbis nobilitatem, et omnes qui sapientes esse uidebantur, consilio inito cum eis, qualiter beatam Margaretam studiosa argumentatione, non occidendo perderet, sed terrificando uinceret.'[141] The Old English is not a translation of this but is clearly relating the same episode.

Other larger-scale departures from the regular *BHL* no. 5303 tradition, however, receive no such external corroboration, though some of them may be thought likely to go back to a Latin source. The representation of Theotimus, Margaret's Christian helper, for example, may come into this category. Theotimus appears in the CCCC version always in the third person: he is not the narrator of the story. Instead, he is presented here as the 'fosterfæder' of Margaret,[142] who finds her when she is cast out by her father, brings her up and teaches her until she is fifteen years old.[143]

Much of ch. 4 in the Old English version has no equivalent in other versions. At this point, in CCCC, in an unparalleled speech of seventy-nine words, the young Margaret preaches the faith to the people, thus establishing her authority and stature at the beginning of the narrative. There is also in this chapter an extended emotive account of the persecution of the Christians at this time, leading up to a powerful prayer by Margaret, which, like the account of the persecution, has no known source. This prayer is unlikely to have been the Old English writer's creation, however, since in giving the first sentence of the prayer in Latin before translating it, 'Domine Deus omnipotens, ego sum ancilla tua',[144] the translator employs the pattern also seen in the prayer in ch. 5, beginning 'Miserere mei, Deus, miserere mei', which *does* appear in the Latin.[145] On the other hand, as explained below,[146] the *sumne . . . sumne . . .* rhetorical structure of Margaret's account of the persecution has a characteristically Old English form and is likely to represent a passage of free adaptation on the part of the Anglo-Saxon writer.

Another possible passage of free adaptation appears in the reference, in ch. 10, to the 'ninth hell'. This is not paralleled in known variants of the

---

[141] Rebdorf version, *ASS*, Iul. V, 36A: 'and calling to himself the whole nobility of the city and all who seemed to be wise, he entered into counsel with them as to how by diligent proofs he should not destroy her by killing her but should overcome her by frightening her.'

[142] CCCC, ch. 12.   [143] CCCC, ch. 3.

[144] CCCC, ch. 4: 'Lord God omnipotent, I am your handmaid.'

[145] P, ch. 5: 'Have mercy upon me, God, have mercy upon me.'

[146] See below, pp. 66–7.

Latin. Remarkably, however, a discussion of the ninth hell appears in a homily in CCCC 303, the manuscript of our St Margaret text. The Old English writer may well have introduced this concept into the text, having derived knowledge of it indeed from this very homily. The concept of nine hells does not appear to occur elsewhere in Anglo-Saxon literature. [147]

One final passage unique to CCCC may also be mentioned at this point. This is the sequence of dialogue in which the persecutor Olibrius and his followers engage with the executioner Malchus before Margaret is put to death:

And se gerefa cwæð to his þeowum Malcum (se ilca dernunga Gode geþenode): 'Gedrah þu þin swurd', cwæð se gerefa, 'and þa fæmne þu ofsleah.' And þa Godes wiðerwinnan þa fæmnan genamon, ut of þære byrig ungerædlice hi togoden, and þa hi þær becomon þær me hio slean scolde and þa leasan witan to Malcum spræcan and cwæðon: 'Drah hraþa þin swurd and þa fæmna þu ofsleah.'[148]

This emotive passage, with its affective repetition of the dreadful command, gives greater prominence to the conventional figure of the unwilling executioner than he has in copies of *BHL* no. 5303. The passage is entirely consonant with the heightened emotionality of the CCCC version, but its content may also be based on inherited material.

As a work of literature the CCCC version is more sophisticated and carefully wrought than the Tiberius. This in itself makes one unwilling to dismiss all peculiarities in the Old English as going back to a Latin intermediary. The CCCC version shows a thematic awareness and coherence which is apparent on various levels of its composition, and some of the departures from *BHL* no. 5303 are to be explained most convincingly as stemming from the Old English writer's concern to express and develop themes suggested by the legend. The Old English version cultivates a rhetoric which is particularly characteristic of the vernacular literary tradition: there is much use of alliteration, word pairing, repetition and cumulation. The syntax demonstrates both variety of construction and freedom from the patterns of Latin composition. The treatment of direct

---

[147] On the concept of the 'nine hells', see below, p. 175, n. 20.

[148] CCCC, ch. 19: 'And the prefect said to his attendant Malchus (who secretly was a servant of God), "Draw your sword and kill the maiden." And God's enemies seized the maiden then and dragged her roughly out of the city, and then they came to where she was to be killed and the deceitful counsellors spoke to Malchus and said, "Draw your sword and kill the maiden."'

and indirect discourse is somewhat more original and varied than that seen in the Tiberius version. Like the Tiberius version, CCCC shows a concern with the abbreviation and simplification of material, but there is more sense in CCCC of a self-conscious writer shaping inherited material to a specific thematic end. The Tiberius version may be seen as a mostly competent but rather insipid translation of the legend from Latin into Old English; the CCCC version, on the other hand, presents something of a reworking of the legend, with new emphases and new preoccupations.

As suggested above, some of the innovation in CCCC has its origins in the particular form of the Latin source used by the translator. The Old English text at the very least, however, transmits the concerns of its source in a sensitive and effective way, and in fact the contribution of the Old English writer clearly must be seen as greater than this: the essential tone and quality of the CCCC version are this writer's distinctive achievement, imposing a particular style on the narrative and giving thoughtful expression to a body of recurrent themes.

One stylistic feature which occurs several times in CCCC is that of a cumulative rhetorical sequence based on the repetition of *sum* (or variant). The first sequence of this kind comes in a passage on the persecution of Christians which has no parallel in other versions of the legend. This passage may possibly owe something to a lost Latin source, but in expression it recalls the *sum . . . sum* lists which occur throughout Old English prose and poetry.[149] The CCCC writer is here drawing upon a familiar vernacular mode of expression in order to heighten the emotional impact of the account:

Sumne hi mid wæpnum acwealdon and sumne mid hatum wætere. Sumne hi onhengon be þan fotum and sumne be þan earmum. Sumne hi pinedon mid wallende leade and mid hatum stanum. Sumne heo mid sweorde ofslogen; sumne mid spiten betweon felle and flæsce þurhwræcon. Eall þæt Godes þeowan geþafodon and geþrowodon for Godes deoran lufan.[150]

---

[149] Such lists provide the central structure of the Exeter Book poems *The Gifts of Men* and *The Fortunes of Men*. Other examples in poetry include *Christ II*, 664–85; *The Wanderer*, 80–4; *Elene*, 131–7. Examples in prose include *Vercelli Homilies*, 4, lines 13–16 (ed. D. G. Scragg, *The Vercelli Homilies and Related Texts*, EETS 300 (Oxford, 1992), 91); Ælfric, *Catholic Homilies* I, 35 (ed. Thorpe, *Ælfric: Sermones Catholici* I, 524); *Catholic Homilies* I, 36 (ed. Thorpe, *ibid.*, p. 540); *The Life of St Mary of Egypt*, 126–9 (ed. Skeat, *Ælfric's Lives of Saints* II, 10).

[150] CCCC, ch. 4; 'One they killed with their weapons and another with hot water. One they hung by the feet and another by the arms. One they tortured with boiling lead

A shorter sequence in this same *sum . . . sum* form occurs in the closing lines of the text,[151] but there is also an even more extended occurrence of it. The translator recasts as a *sum . . . sum* passage the speech of confession which the black demon makes to Margaret in her prison cell, when he catalogues the evil deeds which he perpetrates against humanity. There is a corresponding passage in *BHL* no. 5303, which the Old English follows quite closely in some respects,[152] but the translator freely develops and expands the Latin, and the rhetorical framework adopted in the Old English is not paralleled in *BHL* no. 5303. This *sum . . . sum* sequence continues for eight lines, beginning as follows: 'Sume ic spræce benam and sume heora hlyste, sumen heora fet and sume heora handa, and heo þurh þæt creopeles wurðon.'[153] This sustained passage, in its context of a speech of confession by a demon in the saint's prison cell, provides a remarkable parallel to a passage in the Old English hagiographical poem *Juliana*. The *Juliana* passage begins:

> Oft ic syne ofteah,
> ablende bealoþoncum   beorna unrim
> monna cynnes,   misthelme forbrægd
> þurh attres ord   eagna leoman
> sweartum scurum,   ond ic sumra fet
> forbræc bealosearwum,   sume in bryne sende,
> on liges locan,   þæt him lasta wearð
> siþast gesyne.   Eac ic sume gedyde
> þæt him banlocan   blode spiowedan,
> þæt hi færinga   feorh aleton
> þurh ædra wylm.   Sume on yðfare . . .[154]

and with hot stones. One they slew with the sword; another they thrust through with spits between flesh and skin. All that God's servants endured and suffered for God's dear love.'

[151] CCCC, ch. 23.   [152] Cf. P, ch. 15.

[153] CCCC, ch. 15: 'Some I deprived of their speech and some of their hearing, some of their feet and some of their hands, and through that they became cripples.'

[154] *Juliana*, lines 468–78: 'Repeatedly I have deprived of sight and blinded with wicked thoughts a countless tally of men of the human race, and obscured the light of their eyes with a helm of mist by means of venomous darts in dark showers; and of some I have shattered the feet with vicious snares; and some I have dispatched into the furnace, into the fiery keep, so that the last was seen of their tracks. Some too I have so treated that their bodies spewed blood, so that they relinquished their life suddenly by

Other stylistic features of the Old English version similarly reflect the writer's self-consciously rhetorical approach. [155]

CCCC shows a consistent preoccupation with two main themes, neither of which figures largely, if indeed at all, in other versions of the legend. One of these is the theme of the intense love which Margaret feels for God; the other, linked to the first, is that of the deceit, betrayal, and seduction associated with the devil and his followers. The Old English, of course, also expresses the legend's integral themes of the triumph and glorification of the perfected saint and of the efficacy of Margaret's intercession on behalf of those who pray to her, but it shows a particular concern with these two new themes. As in other respects, we cannot be sure whether these themes are inherited from the immediate source of the Old English or are the contribution of the translator, but they are certainly integrated fully into this vernacular work.

The theme of deceit appears first in the prayer which Margaret offers up when she is apprehended by Olibrius's soldiers. It occurs in a passage which interweaves the idea of the devil's deceit and temptation with that of the saint's fervent love for the Lord and which emphasizes both themes through effective use of repetition and balance: 'And ic þe wille biddan þæt deofle mine sawle ne beswican, ne mine treowðe fram þe ahwerfan, ne mine clæne lichaman gefylan. Drihten leof, æfre ic þe lufode, and þu Wuldorcyning, ne læt þu me naht beswican, ne næfre min gewit fram þe gehwerfan, ne min mægþhad afylan.' [156] The soul-body opposition, the references to the *treowðe* and *gewit* of Margaret, and the concern with her purity are present in the *BHL* no. 5303 text, [157] but not the themes of love or deception.

---

the bursting of their blood-vessels. Some on a sea journey . . .' (trans. S. A. J. Bradley, *Anglo-Saxon Poetry* (London, 1982), p. 313).

[155] CCCC, ch. 4 exemplifies the translator's cultivation of word pairing and balanced phrases: *ægþer ge weres ge wifes, ge cnihtes ge mægdenes, ic eow secge and wissige, ic eow behata and on hand selle, mid Gode and mid his gecorenan, mid wæpnum acwealdon and . . . mid hatum wætere, mid sweorde . . . mid spiten, betweon felle and flæsce, geþafodon and geþrowodon, geherde and geseah, strange and staþolfæste, min hiht and min hope.* Many of these examples also illustrate the writer's fondness for alliteration: *ge weres ge wifes, wæpnum . . . wætere* etc.

[156] CCCC, ch. 5: 'And I wish to ask you that devils do not deceive my soul, nor turn my faith from you, nor defile my pure body. Dear Lord, I have ever loved you; do not let me be betrayed, King of glory, nor ever turn my mind from you, nor defile my chastity.'

[157] Cf. P, ch. 5.

The verb *beswican* 'to deceive' (also *geswican*)[158] is associated in the text with Olibrius[159] as well as with the devil.[160] Also employed is the noun *leasung* 'deceit' and related words: 'mid leasunge',[161] 'þise leasere þrow-unge'.[162] The phrase 'leasum gewitum' (and variants), applied to the advisers of Olibrius, appears throughout the narrative with formulaic regularity.[163] Olibrius's appropriation, rich in irony, of the language of love in his pursuit of Margaret – 'And gif þu woldest me lufian and to minum godum þe gebiddan, þe sceolde beon eall swa wel eall swa me selfan'[164] – illustrates the level of deceit and seduction on which he operates. As against this attachment to betrayal seen in the devil and his acolytes is an awareness of loyalty and an acceptance of true lordship. Margaret accuses Olibrius of trying to seduce her away 'fram minum rihte hlaforde',[165] and later she refers to God as the *hlaford* to whom she is *beweddod*.[166]

As noted by Wolpers,[167] the idea of intense personal love for God as a literary theme is one which we associate with the high rather than the early Middle Ages. The *sponsa Christi* 'betrothed to Christ' motif appears once in *BHL* no. 5303 and several times in the 'Caligula' version of the Margaret legend – it is entirely absent in the Old English Tiberius version – but these texts have no real interest in the theme of love. In the CCCC version, however, the theme of love for God catches the imagination of the writer. It is introduced at the very beginning of the text in the reference to Christ's martyrs, who suffered 'for his þæra micclan leofan lufan',[168] and the insistence on Margaret's love is apparent throughout the text. Almost every utterance of the saint gives expression to this love.

The familiar metaphor of the saint as servant or handmaiden of the Lord is another image which occurs widely in CCCC, but this is employed in a

---

[158] CCCC, ch. 11.   [159] CCCC, chs. 7 and 11.

[160] CCCC, chs. 5 (twice), 14, 15 and 16 (twice).

[161] CCCC, ch. 10: 'with deception'.   [162] CCCC, ch. 10: 'this false suffering'.

[163] CCCC, chs. 7, 9, 10, 17, 19: 'deceitful counsellors'.

[164] CCCC, ch. 7: 'And if you would love me and pray to my gods, it would be as well for you as for myself.' Cf. also CCCC, ch. 17.

[165] CCCC, ch. 7: 'from my proper lord'.

[166] CCCC, ch. 14: 'the *lord* to whom she is *betrothed*'. Here the Old English develops the *sponsa Christi* motif of *BHL* no. 5303 (cf. P, ch. 14).

[167] Wolpers, *Die englische Heiligenlegende des Mittelalters*, p. 154.

[168] CCCC, ch. 1: 'for his great, dear love'.

highly conventional way and does not have emotional impact of the imagery of love. There are eight occurrences of the *{Godes}* *þeow* metaphor, but in only two of these[169] is the phrase applied to Margaret; elsewhere it is applied to other martyrs,[170] to Theotimus[171] and to Christians generally.[172] Greater prominence is given to this motif in the Old English Tiberius version (which, as comparison with Usener's Greek shows, is reflecting its source in this respect). CCCC, on the other hand, prefers the more fervently personal language of love.

Although the theme of love for the Lord, centring particularly on the *sponsa Christi* motif, is widely found in the hagiographical literature of the early Middle Ages,[173] nonetheless the treatment of this theme in CCCC is highly unusual. It is in the extent and ardour with which the imagery of love is employed in the CCCC version of the legend of St Margaret that this text contrasts with what we normally find in other early medieval hagiographical writings. It is significant that references to Margaret's love for Christ occur most typically in CCCC in the speeches, and particularly in the private prayers, of the saint. In most of their occurrences in early medieval literature the *sponsa Christi* motif and its associated imagery appear in external description as elements in the hagiographer's praise of the saint. Where the imagery occurs in direct discourse it is usually in highly public utterances of defiance or encouragement, rather than, as in CCCC, arising from the internal thoughts of the saint herself.

This insistent and developed use of the language of love would in itself incline us to place the date of the composition of CCCC not long before that of the manuscript in which it is preserved. In this context, the influence of Anselmian spirituality on the composition of our text suggests itself, injecting into the prayers of Margaret a personal and emotional fervency unique in extant Old English literature.[174] Thomas H. Bestul has warned

---

169 CCCC, chs. 4 and 14.   170 CCCC, ch. 4 (twice).

171 CCCC, chs. 3 and 4.

172 CCCC, chs. 15 and 16.

173 For a discussion of this imagery, see S. Morrison, 'The Figure of *Christus Sponsus* in Old English Prose', in *Liebe – Ehe – Ehebruch in der Literatur des Mittelalters*, ed. X. von Ertzdorff and M. Wynn, Beiträge zur deutschen Philologie 58 (Giessen, 1984), 5–15.

174 This fervency, expressed in the language of personal love, is illustrated in Anselm's 'Prayer to Christ', in his *Prayers and Meditations*. This prayer is, according to Benedicta Ward, 'the prayer that belongs most completely to the "new style" of devotion of the eleventh and twelfth centuries' (*The Prayers and Meditations of St Anselm*, p. 60). In it

against seeing too great a contrast between Anselmian and Anglo-Saxon spirituality, and he stresses elements of continuity with the Anglo-Saxon past in Norman monasticism.[175] The language of personal love is not mentioned by Bestul, however, in his discussion of devotional traditions, and certainly this language is unparalleled in pre-twelfth-century vernacular literature. The CCCC version of the Margaret legend can be seen as the product of a monasticism which combines Anglo-Saxon tradition with new cultural elements associated with Norman influence. It is notable that the cult of St Margaret itself gathers momentum in England in the period coinciding with the coming of the Normans.

If the Old English writer has merely transferred the love imagery from the Latin source, this source too would presumably have been composed late. Such a Latin version, elaborating the language of love, may have existed, but it is more likely that it was the Old English writer who developed this imagery. As suggested above, many of the peculiarities of CCCC undoubtedly derive from its source, but the mode of expression, with its thoughtful cultivation of a characteristically Anglo-Saxon rhetoric, points to a creative response to inherited material. In the light of such a creative response in other respects, the preoccupation in CCCC with the idea of love – and also with that of deceit, with which the love theme is interwoven – may reasonably be ascribed to the Old English writer.

the speaker exclaims at line 21, 'Conuerte, misericordissime, meum teporem in feruentissimum amorem' (*Oratio* 2, in *Anselmi Opera Omnia*, ed. Schmitt III, 7): 'Most merciful Lord, turn my lukewarmness into a fervent love for you' (trans. Ward, *The Prayers and Meditations of St Anselm*, p. 94); the urgency and intensity of the lover is increased at lines 72–4: 'Quid dicam? Quid faciam? Quo uadam? Vbi eum quaeram? Vbi uel quando inueniam? Quem rogabo? Quis nuntiabit dilecto "quia amore langueo" [Cant. II.5]' (*Oratio* 2, in *Anselmi Opera Omnia*, ed. Schmitt III, 9): 'What shall I say? What shall I do? Whither shall I go? Where shall I seek him? Where and when shall I find him? Whom shall I ask? Who will tell me of my beloved? "for I am sick from love"' (trans. Ward, *The Prayers and Meditations of St Anselm*, p. 97); the prayer ends with an image (line 94) of the speaker weeping until the Lord, the bridegroom of the soul, calls him forth: 'donec audiam: "anima, ecce sponsus tuus"' (*Oratio* 2, in *Anselmi Opera Omnia*, ed. Schmitt III, 9): 'until I hear, "Soul, behold your bridegroom"' (trans. Ward, *The Prayers and Meditations of St Anselm*, p. 98).

[175] T. H. Bestul, 'St Anselm and the Continuity of Anglo-Saxon Devotional Traditions', *Annuale Mediaevale* 18 (1977), 20–41.

5

The cult of St Margaret in Anglo-Saxon England

There is plentiful evidence, especially from late Anglo-Saxon England, for the liturgical celebration of St Margaret, and it comes from a variety of sources: calendars, litanies, masses, relics, inclusion in collections of saints' lives as well as the vernacular evidence of the entry in the *Old English Martyrology* and the three lives (the two edited in the present volume and the lost life once contained in BL, Cotton Otho B. x). As is the case with many saints, other than those of greatest importance to the universal church, the date on which Margaret's feast is celebrated varies from witness to witness and throughout the Anglo-Saxon period dates other than 20 July, the date on which her feast was eventually fixed in the Western church, can be found. In the Eastern church, where the celebration originated, her feast was on 17 July, which, with a dislocation of one day common in the transferral of Eastern feasts to the West, is also found as 18 July in some Anglo-Saxon calendars.

The feast of St Margaret, or Marina, as she is called in the earliest witnesses, does not appear in the enormously influential Hieronymian Martyrology, which lies behind many of the early Insular calendars and martyrologies. She is not mentioned either in the martyrology of Bede. The earliest known entry in a Latin martyrology is that in the Martyrology of Hrabanus Maurus (d. 856), where the saint appears under 13 July.[1] As noted above, a very similar account appears under the name Marina for 18 June.[2] Holweck says of the feast of Marina on this day that she 'is said to have suffered at Alexandria',[3] but that some sources confound her with

---

[1] *Rabani Mauri Martyrologium*, ed. McCulloh, pp. 67–8, lines 120–7. See also above, p. 22.

[2] *Ibid.*, p. 59, lines 202–8, and above, p. 22.

[3] Holweck, *A Biographical Dictionary of the Saints*, p. 658.

72

Margaret and others with that St Marina 'who in male attire lived in a monastery for men'.[4] Hrabanus is clearly among those who confused her with Margaret, despite the inclusion of the very similar Margaret entry in his Martyrology.

The date of 13 July for Margaret reappears in Anglo-Saxon texts, but it is not the only date, nor even the most common. The most commonly attested date is 20 July, though 7 July also occurs frequently in Anglo-Saxon calendars. These are of two kinds: metrical calendars, which were not intended for liturgical use but probably for memorizing as a kind of devotional exercise, and non-metrical calendars, which generally, though by no means always, record the use of the house in which they were compiled. None of the metrical calendars of Anglo-Saxon England (the metrical calendar of York,[5] from the second half of the eighth century, the tenth-century metrical calendar of Ramsey[6] and that of Hampson edited by McGurk[7]) contains the feast of Margaret, whereas the non-metrical calendars almost all include her in some form.

The earliest Anglo-Saxon calendar, that of St Willibrord, which was compiled for private devotional use, has no entry for St Margaret,[8] but the next, that in a northern manuscript, Oxford, Bodleian Library, Digby 63, of the second half of the ninth century, has on 17 July 'Passio Sancte Marie uirginis'. *Marie* here is probably a corrupt form of *Marine*, as Marina's feast in the Eastern church is 17 July, and another English calendar, Salisbury, Cathedral Library, 150, dated to the second half of the tenth century and originating in the south-west (perhaps in Shaftesbury), has the entry 'Sancte Marine uirginis et Cynelmi martiris' on that date.[9] The Salisbury calendar also has an entry for 20 July – 'Sancte Margarite uirginis' – thus

---

[4] *Ibid.*

[5] A. Wilmart, 'Un temoin anglo-saxon du calendrier métrique d'York', *RB* 46 (1934), 41–69.

[6] M. Lapidge, 'A Tenth-Century Metrical Calendar from Ramsey', *RB* 94 (1984), 326–69.

[7] P. McGurk, 'The Metrical Calendar of Hampson: A New Edition', *AB* 104 (1986), 79–125.

[8] *St Willibrord's Calendar*, ed. H. A. Wilson, HBS 55 (London, 1918).

[9] This calendar, and all others discussed in this paragraph, are ed. Wormald, *English Kalendars before A.D. 1100*, except for that in the sacramentary of Robert of Jumièges, which is edited by H. A. Wilson, *The Missal of Robert of Jumièges*, HBS 11 (London, 1896).

entering the saint under both her Greek and Latin names on the Greek and
Latin feast-days. Such a failure to recognize the identity of Margaret and
Marina is by no means uncommon, as we have already seen with Hrabanus:
the legendary in Reims, Bibl. mun., 1395, for example, follows a *Passio S.
Margarite* with a *Passio S. Marinae*, both texts being versions of the same
life, possibly different translations of similar Greek texts.[10] These two
calendars appear to be the only ones to mark the Eastern feast of 17 July in
Anglo-Saxon England, but the feast also occurs on 18 July in Oxford,
Bodleian Library, Bodley 579 ('Leofric Missal' B, perhaps from Glastonbury, *c.* 970) and Cambridge, University Library, Kk. 5. 32 (from the
West Country, perhaps Glastonbury, late eleventh century), both of which
calendars also record the feast of St Marina on 7 July. Even when the
Eastern feast is not noted, the duplication Margaret/Marina continues,
normally on 7 July and 20 July (London, BL, Add. 37517, the 'Bosworth
Psalter', probably a Canterbury manuscript of the second half of the tenth
century; Oxford, Bodleian Library, Hatton 113 (Evesham or Worcester, s.
xi^2); Cambridge, Corpus Christi College 391 (Worcester, s. xi^2); Rome,
Biblioteca Apostolica Vaticana, Reg. lat. 12 (written in Canterbury for
Bury St Edmunds, second quarter of the eleventh century); Oxford,
Bodleian Library, Douce 296 (perhaps Crowland, second quarter of the
eleventh century) and Rouen, Bibl. mun., 274 (the Sacramentary of
Robert of Jumièges, produced under the patronage of Cnut and Emma, *c.*
1020)),[11] but also on 7 July and 13 July (London, BL, Cotton Nero A. ii
(Wessex, s. xi^1)). London, BL, Cotton Vitellius A. xii (Exeter, s. xi^{ex}) reads
'Sanctarum uirginum Margarete et Mildrade' on 13 July and 'Sancte
Margarete uirginis et martiris' on 20 July. London, BL, Cotton Vitellius
A. xviii (Wells, 1061–88) has 'Sancti Wlmari confessoris et Sancte
Margarete uirginis' on 20 July, as does London, BL, Arundel 155
(Canterbury, Christ Church, s. xi^1) and Arundel 60 (Winchester, s. xi^2).
Margaret was added on 20 July in a Canterbury hand of the end of the
eleventh century to the Winchester manuscript, Cambridge, Trinity
College R. 15. 32, presumably when the manuscript, written in the first
half of the eleventh century, was transferred to St Augustine's, Canter-

[10] See Cross, 'St Marina'. See also above, pp. 8–9 and n. 17.
[11] See Heslop, 'The Production of *De Luxe* Manuscripts'.

bury.[12] Finally, the Worcester calendar of the second quarter of the eleventh century in Cambridge, Corpus Christi College 9, has 'Sancte Marie (*sic*) uirginis' for 7 July and no separate entry for St Margaret; a Winchester manuscript of *c.* 1030, London, BL, Cotton Titus D. xxvii, has no Margaret or Marina entries; Margaret was added only in the thirteenth century to the Winchester manuscript, London, BL, Cotton Vitellius E. xviii of the mid-eleventh century; and in the twelfth century to Cambridge, Corpus Christi College 422, a Sherborne manuscript of the mid-eleventh century.

In the Canterbury manuscript Arundel 155 the entry for 20 July is marked 'xii lc', as a feast of twelve lections, which is more likely to be in honour of Margaret than in honour of the first saint mentioned on that day, St Wulfmar; the same note is found in CCCC 391, from Worcester. The highlighting of the day in the calendar in Douce 296, possibly from Crowland, moreover, is unambiguously in honour of Margaret, the only saint commemorated: the words 'SANCTAE MARGARETE VIRGINIS ET MARTIRIS' are entered in blue capitals as a mark of her importance.

We have, therefore, one ninth-century northern manuscript and a (possibly) Shaftesbury manuscript of the second half of the tenth century with Marina on 17 July; a Glastonbury calendar of *c.* 970 and a late eleventh-century West Country manuscript with Margaret on 18 July; and with Margaret on 20 July we have manuscripts from the south-west (Glastonbury and perhaps Shaftesbury) and Canterbury of the second half of the tenth century; from Bury St Edmunds, perhaps Crowland, Canterbury, Worcester and the Sacramentary of Robert of Jumièges from the first half of the eleventh century; and Evesham, Worcester, the West Country, Exeter, Wells, Winchester and Canterbury from the second half of the eleventh century. St Margaret features, therefore, in almost all of the surviving calendars of the Anglo-Saxon church, possibly, as Ortenberg suggests, 'from the late tenth century onwards . . . as a result of an intensification of the Roman pilgrimage'.[13] While the south-western monastries, as she points out, appear to have adopted the cult from an early date,[14]

---

[12] For the transferral of the manuscript, see S. Keynes, *Anglo-Saxon Manuscripts and Other Items of Related Interest in the Library of Trinity College, Cambridge*, Old English Newsletter Subsidia 18 (Binghamton, NY, 1992), 31.

[13] Ortenberg, 'Aspects of Monastic Devotions to the Saints', pp. 335–6.

[14] *Ibid.*, p. 337.

Canterbury is very important too, with the feast recorded in the second half of the tenth century in the Bosworth Psalter, in the first half of the eleventh in Arundel 155 (where it is marked as a feast of twelve lections) and in the second half of the eleventh in Cambridge, Trinity College R. 15. 32.

The other date for Marina, 7 July, is difficult to explain, as it does not appear to occur outside England. Ortenberg says that a different Marina is concerned and does not consider the date in her discussion of St Margaret,[15] but the entry for Marina in the *Old English Martyrology* is on 7 July and this Marina is undoubtedly the same as Margaret: the *passio* from which the entry was derived is a version of the *passio* of Margaret.[16] Eight Anglo-Saxon calendars have an entry under 7 July for Marina and two Worcester calendars (CCCC 9, of the mid-eleventh century, and CCCC 391, of the second half of the eleventh century) enter 'sancte Marie uirginis' for the same date, where 'Marie' is obviously a corruption of 'Marina'. The duplication of Marina and Margareta, both in the calendars and the litanies, certainly suggests that the Anglo-Saxons considered them separate saints. It is possible that the Marina of 7 July is a saint different from the Marina who is identical with Margaret and that the author of the *Old English Martyrology* was the only one to confuse them, combining an account of the Marina of 17 or 20 July with a date of 7 July suggested by the entry for a different Marina in his calendar, but in this case we would be obliged to account for an otherwise unknown Marina, and there does not seem to be any suitable candidate.

Margaret features also in the litanies of Anglo-Saxon England, under both Margareta and Marina, beginning with Marina in a late tenth-century manuscript and Margareta from the first half of the eleventh century onwards.[17] Those to contain her under the name 'Margareta' are the second litany in BL, Cotton Galba A. xiv, of the first half of the eleventh century, possibly from Winchester; Cambridge, Corpus Christi College 44, from the second quarter of the eleventh century, perhaps from Canterbury; Oxford, Bodleian Library, Douce 296, of the second quarter of the eleventh century, perhaps from Crowland; Vatican City, Biblioteca Apostolica Vaticana, Reg. lat. 12, produced in Canterbury but probably for Bury St

---

[15] *Ibid.*, p. 335, n. 131.

[16] *Das altenglische Martyrologium*, ed. Kotzor II, 141–4; see also the discussion of the date of 7 July for Marina by Cross (as cited above, n. 10).

[17] The litanies are ed. M. Lapidge, *Anglo-Saxon Litanies of the Saints*, HBS 106 (London, 1991), from which edition all the information in this paragraph is taken.

Edmunds in the second quarter of the eleventh century; the first litany in Cambridge, Corpus Christi College 163, of the mid-eleventh century, which was probably copied from a German exemplar; London, BL, Cotton Tiberius A. iii, a Canterbury manuscript of the mid-eleventh century, where 'Margareta' is written in capital letters; the first litany in Cambridge, Corpus Christi College 422, a mid-eleventh century manuscript possibly written in Winchester for use at Sherborne; Paris, BN, lat. 8824, a mid-eleventh-century English manuscript of uncertain origin; Cambridge, Corpus Christi College 391, a Worcester manuscript of the second half of the eleventh century; the first litany in London, BL, Add. 28188, written in Exeter in the second half of the eleventh century; Oxford, Bodleian Library, Laud lat. 81, from the second half of the eleventh century; London, BL, Harley 863, written in Exeter in the third quarter of the eleventh century; and Rouen, Bibl. mun., 231 (A. 44), a late eleventh-century manuscript from St Augustine's, Canterbury. The saint is included under the name Marina in Orléans, Bibl. mun., 127 (105), a late tenth-century manuscript probably written in England; in the second litany in London, BL, Cotton Galba A. xiv, of the first half of the eleventh century; in the first litany in London, BL, Cotton Vitellius A. vii, a Ramsey or Exeter manuscript of the first half of the eleventh century; in Paris, BN, lat. 8824, of the second quarter of the eleventh century; in London, BL, Arundel 60, a Winchester manuscript of the second half of the eleventh century; in Oxford, Bodleian Library, Douce 296, perhaps from Crowland and written in the second quarter of the eleventh century; and in London, BL, Harley 863, of the third quarter of the eleventh century from Exeter. Galba A. xiv, Harley 863, Douce 296 and Paris, BN, lat. 8824 all, therefore, enter the saint under both names. She is absent from many other litanies, sometimes presumably because of their brevity (as in those in CCCC 146 or Cotton Tiberius C. vi) or their very early date (Harley 7653 and Royal 2. A. XX), but often for no obvious reason. The only litany in which she is inserted in capitals is that in the Canterbury manuscript, Tiberius A. iii, which also, of course, contains one of the vernacular lives edited here.

Few Anglo-Saxon liturgical books contain a mass for Margaret. Her feast, insofar as it was celebrated, would presumably have been kept with the mass for the Common of Virgins. This would undoubtedly have been the case up to the eleventh century and until then the calendar entries may not even represent a feast actually celebrated; once the feast became more established, then it would, presumably, have been kept. Two manuscripts, however, do have a mass. One of these is the mass for Margaret preserved on fol. 341 of section C of the Leofric Missal, that part of the missal written in Exeter. It was copied into the manuscript by the scribe whom Drage terms scribe 10: this scribe worked on the manuscript both before and after Leofric's death in 1072 and was probably a canon of Exeter cathedral. [18] For 'XII Kal aug S. Margaretae uirg. et mart.' (21 July) it runs:

Deus, qui beatam uirginem Margaretam ad caelos per martyrii palmam peruenire fecisti, concede propitius ut sicut illa, te adiuuante, tyrannicam meruit seuitiam triumphare; ita nos, ipsa intercedente, uisibilium et inuisibilium hostium insidias ualeamus superare. Per.

[*Secreta*]

Haec uictima, Domine, quesumus, pro beate uirginis Margaretae martyrio oblata, et mentium nobis sanctitatem et corporum optineat sanctitatem. Per.

Pro cuius nomine penarum *require de S. Agatha*

[*Postcommunio*]

Purificent nos, Domine, quesumus, diuina sacramenta quae sumpsimus, et, beata intercedente uirgine martyreque tua Margareta, ad presentis uitae prosperitatem, et futurae beatitudinem sempiternam nobis ea prouenire concedas. Per. [19]

The text from the mass for St Agatha, the *Praefatio*, is found elsewhere in the Leofric Missal and reads:

Pro cuius nomine poenarum mortisque contemptum in utroque sexu fidelium cunctis ætatibus contulisti, Ut inter felicium martyrum palmas Agathen quoque beatissimam uirginem uictrici pacientiae coronares, Quæ nec minis territa, nec suppliciis superata, de diaboli seuitia triumphauit quia in tuæ deitatis confessione permansit. Et ideo cum angelis. [20]

---

[18] Drage, 'Bishop Leofric and the Exeter Cathedral Chapter', pp. 122 and 164.

[19] *The Leofric Missal*, ed. Warren, p. 253: 'Lord, who caused the blessed virgin Margaret to come to heaven by means of the glory of martyrdom, graciously grant that as she, with your help, deserved to triumph over a savage tyranny, so we, through your intercession, may be able to overcome the snares of enemies seen and unseen. *Secret*. May this sacrifice, Lord, we beg, offered for the martyrdom of the blessed virgin Margaret, obtain for us the sanctity of our minds and the sanctity of our bodies. *Pro cuius nomine penarum* to be sought for from [the mass] of St Agatha. *Postcommunion*. May the divine sacraments which we have received, Lord, we beseech, purify us and, by the intercession of your blessed virgin and martyr Margaret, may you grant good fortune in the present life and that we attain everlasting happiness by means of her in the future life.'

[20] *Ibid.*, p. 137: 'Through whose name you have bestowed contempt of punishments and death on both sexes of the faithful of every age, so that you crowned the blessed virgin

The unpublished Wells sacramentary, London, BL, Cotton Vitellius A. xviii, of the second half of the eleventh century, also has a mass for Margaret on 109r–v, again for 'XII Kal aug', 21 July:

Deus, qui beatam uirginem Margaretam hodierna die ad celos per martyrii palmam uenire fecisti, concede nobis, quesumus, ut eius exempla sequentes ad te pertingere mereamur. Per.

Haec uictima, Domine, quesumus, pro beate uirginis Margarete oblata martyrio et mentium nobis conferat sanctitatem et corporum obtineat iugiter castitatem. Per.

Percipiat, quesumus, Domine, plebs tua beate Margarete uirginis tue et martyris natalitia celebrando letitiam et quam celestis mense refecisti conuiuio eternitatis tue facias ascribi consortio. Per.[21]

The first two prayers are very similar to those in the Leofric Missal, but the last, the postcommunion prayer, clearly comes from a completely different source. This mass is written in a hand different from the remainder of the sacramentary, though it does not seem to be over an erasure. The initial D of the mass, which should have been written in blue ink to fit in with the pattern of the other masses, was never filled in and the mass was also written further into the bottom margin of 109r than is any other text in the manuscript. It is difficult to know why this should be the case, unless a gap had to be left when the manuscript was being copied, because no mass for Margaret was available at the time, and that the intention to supply one was fulfilled when a text was found.

The Missal of St Augustine's, Canterbury, now Cambridge, Corpus Christi College 270, of *c.* 1100, must also have contained a mass to Margaret, but it is now lost. The principal reviser, according to Rule,

Agatha among the glories of the fortunate martyrs for her victorious endurance, she who, neither frightened by threats nor overcome by punishments, triumphed over the savagery of the devil because she persisted in acknowledgement of your godhead. And therefore with the angels . . .'

[21] 'Lord, who caused the blessed virgin Margaret to come today to heaven by means of the glory of martyrdom, grant us, we beg, that, following her example, we may reach you. May this sacrifice, Lord, we beg, offered for the martyrdom of the blessed virgin Margaret, bestow sanctity on our minds and obtain the chastity of our bodies perpetually.

May your people, Lord, we beg, obtain happiness, celebrating the festival of your blessed Margaret, virgin and martyr, and may you cause those whom you have refreshed by the banquet of the celestial table to be included for ever in your company.'

wrote a note after the mass for Deusdedit, which reads: 'De sancta Margareta. Require in principo (*sic*) libri huius post aliquas orationes.'[22] Another hand has added 'que sunt ante Kalendare. post Credo in unum.'[23] The calendar itself has been removed and with it, presumably, the mass for Margaret, which is not now found in the manuscript.

Ortenberg says that there is a group of collects to Margaret at the end of London, BL, Cotton Galba A. xiv: this is presumably on 153r, which is very badly burnt, where the letters 'gare' appear and where a modern hand has written 'Margaret' on the mounting.[24] Muir, however, the editor of the manuscript, transcribes what can still be read on this very badly damaged folio and regards it as 'apparently a prayer for the intercession of the Blessed Virgin';[25] this fits the remaining words better and it is unlikely, therefore, that we have here a prayer to Margaret.

No dedications to Margaret are attested in the Anglo-Saxon period and it is only after the Conquest that we begin to find them. King's Lynn in Norfolk was dedicated to Margaret around 1100 by Bishop Herbert Losinga (bishop of East Anglia from 1093 to 1119), as was Isleham in Cambridgeshire, which was founded before 1100 as a dependency of the French house, Saint-Jacut-de-Mer.[26]

Relics of Margaret are attested in all three of the manuscripts containing lists of relics in Anglo-Saxon monastic houses. The list from Bath, which was added to Cambridge, Corpus Christi College 111 in the second half of the eleventh century, includes a relic 'of sancta Margaretan':[27] although the list itself is quite late, the relics themselves must have been older, as it is prefaced by an account of how Abbot Ælfsige and the monks opened the shrines when they were uncertain of what relics they had. The Old English list from Exeter, which takes the form of a kind of sermon, was added in Exeter in the second half of the eleventh century to a tenth-century Breton gospelbook, Oxford, Bodleian Library, Auct. D. 2. 16, but again at least

---

22 *The Missal of St Augustine's Abbey, Canterbury*, ed. Rule, p. 98, n. 2: 'Concerning St Margaret. Look in the beginning of this book after some other prayers.'

23 *Ibid.*, p. 98, n. 2: 'which are before the calendar, after the creed'.

24 Ortenberg, 'Aspects of Monastic Devotions', p. 334.

25 *A Pre-Conquest English Prayer-Book*, ed. B. J. Muir, HBS 103 (London, 1988), 192.

26 A. Binns, *Dedications of Monastic Houses in England and Wales 1066–1216* (Woodbridge, 1989), pp. 77 and 100.

27 *Two Chartularies of the Priory of St Peter at Bath*, ed. W. Hunt, Somerset Record Society 7 (London, 1893), 3–4.

some of the relics had been given to Exeter by Athelstan and must have been considerably older than this record of them. The relics of holy virgins are introduced by a general statement:

Eac her beoð reliquiae of manegum halgum fæmnum and of þam halgum Cristes mædenum, þæge þurh Godes gife þone ealdan deofol and ealle flæsclice unlustas oferswiðdon and sume þurh haliges lifes drohtnunge, sume þurh sigefæstne martyrdom þam heofonlican bridguman Criste beoð geþeodde.[28]

Again, the relic is unspecified, being entered merely as 'of sancta Margareta'.[29] The Latin lists from Exeter, entered by the same scribe in the Leofric Missal, Bodley 579, and London, BL, Royal 6. B. VII also contain a relic of the saint, clearly the same one, this time specified as 'De capite Sanctae Margarete uirginis.' These lists were all copied by the same scribe, scribe 10 of the Leofric Missal, who was also responsible for the Margaret mass in that manuscript.[30]

In the *Liber uitae* of the New Minster, Winchester, now preserved as London, BL, Stowe 944, there are six lists of relics, two of which include Margaret. The three lists which are entered in a hand of the middle of the eleventh century, however, include no relics of the saint and it is only in the lists which are in twelfth-century hands that we find her mentioned. The list of the relics in the great cross donated by Cnut and Emma [Ælfgifu] includes 'item de reliquiis Sancte Margarete'[31] and the relics 'in gestatorio ligni domini' (a shrine containing a portion of the wood of the true cross) also include a relic 'de sancta Margareta'.[32] We do not know whether the relics in Cnut and Emma's cross (and both the king and queen were intensely interested in relics and the cults of saints[33]) date back to their day or whether they were enshrined there at a later date. Birch considered that these were relics of Margaret of Scotland, who died in 1093, but they are far more likely to have been relics of the virgin martyr.[34]

---

[28] Förster, *Zur Geschichte des Reliquienkultes*, pp. 78–9: 'Also there are here the relics of many holy virgins and of the holy maidens of Christ, who through God's grace overcame the old devil and all carnal lusts and are joined with the heavenly bridegroom Christ, some through the conduct of a holy life, some through victorious martyrdom.'

[29] *Ibid.*, p. 79.

[30] Drage, 'Bishop Leofric and the Exeter Cathedral Chapter', pp. 81, 163–4 and 228–9; Warren, *Leofric Missal*, p. 5.

[31] *Liber Vitae*, ed. Birch, p. 152.   [32] *Ibid.*, p. 159.

[33] See Heslop, 'The Production of *De Luxe* Manuscripts', pp. 156–8.

[34] *Liber Vitae*, ed. Birch, p. 152, n. 16.

The presence of relics of Margaret in England is not surprising, given that her relics had been translated from the East to San Pietro della Valle near Lake Bolsena in Italy in 908 and that Bolsena was on the route which English pilgrims commonly took to Rome.[35] When Archbishop Sigeric went to Rome in 990 to receive his pallium, for example, his route took him through Bolsena, and Ortenberg connects this stop with the introduction in England of the cults of both SS Christina and Margaret: '[Christina] was the first example of a popular saint in England, whose cult had presumably been brought back by pilgrims from Rome who had stopped at Bolsena. Another virgin saint whose cult was a flourishing one in England from the tenth century onwards, St Margaret of Antioch, was also venerated in the area of Bolsena, to where some of her relics had been translated.'[36]

It is possible that veneration of Margaret in the second half of the eleventh century may have had something to do with respect for a member of the Anglo-Saxon royal house, that Margaret who became queen of Scotland and a saint in her own right. She was a granddaughter of Edmund Ironside, king for a brief period in 1016, and daughter of Edward the Exile and sister of Edgar Ætheling; brought up in Hungary and Germany, she went to England in 1057, living at the English court until she married Malcolm Canmore in 1070.[37] That she was called Margaret is clearly the result of her continental birth: she is the only Anglo-Saxon to bear this name. The only other Margaret in Searle's *Onomasticon* is Estrith or Margaret, sister of King Cnut, and again she was not of English birth.[38] Margaret of Scotland may have been betrothed to Malcolm Canmore from 1059, as Margaret Gibson conjectures,[39] and, if so, her importance at the English court would undoubtedly have been heightened from this date. She was exceptionally pious, as her career as queen of Scotland proves, and the Norman Lanfranc, archbishop of Canterbury, seems to have been her spiritual adviser, helping her also in her attempts to reform the Scottish

[35] On the route to Rome, see Ortenberg, 'Archbishop Sigeric's Journey to Rome in 990', p. 229.

[36] *Ibid.*

[37] On her background, see G. Ronay, *The Lost King of England: The East European Adventures of Edward the Exile* (Woodbridge, 1989); for Margaret, see Gibson, *Lanfranc of Bec*, pp. 126–9.

[38] W. G. Searle, *Onomasticon Anglo-Saxonicum* (Cambridge, 1897), p. 349.

[39] Gibson, *Lanfranc of Bec*, pp. 126–7.

church. She founded Holy Trinity, Dunfermline, as the first regular Benedictine house in Scotland, establishing it with three monks from Christ Church, Canterbury: 'Lavishly endowed with property, furnishings and plate, linked in confraternity with Christ Church and deliberately sharing its other name of Holy Trinity, the new house at Dunfermline was a firm basis for the influence of Canterbury in the far north.'[40] Both manuscripts containing Old English lives of Margaret have Canterbury connections and, while Tiberius A. iii is probably too early for its inclusion of the *uita* to have any link with Margaret of Scotland, her presence in CCCC 303, written in the first half of the twelfth century, may not be unconnected with the queen's links with the archiepiscopal see: the popularity of the saint could be an indirect tribute to the Scottish queen. Indeed, the composition of the CCCC life itself, which linguistic evidence and its similarities with the probably late lives of Giles and Nicholas suggest could be post-Conquest, may even in some way be linked to the growing importance of the saint's namesake, Margaret of Scotland. Schipper suggests that the composition of the lives of Giles and Nicholas was influenced by the Normans, who introduced the cult of these saints in England;[41] while the cult of Margaret was known and gave rise to vernacular versions of her life before the Conquest, the Normans may also have given an extra boost to the cult of Margaret in England.[42]

[40] *Ibid.*, p. 127.
[41] Schipper, 'The Normans and the Old English Lives of Saint Giles and Saint Nicholas'.
[42] See also above, p. 71.

6

Manuscripts

Each of the vernacular lives of Margaret is extant in a single manuscript only: one in London, British Library, Cotton Tiberius A. iii and the second in Cambridge, Corpus Christi College 303. In addition we have the *incipit* and *explicit* of an otherwise destroyed life in a burnt manuscript, London, British Library, Cotton Otho B. x. The Latin *uita* edited here (Appendix 2) has been chosen because it has been preserved in a manuscript from Anglo-Saxon England, and this manuscript, Paris, Bibliothèque nationale, lat. 5574, fols. 1–39, is also described below.

LONDON, BRITISH LIBRARY, COTTON TIBERIUS A. iii

Cotton Tiberius A. iii is a large and varied collection of texts, written around the middle of the eleventh century by five different hands.[1] It is assigned to Christ Church, Canterbury, because its contents agree closely with those of a manuscript described in the medieval catalogue of Christ Church and because several of the saints invoked in its litany were culted at Christ Church. Dewick suggested that the manuscript was written after 1031 because of St Martial's position in the litany, where he is among the apostles and evangelists.[2] The order of the texts in their present binding is not original, as Ker has shown; in their original order the contents include the *Regula S. Benedicti*, with an Old English gloss; supplements to the *Regula*, most of which are glossed; the *Regularis concordia*, again with an Old English gloss; collections of prognostics, short notes, prayers and

---

[1] Ker, *Catalogue*, no. 186.
[2] *Facsimiles of Horae de Beata Virgine from English Manuscripts of the Eleventh Century*, ed. E. S. Dewick, HBS 21 (London, 1902), xiv.

devotions; Ælfric's *Colloquy* and his *De temporibus anni*; the Margaret *passio*; Ælfric's Palm Sunday homily; a Sunday Letter; some short homilies, the *ordo* for the ordination of a bishop, directions for confessors, a text on monastic sign language, a lapidary, part of one of Ælfric's pastoral letters and an Office of the Virgin (of which the litany forms part). Three saints in the litany are in capitals: Augustine of Canterbury, Dunstan and Margaret. There are two miniatures, forming frontispieces to the *Regula S. Benedicti* and the *Regularis concordia*.[3] The miniature accompanying the *Regula*, probably a copy of a lost Winchester archetype, shows an enthroned St Benedict expounding the *Regula* to a group of monks, while below one kneeling monk kisses Benedict's feet and another girds himself with a scroll representing the *Regula*.[4] The *Regularis concordia*'s line drawing, which was probably copied from a tenth-century dedication copy of the text, depicts King Edgar, with Bishop Æthelwold on his left and Archbishop Dunstan on his right, all three co-enthroned and holding a long scroll representing the text of the customary, while below them a genuflecting monk represents those for whom the text was written.[5]

The Margaret *passio* on 73v–77v is the only saint's life in the manuscript. It was copied by Ker's scribe three (A in this discussion): this scribe was responsible for glossing the *Regularis concordia* in Old English, for writing some of the prognostics, for the gloss to Ælfric's *Colloquy* and for the Old English texts on 65v–95v (Ælfric's *De temporibus*, homilies and directions for a confessor). Punctuation in the homily is restricted to the point, except for one instance of the *punctus elevatus* (in ch. 15). A very large number of additions and alterations has been incorporated in the text 'in brown ink, in a small upward-sloping hand of s. xi^2'[6] (scribe C in this discussion). A second correcting hand is also at work in the Margaret text, but, because so many of the corrections are very brief (often a single letter), it is not always possible to distinguish which hand has made a particular alteration.[7] The scribe of the small hand and the brown ink also worked on other texts in the manuscript, but the other, larger hand appears to have been at work only on the Margaret *passio*.

The manuscript is in many ways an odd compilation and it is difficult to

---

[3] Both miniatures are discussed by Deshman, '*Benedictus monarcha et monachus*'.

[4] For a reproduction, see Temple, *Anglo-Saxon Manuscripts 900–1066*, fig. 314.

[5] For a reproduction, see Temple, *ibid.*, fig. 313.   [6] Ker, *Catalogue*, p. 240.

[7] This was first pointed out by Herbst, *Die altenglische Margaretenlegende*, pp. 1–3.

see how the different parts cohere. The monastic rules with which it begins clearly form a planned collection of monastic materials, both traditional and English, and Deshman points out how the very structure of the manuscript 'is laden with meaning'.[8] The supplements to the *Regula S. Benedicti* are standard in manuscripts produced as a result of the Benedictine Reform, but 'it seems to have been the innovation of the redactor of the Tiberius manuscript to append the *Regularis concordia* to the supplemented edition of the Rule' and 'as a result, the three texts associated with the Carolingian reform have assumed the place of mediators, so to speak, between the Benedictine Rule and the *Regularis concordia*, with the latter's frontispiece picture coming after the Carolingian monastic legislation.'[9] After the *Regularis concordia*, and surprisingly in view of the attention devoted to planning the manuscript up to this point, it then takes on a much more miscellaneous character, giving to some extent the impression that texts were gathered according as they came to hand, though with an emphasis on vernacular devotional materials. While some of the texts, such as the directions for confessors and the Office of the Virgin, were written for a particular practical purpose, it is difficult to imagine this manuscript as having been intended for direct use in practical contexts, as texts for very different situations are placed side by side. The manuscript perhaps came to be viewed primarily as a type of reference book, preserving texts of interest to the community and serving as a handy repository for such diverse items as the lapidary and the guide to monastic sign language. The Old English homilies are perhaps the most likely to have been put to practical use for preaching from this manuscript, and that many of them are glossed in a hand of the second half of the eleventh century indicates a continuing interest. The texts thus glossed are the two short Ælfric texts on confession, the Margaret *passio* and a series of twelve short homiletic pieces by Wulfstan or drawn from his writings. The first ten are headed *To eallum folce*, the last two *To mæssepreostum*, and they principally contain exhortation and advice of a very basic level. The first ten are clearly for preaching to a general congregation and, as the same glossator worked on them and the Margaret text, it suggests that the *passio* could have been regarded in the same fashion. On the other hand, it is a much longer text and, of course, of a different nature.

The importance granted to Margaret in the manuscript is puzzling: hers

---

[8] Deshman, '*Benedictus monarcha et monachus*', p. 229.   [9] *Ibid.*

is the only saint's life in the collection and the Tiberius litany is the only Anglo-Saxon litany in which her name is entered in capitals, according her the same status as the Canterbury saints Augustine and Dunstan.

We may now turn to a detailed examination of the text of the *passio* of Margaret as it is preserved in Tiberius A. iii. Three scribes were at work on the version of the Margaret text in this manuscript. The original scribe, A, copied the text and made some corrections, probably based partly on the exemplar and partly on his own initiative, since it is clear that his dialect differed from that of the exemplar.[10] Two further scribes, termed B and C by Herbst and in this discussion, subsequently revised and corrected the text. Herbst argues convincingly, on the basis of two passages in the text, that B worked before C.[11] In ch. 2, A wrote *gesealde*; B then erased *g* and wrote *h* on the erasure, producing *he sealde*. Between *he* and *sealde* C has inserted *ge*, which makes sense only after B's erasure. In ch. 9, A wrote *we seoþ hnacod þinne lichama beon cwylmiend*. B added *ge* to *seoþ*, added *þe*, *-e* to *hnacod* and *ge* to *cwylmiend*, of which the *i* and *n* were erased, giving therefore *we geseoþ þe hnacode þinne lichama beon gecwylmed*. C then added a contraction stroke to *lichama* and 7 before *þinne*, resulting in *we geseoþ þe hnacode and þinne lichaman beon gecwylmed*. As Herbst points out, C's *and* is necessary only because of B's introduction of *þe*.

The work of the two correctors can, in most cases, be clearly distinguished in the text, as their hands are very different. B, the first corrector, adds case endings on possessives, adjectives and nouns, adds or alters verb-endings, adds *ge* to the preterite of verbs, changes *beo* and *bist* to *eom* and *eart*, adds *-o* to some feminine *se* articles and sometimes alters *on* to *to*. This scribe also makes some more substantial changes, inserting, for example, *he cwæþ ne* before the executioner's speech (ch. 22), where the sense of the passages clearly demands such an addition; altering *snyttro* to *gesælþe* (ch. 15) and *gecwille* to *ofsleh* (ch. 22); inserting *þe on þe gelevat* on an erasure, probably of something similar (ch. 10).

C makes many of the same kind of grammatical corrections as B, whose alterations and additions had been far from entirely systematic, and also makes lexical substitutions: *forspillan* for *forleosan* (ch. 9); *anlyht* for *gefeonde* (ch. 13); *fram geleafan* for *hera sefan* (ch. 15); *geswinge* for *gewinne* (ch. 19); *godes wifes* for *siþwifes* (ch. 24); *beon bliðe* for *wesaþ onbryrdad* (ch. 24). New words and phrases, often making the meaning more explicit, are also

---

[10] See below, pp. 97–103.   [11] Herbst, *Die altenglische Margaretenlegende*, pp. 1–3.

added: where the A text says merely that *Crist geþrowade*, C adds *deað for eall mankin* (ch. 2); to A's *forþgefaren*, C adds *of þisan life* (ch. 3); to A's *þus gebæd*, C adds *hig to Crist* (ch. 13); and to A's *gecyþ hine, Drihten*, C adds *his bene* (ch. 19). C occasionally adds emotive details, e.g. *swiðe* in *swingan swiðe* (ch. 8) and *wælhreowan* in *þone wælhreowan deofol* (ch. 16). C regularly inserts short temporal adverbs (*þa* seven times and *nu* three). At the end of the text C reduces what this corrector seems to have regarded as the excesses of the A text with regard to Margaret's cult: while in the A text the dove tells Margaret that God will set three hundred angels in her church to receive men's prayers, in C this is reduced to three angels (ch. 20); in A a thousand angels bless Margaret's body, but in C this becomes *manega* (ch. 22); and in A *twelf englas* come to take her head to heaven, but *twelf* is marked for deletion, leaving only *englas* (ch. 23). It is hardly too much to assume that the C corrector was responsible for the underlining of *twelf*.

As well as corrections made by altering the text, there are many accomplished by erasure and deletion marks. *Hire*, for example, is used in the original text for the accusative feminine singular as well as the dative, but the *-re* is regularly erased in the accusative. There are many such alterations by erasure to the grammar and word-forms of the text. It is, of course, impossible to know whether A, B or C was responsible for these. Other passages are marked for omission by underlining. Margaret's address to Olibrius in ch. 10 as *þu ungefylledlican dracan, mannes ofen*, for example, is so marked: here *mannes ofen* is a puzzling epithet and the deletor may also have wished to avoid the possible confusion of a dragon image shortly before the dragon appears in the narrative. Similarly, *and þu ane wiþ me and wið eall hire cneo ʿcingʾ rise, Cristes gefylgendum, þurh þono deofla magen eall to nahte gebiþ* (ch. 15) is underlined. This passage has been added to by C, who inserted *cing*, but this addition does not aid the sense of the passage and C may therefore have first attempted to produce a more satisfactory meaning and then, giving up, decided to delete. The Old English is clearly corrupt at this point. The final substantial passage to be cancelled is *and nænig on neorxnawonge mare gemetod mid meder ealra Gescippendes nimþe þreo fæmnan* (ch. 20) and, again, the reasons for the deletion can be surmised. While the meaning of the sentence appears to be that only three saints deserve to be compared with the Virgin Mary, this is not self-evident and one of the correctors obviously felt that the possibility of confusion outweighed any other considerations.

Because of this extensive re-working, an edition of the Margaret *uita* in this manuscript presents us with far more problems than that in CCCC 303. The procedure we have chosen is, accordingly, a more complicated and, perhaps, more questionable one. We have decided to print two texts, one of the *uita* as it was copied into the manuscript by the first scribe, A, which is presented here in Appendix 1, and the second, to which we have given priority, a composite text produced by incorporating the additions and corrections of the second and third scribes and following their instructions to delete parts of the A text. By thus producing two versions (albeit one of them as an appendix), we realize that we are laying ourselves open to the charge of refusing to assume what is commonly perceived as the editorial responsibility to produce a single edited text. Printing two texts of a *uita* which exists in only one manuscript of course makes this decision even more unusual.

Our decision was guided by several factors. Had we to produce a single text, the obvious basis in terms of traditional editing procedures would have to be A's text, as it was originally copied into Tiberius A. iii. Because, however, many of the corrections in the manuscript were effected by erasure, this text cannot be recovered in its entirety. A, moreover, appears to have been responsible for some corrections which seem to have been made in order to bring the text more into conformity with this scribe's own dialect and these, too, obscure the integrity of the text. The version of the Margaret legend in the A scribe's exemplar cannot, therefore, be fully recovered. In addition, the A text has been edited twice already, albeit in not easily accessible editions, and our text, while it differs from its forebears in some respects, is naturally similar to them. Our edition of the composite text, on the other hand, is a new undertaking, which is particularly revealing about the reception of and response to an Old English text in the eleventh century.

The composite text is, in fact, an Old English edition of an Old English text. For this reason it is interesting and important enough to be highlighted here, rather than being presented as apparatus to an A text, where it would be too fragmented and difficult to appreciate fully. While most Old English manuscripts do, of course, by their very nature as documents transmitted by different scribes, offer us Old English editions of Old English texts, this procedure can be seen far more clearly here than in most manuscripts. The successive corrections and additions, clearly traceable in the manuscript, allow us to see two Old English correctors in the process of intelligent interpretation of the A text and many of their emendations correspond to those which would be made by any modern editor of the text (e.g. *risaþ* to *rixaþ* (ch. 21) [B], *mægþ* to *mægþhad* (ch. 6) [C], *inre* to *hyre* (ch. 11) [C], *ofastag* to *ofastang* (ch. 22) [C]). Since the author's text cannot be reconstructed with certainty from the A scribe's version, it has, then, seemed legitimate to us to present that text as faithfully as possible in an appendix and to offer as our main text the version which has the advantage of having been mediated and, to some extent, elucidated by two Anglo-Saxon scribes working within a fairly short period of the copying of the legend into Tiberius A. iii. As evidence for the reception of the text at a particular time, their work is invaluable. They are far closer to the original in time and in their knowledge of the language than any modern reader and we have, therefore, felt it essential to give their text in as full a fashion as possible.

We have not felt it justifiable to present the composite text as our only text, however, because there can be no doubt that it sometimes misrepresents the original quite radically, as in the C scribe's treatment of the number of angels in Margaret's church and in attendance on her body. Here the C scribe's alterations are clearly guided by doctrinal considerations and are not simply the result of a desire to make sense of the A text. On the other hand, it could perhaps be argued that we have not gone far enough for those interested in the different stages of the reception history of the work and that we should have produced a different text illustrating each stage in this process. Against this we would argue that the B and C scribes' alterations complement each other, that C has been content to keep the B readings and that there is, therefore, good reason for thus combining their alterations in a single text. C often carries out more systematically what B does sporadically, as, for example, the alteration of *se* to *seo*, adds to B's lexical substitutions and, in addition, goes beyond B in amplifying the text. As B's editorial input is so much less extensive than C's, while following basically the same principles, it has not seemed to us to merit separate presentation. There is, in any case, no difficulty in distinguishing the two scribes' work from the apparatus. We have, too, no means of discerning which scribe was responsible for most of the erasures and this is a further argument for combining both scribes' work in the type of composite edition presented to us in the manuscript itself.

By offering both Old English texts, therefore (that of the A scribe, insofar as it can be recovered, and that which is the result of the combined efforts of all three scribes), we are offering the reader the opportunity to see in a dynamic way the successive stages of the evolution of the text in this manuscript and to read the legend in two very different linguistic forms.

It is the policy of this series to produce critical texts, rather than diplomatic editions, but, since we are offering two texts of the same manuscript, we have decided to vary the editorial procedure somewhat in our two texts. Our version of the A text is a semi-diplomatic one and we have used square brackets, angle brackets, insertion marks and obeli in the text, with none but the most probable conjectures being included. The composite text, on the other hand, is much more thoroughly edited. We have chosen the A text for the very conservative treatment because it seems to us important that the reader should have the opportunity to encounter in a very faithful form the text closest, we presume, to the authorial text.

Our version of the A text is based only on what the A scribe wrote; additions and alterations clearly made by the B or C scribes are not noted. Where the hand responsible for a correction cannot be determined, however, the alteration has been noted in the A apparatus. Erasures, by their very nature, cannot usually be assigned to a particular scribe and, unless there is a clear indication that they are the work of B or C (if, that is, either B or C has replaced the erased reading by an alternative), they have been included here. Where there is a possibility of an erasure having been made by A, then that fact is noted in the apparatus. All such erasures have been indicated in the text. In some cases the erased letters are still visible and they are given here in double square brackets. Where erased letters are indecipherable, dots (corresponding in number up to three to the erased letters) are inserted in double square brackets. Double square brackets are also used for letters which have been altered to other letters, as this represents a type of deletion. Where the text cannot be read but can be guessed with reasonable probability, conjectured letters or words are given in angle brackets inside double square brackets. Angle brackets, when they enclose a blank, indicate that something has been omitted in transmission. Where it is clear that the A scribe has corrected the text, a choice has been made on the basis of superiority of reading. Obeli mark readings which are corrupt, but in cases where an unattributable erasure has resulted in a correct reading there is no obelus, as in such cases the A scribe may have been responsible for the corrected reading. Manuscript abbreviations have been expanded and punctuation and capitalization are acccording to modern convention. Chapter numbers follow Assmann's edition of the CCCC text and of the Latin.

The version of the composite text, on the other hand, relegates all indications of erasures, alterations and additions to the apparatus, and the text has been emended at points where it is obviously corrupt. The only signals used are the superscript letter and number, and the apparatus criticus and commentary are thus keyed to the text. As we have pointed out above, the composite text has already been edited by two Anglo-Saxon scribes and we have added some further emendations to their edition. Other editorial problems are solved, in a manner, by the directions of the Anglo-Saxon scribes to delete in the case of what they regard as a *locus desperandus*, and we have respected their instructions and deleted those passages from our version of the text. They are, of course, preserved in the A text and discussed in the notes. We have chosen not to emend in an effort to carry through systematically the B and C correctors' emendations to the A text where it is not in error: while B and C, for example, add *-o* to almost all instances of A's use of *se* as the feminine article, a few cases have been missed, and we have left these as they stand in the manuscript. As both *se* and *seo* are legitimate forms, we have decided against emendations based on the correctors' principles, rather than their practice. In the composite text's apparatus we have not marked those places where the A scribe has corrected his own formation of a letter, as these corrections are noted in the A apparatus.

CAMBRIDGE, CORPUS CHRISTI COLLEGE 303

CCCC 303 is a large collection, simply produced, of homilies and saints' lives, mainly by Ælfric, from the first half of the twelfth century, forming an ordered vernacular homiliary.[12] The manuscript is very plain, with minuscule rubrics and large red initials at the beginning of the pericopes and homilies and some red initials and black initials highlighted in red within the texts. Forty-four leaves appear to be missing from the beginning and an unknown number from the end of the manuscript, but the remaining texts fall into five groups:

(a) pp. 1–75: homilies for the *temporale* from the second Sunday after Epiphany to Easter.

(b) pp. 76–185: texts for the *sanctorale* from 3 May, the Invention of the Cross, to 6 December, the feast of St Nicholas. All but four of the texts

[12] Ker, *Catalogue*, no. 57.

are by Ælfric, the others being anonymous texts for the Invention of the Cross and SS Margaret, Nicholas and Giles. The last three items are unique.

(c) pp. 203–90: texts for the *temporale* from Rogationtide to the twenty-first Sunday after Pentecost.

(d) pp. 290–360: miscellaneous items, largely by Ælfric.

The work of three scribes can be seen in the manuscript: one writing pp. 1–50 and most of pp. 203–362, the second pp. 51–202 and the third two short passages (p. 226, line 27 – p. 231, line 28 and p. 251, line 10 – p. 254, line 5). Different exemplars lie behind the manuscript, as is obvious from the Ælfric texts which are drawn from different strands of transmission.[13] The Margaret text, on pp. 99–107, is by the second scribe and comes between the texts for the feast of St Paul (29 June) and that of St Laurence (10 August). The main mark of punctuation in the text is the point but the *punctus elevatus* is sometimes used at the end of clauses where the following clause clearly continues the construction (i.e. between syntactically connected clauses). The *punctus interrogativus* is used also, although not consistently. The abbreviations used are 7 for *and*; þ with a stroke through the ascender for *þæt*; *g* with a stroke over it for *ge*; *cw* for *cwæþ*; a stroke over a vowel for a following *m* or *n*; a stroke over a consonant for a vowel followed by *m* or *n*; a stroke over *t* for *ter* and through the ascender of *d* for *der*; *þon* for *þonne* or *þone* and *þin* for *þinne*; *ig* with a stroke over the *g* for *igne*; and *hæl* with a stroke through the *l* for *hælend*. Standard abbreviations are used in Latin names and quotations.

Ker assigns the manuscript to Rochester on the basis of the script ('the "prickly" kind often found in Rochester')[14] and its relationship to Oxford, Bodleian Library, Bodley 340 + 342, an early eleventh-century collection whose provenance is Rochester. Items in CCCC 303 are also related to some in CCCC 162, again probably a Rochester manuscript, so that the compiler of the twelfth-century collection clearly made use of the materials at hand in Rochester.[15] Mary Richards notes that, of the three anonymous

[13] See the discussions by P. A. M. Clemoes, 'The Chronology of Ælfric's Works' in *The Anglo-Saxons: Studies in Some Aspects of their History and Culture Presented to Bruce Dickins*, ed. P. Clemoes (London, 1959), pp. 212–47, at 236; *Homilies of Ælfric*, ed. Pope I, 18–20; *Ælfric's Catholic Homilies*, ed. Godden, pp. xxxiii–xxxvii.

[14] Ker, *Catalogue*, p. 105.

[15] *Ælfric's Catholic Homilies*, ed. Godden, pp. xxxv–xxxvii.

Old English saints' lives in the manuscript, two can be related to
Rochester: Margaret was the patron saint of a local church owned by the
priory and there was 'an important altar for the laity' dedicated to Nicholas
in Rochester Cathedral.[16] Richards points out, too, that two saints with
Rochester connections (Augustine, the founder of the see, and Nicholas)
have been added to the forms of excommunication found in the manuscript.[17] Schipper has suggested that the lives of SS Giles and Nicholas in
the manuscript 'came into existence because the cults of these saints,
introduced into England by the Normans after 1066, created a demand for
vernacular versions of their lives'[18] and that the frequency of late linguistic
forms supports this conjecture. The manuscript would seem to have been
part of the pastoral activities of the monks of Rochester Cathedral, who
were clearly concerned, well into the twelfth century, to cater for the laity
of the town by preaching in the vernacular.[19]

The text of the life of Margaret in CCCC 303 was written and corrected
by one scribe and is very straightforward from the editorial viewpoint. In
the present edition, alterations by the scribe have been incorporated in the
text and are indicated in the apparatus. What we have judged to be
corruptions in the text have been emended and the manuscript readings are
likewise indicated in the apparatus. Capitalization and punctuation follow
modern conventions and the manuscript abbreviations have been silently
expanded. Chapter numbers follow Assmann's edition of the Latin and Old
English texts.

LONDON, BRITISH LIBRARY, COTTON OTHO B. X, FOL. 195

Section C of Otho B. x[20] contained a life of Margaret, of which now only
the *incipit* and *explicit*, recorded by Wanley, are preserved.[21] The manuscript itself, of the first half of the eleventh century but of unknown origin,
was burnt and very badly damaged in the fire in the Cotton Library in
1731, and the portion containing the Margaret text was completely lost.

---

[16] Richards, *Texts and their Traditions*, p. 91.   [17] *Ibid.*

[18] Schipper, 'The Normans and the Old English Lives of Saint Giles and Saint Nicholas',
p. 98.

[19] Richards, *Texts and their Traditions*, pp. 92 and 94.

[20] Ker, *Catalogue*, no. 177.

[21] Wanley, *Librorum Veterum Septentrionalium*, pp. 192–3.

The main part of the manuscript (A) contains lives of saints, most by Ælfric, but it is not clear whether the Margaret text, which is the only text in part C, originally formed part of the same manuscript or not.[22]

The surviving portions of the text, as copied by Wanley, read:

XVII. KL. Agusti. Passio in Anglice De Sancta Margareta Christi Virgine. Post Christi Passionem et Resurrectionem Et Ascensionem Eius Ad Patrem.

Incip. Æfter æriste ures drihtenes hælendes cristes. and his wuldorfæstan upastigenesse on heofonas to þam ælmihtigan gode. On his nama andetnysse maniga martyros wæron þrowiende. and his apostoli geliffæste . . .

Expl. Nu ge gebroðra mine ge gehyrdon be þære eadigan Margaretan þrowunge. hu heo ofer swiðe ealra deofla mægen. gelyfað on hi. 7 on God ælmihtine. 7 doþ gemynd þare halgan fæmnan. Sancta Margaretan. 7 Sancta Marian. 7 on heora ðanc ælmessan syllað. þæt hi eow onfon on gesihþe hælendes cristes. Him is lof. 7 wuldor. 7 weorþmynt. 7 a he lyfaþ mid englum. 7 mid heah fæderum. and mid witegum. 7 mid apostolum. and mid haligum fæmnum. in ealra worulda woruld. abuton ende. Amen.[23]

PARIS, BN, LAT. 5574, FOLS. 1–39

Paris, BN, lat. 5574 is a small collection containing a *uita* of St Christopher, an account of the Invention of the Cross and the *uitae* of SS Margaret and Juliana.[24] It is in Anglo-Saxon minuscule, with some Caroline majuscule forms and with the characteristically Insular arrangement of quires (hair facing flesh). It has been attributed to Mercia on the basis of the similarity of its decoration to that of London, BL, Royal 5. F.

---

[22] Ker, *Catalogue*, p. 224.

[23] 'XVII Kalends of August: The passion of Christ's virgin St Margaret, in English. After the Passion and Resurrection of Christ and his Ascension to the Father: after the Resurrection of our Lord the Saviour Christ and his glorious Ascension to heaven to the Almighty God, many martyrs suffered for confessing his name and his apostles gave them life . . . (?) Now, my brothers, you have heard about the passion of the blessed Margaret, how she overcame the power of all the devils. Believe in her and in God Almighty and commemorate the holy virgins St Margaret and St Mary and give alms for their sakes so that they may receive you in the sight of the Saviour Christ. To him be praise and glory and honour and he lives eternally with the angels and with the patriarchs and with the prophets and with the apostles and with holy virgins for ever and ever, world without end. Amen.'

[24] Described and dated in Avril and Stirnemann, *Manuscrits enluminés*, p. 11 (no. 12 bis).

III.[25] The Royal manuscript is dated *c.* 900 and contains Aldhelm's prose *De laude uirginitatis*; its provenance is Worcester and it is written in several hands 'more or less of Mercian type'.[26] BN lat. 5574 is also thought to date from *c.* 900, again because of its similarity to the Aldhelm manuscript.

The manuscript contains three decorated initials (fols. 1, 18 and 32), sketched in brown ink. The initial on the opening folio is composed of a T whose upright is comprised of a bird's head and two wings and whose cross-stroke has animal head terminals with foliage being emitted from the animals' mouths. Further letters and whole words decorated with leafy frills on the stems and in the bowls are found on fols. 1, 13, 18 (where there is also a pendant heart shape suspended from the capital P) and 32. These frilly foliate motifs are probably indebted to the school of Metz or Tours, where we find similar features from the middle of the ninth century onwards.[27] There are marginal corrections and notes in a twelfth-century French hand.

---

[25] On this manuscript, see J. Morrish, 'Dated and Datable Manuscripts Copied in England during the Ninth Century: A Preliminary List', *Mediæval Studies* 50 (1988), 512–38, at 535; there are facsimiles in Temple, *Anglo-Saxon Manuscripts 900–1066*, no. 2 and ills. 5, 6 and 9. On the decoration, see Wormald, 'Decorated Initials', pp. 52–3 and 174, n. 21.

[26] G. F. Warner and J. P. Gilson, *Catalogue of Western Manuscripts in the Old Royal and King's Collections* I (London, 1921), 120.

[27] See Wormald, 'Decorated Initials', p. 174, n. 21.

7

The language of the Old English texts

Given the mutual independence of the two Old English versions of the legend of St Margaret and their differing manuscript histories, it is appropriate to discuss the language of our two texts separately. Where relevant, however, comparisons will be made below concerning the language of the two versions.

THE TIBERIUS VERSION

The language of the Tiberius version of the legend, as preserved in our unique manuscript, is predominantly late West Saxon, but with a remarkable proportion of non-West Saxon elements and of features associated with the transition from Old to Middle English. This non-standard West Saxon aspect of the language of the *Legend* is not reflected to anything like the same extent in the other texts in Cotton Tiberius A. iii copied by Scribe A, Ker's 'Scribe 3'.[1] It is likely, therefore, that the linguistic idiosyncrasy of the Margaret text has been largely inherited from the copyist's exemplar containing the *Legend of St Margaret*. Many of the interventions of the correctors B and C in the *Legend* are in the direction of harmonizing the language of this text with more regular West Saxon practice, as reflected elsewhere in the manuscript.

The language of the Tiberius version has been studied in detail by Herbst, to whose analysis the present account is much indebted. Herbst discerns some Kentish influence in the *Legend*, which *is* reflected more widely in the manuscript and which may arise from Cotton Tiberius A. iii having been copied at Canterbury.[2] Herbst's analysis of the language of the

---

[1] See Ker, *Catalogue*, p. 248.   [2] Herbst, *Die altenglische Margaretenlegende*, p. 46.

Legend leads her to conclude that this text had a Mercian and a Northumbrian stage in its transmission.[3] We already know that a version of the Latin *passio* similar to that used by the translator of the Tiberius version existed in Anglo-Saxon England in the Anglian dialect area, as this served as source for the *Old English Martyrology* analogue.

This knowledge of the Latin version in the Anglian area might itself encourage us to consider the possibility of an Anglian origin for our Old English text. The linguistic evidence also leans in this direction. In the light of his exhaustive study of Anglian vocabulary, Wenisch comes to the conclusion that the Tiberius version is probably of Anglian origin.[4] This view is endorsed by Hofstetter,[5] who points out in particular the fundamental deviation from Winchester lexical usage apparent in the *Legend*. So extraordinary to Hofstetter is the single occurrence in the Tiberius version of the Winchester word *wuldorbeah* 'crown of glory (in heaven)' (ch. 2)[6] that he concludes that this must represent a substitution for a different original reading. Hofstetter adds that it is impossible to tell whether this substitution was introduced in Cotton Tiberius A. iii itself ('probably in Canterbury') or at an earlier stage in the transmission.[7] As against *wuldorbeah*, the *Legend* has the non-Winchester *gesygefæst* (ch. 10: translating Latin *coronata*[8]); it also has the phrase *wuldres beh* (ch. 18).

The distinctive elements of Anglian vocabulary have been established most fully by Wenisch, building on the earlier researches of Jordan and others.[9] Among the 'Anglian' words identified by these scholars we find in the *Legend* the prepositions *nimþe* 'except' (ch. 20; A text only) (as well as *buton*) and *in* 'in, on' (chs. 6, 7, 10) (as well as *on*); *nænig* 'no one' (ch. 20; A text only) (as well as *nan*); and *eþian* 'breathe' (ch. 12) instead of WS *orþian*.[10] There are also in the *Legend* occurrences of a number of words

---

[3] *Ibid.*, p. 45.   [4] Wenisch, *Spezifisch anglisches Wortgut*, p. 327.

[5] Hofstetter, *Winchester und der spätaltenglische Sprachgebrauch*, p. 236.

[6] References in this chapter to the Tiberius version are to the Comp text unless otherwise specified.

[7] Hofstetter, *Winchester und der spätaltenglische Sprachgebrauch*, p. 236.

[8] Cas, p. 228.

[9] Wenisch, *Spezifisch anglisches Wortgut*; Jordan, *Eigentümlichkeiten des anglischen Wortschatzes*; see also R. J. Menner, 'Anglian and Saxon Elements in Wulfstan's Vocabulary', *Modern Language Notes* 63 (1948), 1–9, and 'The Anglian Vocabulary of the *Blickling Homilies*'; *The Life of St Chad*, ed. Vleeskruyer, pp. 23–37.

[10] See Jordan, *Eigentümlichkeiten des anglischen Wortschatzes*, p. 54. Herbst notes also *sopfæst* and *gewinne* (*Die altenglische Margaretenlegende*, p. 25).

which are found in early West Saxon as well as Anglian, but not in late West Saxon. Herbst notes the following: *hwæthwugo* 'some, a certain amount' (ch. 2) instead of *sum, ænig*; *tid* 'time' (ch. 4 etc.) instead of *tima*; *carcern* 'prison' (ch. 6 etc.) as well as 1WS *cweartern* (ch. 15: one occurrence of the latter form, as opposed to five of *carcern*); *snyttro* 'wisdom' (ch. 15: A text only) instead of *wisdom* (here B emends *snyttro* to *gesælþe*); *gefeon* 'rejoice' (ch. 18; A text only) instead of *fægnian* (here C emends *gefeonde* to *anlyht*); *cigan* 'call' (chs. 17, 20) instead of *clipian*: Anglian preserves this meaning for *cigan*, but in late West Saxon the sense, found only once in the *Legend* (ch. 6), is normally 'name, call by name'.[11]

Phonological forms which might suggest Anglian influence are *saga* (imperative sing. of *secgan*: ch. 16, twice) and *eam* (1 sing. pres. indic. of the verb 'to be': chs. 15, 22), which occurs alongside West Saxon and Kentish *eom*. As Herbst points out,[12] these forms are indeed normally regarded as specifically Mercian. It should be noted, however, that *eam* also appears in Kentish texts.[13] The *eam* forms are not corrected in the manuscript, but B, in two substitutions where A had *beo*, writes *eom*, not *eam* (chs. 5, 11). *Saga* is emended by C to the normal late West Saxon form *sege* (ch. 16) and by B to the hybrid-looking *sage* (ch. 16).

The adjectival form *gingre* (ch. 15) looks distinctively Northumbrian: in West Saxon *i* appears in the stem of this adjective in the comparative and superlative forms, but not in the positive (WS *geong*). *Gingre* could conceivably be a comparative form but Herbst argues persuasively that the occurrence in the *Legend* is positive (dat. sing. fem.), translating perhaps *paruula puella*.[14]

A number of other phonological features of the *Legend* might be mentioned which appear to reflect the non-West Saxon aspect of our text's language.

The form *hio*, not found in 'regular' late West Saxon, appears as acc. sing. fem. personal pronoun (ch. 11).[15] *Hio* also appears, in corrections (thus suggesting Kentish influence), as nom./acc. pl. (chs. 17, 24). And it occurs once as nom. sing. fem. (ch. 11), alongside *hi* (ch. 24) and the more

---

[11] Herbst, *Die altenglische Margaretenlegende*, pp. 27–8.   [12] *Ibid.*, p. 9.

[13] Campbell §768 (d); as noted below (p. 105), *eam* occurs in CCCC.

[14] Herbst, *Die altenglische Margaretenlegende*, pp. 13–14.

[15] Campbell §703, has one citation of *hio*, acc. sing. fem., in 'Martyrology fragment'.

usual *heo* (ch. 11 etc.). *Hio* and *hi*, nom. sing. fem., occur in the *Kentish Glosses*.[16]

The pres. subjunctive form *cyme* (ch. 10), with *y* instead of *u*, is restricted to the earlier period in West Saxon but in Anglian it appears in later texts as well.[17]

Such forms as *ongete* (ch. 11) and *deofolgeld* (ch. 3) lack the characteristic West Saxon diphthongization triggered by a preceding initial consonant; the non-West Saxon form *get* (ch. 20) has itself been altered in the manuscript, probably by B, from *git*, in what appears to be a reverse spelling.

The forms *weorlde* (chs. 11, 18) and *weorulde* (ch. 10) show simple *u*-Umlaut, where late West Saxon normally has combinative *u*-Umlaut (as in the *woruld* forms in the *Legend*, ch. 21 etc.).

Though found in early West Saxon and early Kentish, the *o* spellings in such forms as *gongaþ* (ch. 5) (as well as *gangaþ*, ch. 9), *hond* (ch. 7 etc.) (as well as *hand*, ch. 5 etc.), and *noman* (ch. 21) (as well as *nama*, ch. 6 etc.) are likely to reflect Anglian influence in the period of our manuscript.[18]

ē for WS *īe* (1WS *ȳ*) appears in *geheran* (ch. 9), *geheraþ* (ch. 2) etc., and, represented by *æ*,[19] in *gehærþ* (ch. 2); *y* forms of this verb also occur (chs. 7, 9 etc.). *ē* for WS *īe* also appears in the pres. indic. pl. form *geleuat* 'believe' written by B (ch. 10).[20] Most occurrences in the *Legend* of this verb (1WS *gelīefan*) have *æ* instead of *e* as their stem vowel (chs. 2, 8 etc.); the diphthong *ea* appears once (*geleafaþ*, imperative pl., ch. 9), and *i* twice (*gelifaþ*, pres. indic. pl., ch. 24; *gelifde*, pret. indic. 3 sing., ch. 2).

The *Legend* exhibits the form *cwyllere* (ch. 19 etc.), as well as regular WS

---

[16] Campbell (*ibid.*).   [17] Campbell §742.

[18] See Herbst, *Die altenglische Margaretenlegende*, pp. 9–10; Campbell §130.

[19] Confusion of *æ* and *e* in late Old English can arise particularly under Kentish influence, because of Kentish raising of *æ* to *e*: see Campbell §§169, 288–90.

[20] Here the medial *u* and the suffix are notable. In discussing orthographic practice in the late Old English and early Middle English period, D. G. Scragg comments on *u/v* for *f*: 'Since scribes became used to ⟨v⟩ to represent Latin /v/, they tended occasionally to extend it to native words containing [v] medially, and with the arrival in subsequent centuries of many French loanwords with /v/ initially, so that voiced and voiceless sounds became phonemic, /v/ and /f/ came to be distinguished regularly graphemically', *A History of English Spelling* (Manchester, 1974), p. 13, n. 4.

In discussing variant 3rd sing. pres. indic. endings, Campbell notes the occurrence of endings in *-et*, *-it* in the *Kentish Glosses*, though he cites no examples of *-at*. In Tib, note also the 3rd sing. form *gesættet* (ch. 20) and the pl. *gemundyt* (ch. 24, addition by B).

cwelleras (ch. 9). The former may represent Kentish reverse spelling, with the scribe assuming that *e* forms of this word would require *y* in West Saxon. The *Legend* has eight occurrences of the *y* spelling but only one of the *e*.

With regard to some of these phonological features, as with others which could be noted as well, it is impossible to be categorical concerning the origins of the divergence from usual late West Saxon. There is nothing in the phonological evidence, however, inconsistent with the view that the translation itself was done in the late Old English period, but outside the West Saxon sphere. This view is supported also by aspects of the morphology of the *Legend*. The non-West Saxon morphological features include the use of unsyncopated (as well as the more usual West Saxon syncopated) forms of the 2nd and 3rd sing. pres. indic. of verbs (e.g. *gehyrest*, ch. 7; *gefihtaþ*, ch. 10) and the use of endingless imperative singulars in the verbs *biddan*, *secgan* and *sittan*. *Bid* (ch. 19) and *sit* (ch. 20) are 'regularized' by C, but *sæcg* (ch. 16) remains unchanged. There is indeed a considerable variety of forms of the imperative singular of *secgan* in our text: *sægæ* (ch. 6), with *æ* for *e* in both syllables; *saga*, corrected by C to *sege* (ch. 16) and by B to *sage* (ch. 16); *sæcg* (ch. 16), uncorrected; and *secgæ* (ch. 16), which appears to be a scribal correction of an erroneous reading *secgan*, with *æ* for *e*.

The breakdown of the Old English inflexional system is unusually far advanced in this text, considering that it is written in a manuscript of the mid-eleventh century. Levelling of vowels in suffixes is widely exemplified. Notable instances in noun phrase elements are *martyres*, nom. pl. (ch. 1), uncorrected in the manuscript; *halgæ fæmnæ*, nom. sing. (ch. 12), altered, probably by C, from *halga fæmna*; *hira*, gen. sing. fem. (ch. 17); *minra*, dat. sing. fem. (ch. 7), written by B; *þearfendra and earfoþra*, also dat. sing. fem. (ch. 12); *þære hæþenre*, gen. pl. (ch. 3); the demonstrative form *þono*, acc. sing. masc. (ch. 19); C also writes *minna*, acc. sing. masc., correcting *min* (chs. 5, 19).

Final -*e* and -*ne* are widely omitted in possessive adjectives and the required endings are supplied, with some inconsistency, by B and C. Final -*e* is also frequently omitted in trisyllabic forms with stressed first syllable: for example, *karcern*, dat. sing. (ch. 12), with -*e* added by B; *innoþ*, dat. sing. (ch. 13), with -*e* added by C. Notable as well are the endingless dat. sing. forms of monosyllabic stems: *word* (ch. 10), with -*e* added by C; *bæþ* (ch. 18), with -*e* added by B; etc. Such forms are usually corrected in the

101

manuscript, but *tid* (ch. 18, twice) remains unaltered. There even appears to be one instance of an endingless dative in an addition by C: at the beginning of ch. 13 this reviser inserts the phrase *to Crist*.

Datives in *-um*, however, are conservatively preserved, with 'strong' *-an* being confined to corrections, as in C's correction of *cwylleras* (the latter form is best taken as a simple scribal error) to *cwylleran*, dat. pl. (ch. 5) and insertion of *butan wifan and cildan* (ch. 18). Another conservative feature is the preservation of *-u* in the nom. and acc. pl. of neuter nouns: exceptions are *deofle*, acc. (ch. 12), and *wæpne*, nom. (ch. 15).

Oblique cases of weak nouns sometimes lack the expected nasal ending. Although B and C are active in correcting such irregularities, some instances remain unaltered, e.g. *lichoma*, acc. (ch. 17), *fæmne*, acc. (ch. 22). In the reading *þinne sweora* (ch. 19) *-ne* has been added by B to the possessive to provide the required acc., but *sweora* has not been emended. The reading *eorþan* (ch. 23), where we would expect *eorþe*, may represent a reverse spelling of this. The verb form *beeode*, in a context which requires the plural number (ch. 1; A text only), also lacks final *-n* (C alters this to *beeodan*), but this unusual form may simply be due to a scribal lapse.

Quite apart from *beeode*, however, verb suffixes in the *Legend* show considerable variation, indicating levelling of inflexion. We find pret. pls. in *-en* as well as *-an* and *-on*: *stoden* (ch. 9), *weopen* (ch. 9), and *dyden* (ch. 18) are all indicatives. Past participles occur in *-an* as well as *-en*: for example, *ahangan* (ch. 6), *forlætan* (ch. 22); and infinitives in *-on* and *-en*: *gelædon* (ch. 6), *ælen* (ch. 18), corrected by C to *ælan*. The form *aþenoda* occurs as a pret. sing. (ch. 12).

Many of these features indicating the breakdown of the inflexional system can be paralleled readily enough in other eleventh-century manuscripts, but two significant transitional features of the *Legend* are worthy of particular note as highly exceptional in manuscripts of this period. The first of these, a phonological feature, is the monophthongization of *eo* to *e* (long and short) resulting in the forms *se*, demonstrative nom. sing. fem. (found throughout the text and almost always corrected to *seo*) and *be*, imperative sing. of *beon* (ch. 23; corrected to *beo*, probably by B).[21] This

---

[21] Cecily Clark discusses confusion between *se* and *seo* in the twelfth-century *Peterborough Chronicle*: see *The Peterborough Chronicle 1070–1154*, ed. C. Clark, 2nd ed. (London, 1970), pp. lix–lxi.

sound change leads to reverse spellings in *feolde* (ch. 5: changed to *felde* by C; ch. 19), *ableonde* (ch. 15) and *gesweotte* (ch. 24).

The second significant transitional feature, a morphological one, is the use of *hire* for the acc. sing. fem. of the third person pronoun. This is the form used regularly in the *Legend*, though it is always corrected in the manuscript to *hi* or variant (see, for example, chs. 3, 5, 12).

These two features are not typical of the manuscript as a whole. Their early occurrence in our text of the *Legend* has been seen as suggesting a Northumbrian influence, as they were introduced in the Northumbrian speech area earlier than elsewhere.[22] Like other aspects of our text, the presence of these features leads to the conclusion that the *Legend* was introduced into the south in the eleventh century through a copy whose language had a distinctive Northumbrian orientation (as well as the Mercian elements mentioned above). As noted at the beginning of this section, the lexical evidence suggests an Anglian origin for the translation itself.

THE CCCC VERSION

The language of the CCCC 303 version is also predominantly late West Saxon, though again with a significant proportion of non-West Saxon features. In many respects the language of the St Margaret text is consistent with that of the lives of SS Giles and Nicholas copied in this manuscript by the same hand, Ker's 'second hand' of the three that he identifies.[23] Schipper points out, however, that the 'non-standard' features of these saints' lives are absent from the Ælfrician items in the collection copied by this scribe.[24] This suggests that they go back to the scribe's exemplar(s). It is also notable that, although the non-West Saxon aspect of this version of the legend of St Margaret is clearly evident, the language of this text approximates more closely in some ways to 'standard' late West Saxon than does that of the considerably earlier Cotton Tiberius analogue. For example, syncopated forms of the 2nd and 3rd person sing. present indic. of verbs are used throughout (*gelefst*, ch. 4; *hæfð*, ch. 6 etc.), and *ea*

---

[22] See Herbst, *Die altenglische Margaretenlegende*, p. 30.   [23] Ker, *Catalogue*, p. 105.

[24] Schipper, 'The Normans and the Old English lives of Saint Giles and Saint Nicholas', p. 102. On the language of this manuscript, see also Picard, *Das altenglische Aegidius-leben*, pp. 17–34.

spellings are preserved in such words as *beseah* (ch. 5), *geseah* (ch. 5), and *spearwe* (ch. 5): Tiberius has *gesæh/geseh* (chs. 12/5 etc.), *besæh* (ch. 7 etc.), and *spærwe* (ch. 5).[25]

There is no widespread Anglian element in the vocabulary of the CCCC version. Anglian influence is possibly present in the use of the noun *carcern* 'prison', instead of WS *cweartern*,[26] but the vocabulary generally accords with West Saxon practice, although there is no evidence of influence of the stricter usage associated with Bishop Æthelwold and his circle. The general West Saxon character of the vocabulary of CCCC is reflected in the employment of such words as *tima* (ch. 22), *wisdom* (ch. 5), *nan* (ch. 6 etc.) and *clipian* (ch. 9 etc.) (whereas Tiberius has *tid, snyttro, nænig* and *cigan*).[27] CCCC uses *tid* only in the sense 'hour' (ch. 9). The use of *cerdon* (ch. 6), as well as *ahwerfan* (ch. 5) and *gehwerfan* (ch. 5), and of *andwyrde* (ch. 6), as well as *andswerode* (ch. 7 etc.), perhaps suggests a conscious conservatism in vocabulary.[28] On the other hand, we should note the occurrence of *bread* instead of *hlaf*: *bread* in the sense 'bread' is extremely rare in Old English. Its occurrence in the CCCC St Margaret supports the belief that this is a late composition. The *Oxford English Dictionary* comments (s.v. *bread*) that 'before 1200 *bread* had quite displaced *hlaf*'. Also notable is the occurrence of *seagntes* (ch. 1), as well as OE *sancte* (ch. 4 etc.): the spelling of this word may suggest Anglo-Norman influence.[29]

Among non-West Saxon phonological features is the use of the form *eorre* 'angry' (ch. 10 etc.) as well as *yrre* (ch. 11 etc.); *eo* for WS *y* also appears in *creopoles* 'cripples' (ch. 15) (*crypol* and *crypeles* also occur, chs. 19 and 23); *y* for *eo* appears in *gefyll* 'fell' (ch. 22) (*feol* also occurs, ch. 22): here the *y* form may be due to reverse spelling, but Picard suggests Anglo-Norman scribal influence in the employment of such *y* forms in this manuscript, as they are

---

[25] The spellings *feagre* (ch. 21) (alongside *fægre*, ch. 6 etc.) and *pear* (ch. 23) (alongside *þær*, ch. 4 etc.) may represent reverse spellings, or they may be transitional features. *Pear* is rare in Old English, occurring notably in the Worcester Chronicle (*c.* 1050) and the Peterborough Chronicle (written in the first half of the twelfth century). The only parallel to the spelling *feagre* is in the *Life of St Nicholas* in CCCC 303 (*DOE* transcript, line 1).

[26] See Menner, 'The Anglian Vocabulary of the *Blickling Homilies*', p. 59; Vleeskruyer, *The Life of St Chad*, p. 26. *St Nicholas* has *cwærtern* (*DOE* transcript, line 395 etc.).

[27] See above, p. 99.   [28] See Vleeskruyer, *The Life of St Chad*, p. 26.

[29] Spellings similar to *seagntes* are not recorded for this word in *MED* (see s.v. *seint(e)*). For *bread*, see also *MED* (s.v. *brēd*).

not reported as recorded elsewhere in Old English or Middle English.[30] Notable also in the Margaret text are the present tense Class V verb forms *geofa* (ch. 20) (as well as *gife*, ch. 7) and *geofð* (ch. 9) and the Class VII preterites *aheongan* (ch. 6) (as well as *ahengan*, ch. 6) and *underfeongan* (ch. 22) (as well as *onfenge*, ch. 23). The *eo* spellings in the preterites of *(-)hon* and *(-)fon* are confined to the present text.

Specifically Kentish features are apparent in the *e* spellings of such words as *selle* (ch. 4), *cerdon* (ch. 6), *eldan* (as well as *yldran*, ch. 6) (ch. 6 etc.) and *self* (ch. 10 etc.),[31] and in the back-mutated form *sioððan* (ch. 15; note also *siððan*, ch. 15).[32] On the other hand, Anglian influence is suggested by the unbroken stem vowels in *gewald* (ch. 9) and *wallende* (chs. 4, 18) (contrast *wealden*, ch. 7 etc.; *weallende*, ch. 18). The past participle *gesegon* 'seen' (ch. 15) is also Anglian, and the preterite forms *geseage* (ch. 12) and *geseagan* (ch. 18) also derives from the Anglian paradigm of this verb, with *e* appearing as *ea*.[33]

Kentish inflexional patterns can be seen in the use of the pres. subjunctive 3 sing. forms *sio* (ch. 20) and *seo* (ch. 5, twice) of the verb 'to be' (as well as *sy*, ch. 13 etc.)[34] and probably also in the 1 sing. pres. indic. *eam* (ch. 14 etc.) (as well as *eom*, ch. 6 etc.), though *eam* also occurs in Mercian.[35] The appearance, alongside *hio/heo* (chs. 5, 15 etc.), of *hi* as the nom. sing. fem. of the third person pronoun (ch. 3 etc.) is also in accordance with Kentish practice, as is the appearance of *hio/heo* instead of *hie* (*hio*, acc. sing. fem., ch. 10 etc.; nom. pl., ch. 15 etc.; *heo*, acc. sing. fem. (?), ch. 23; nom. pl., ch. 3 etc.).[36] As against these Kentish features, however, the occurrence of 1 sing. pres. indic. verbs in *-a* is normally taken as indicating Northumbrian influence. In the *Legend* we find *behata* (ch. 4), *gelefa* (ch. 6), and *geofa* (ch. 20).

Thus the specifically Kentish influence on the late West Saxon language of our text, an influence which accords with the palaeographical pointers that the manuscript was probably written at Rochester,[37] can be seen as accompanied by some admixture of other dialect forms. This mixture of

[30] Picard, *Das altenglische Aegidiusleben*, p. 18.
[31] Campbell comments, 'It is plain that all front vowels except *ī* appeared in late Kentish as *ē*' (Campbell §288).
[32] Campbell §217.   [33] Campbell §743.   [34] Campbell §768 (d).
[35] Campbell (*ibid.*). On *eam* forms in Tib, see above, p. 99.
[36] Campbell §703.
[37] See Richards, 'Innovations in Ælfrician Homiletic Manuscripts', p. 17.

forms and the lateness of the text itself make it impossible to be certain about the geographical origin of the translation. The lack of a clear-cut Anglian component in the vocabulary of the piece would incline us to assign the composition to the south. One should add the caveat, however, that if, as seems not unlikely, the CCCC St Margaret was composed as late as the late eleventh or early twelfth century, we can hardly place complete confidence in dialectal lexical criteria.

There is little positive linguistic evidence for precise dating of this version of the legend, as it is often difficult to distinguish in our text between authorial and scribal contributions. CCCC is itself a copy, and we do not know at how many removes it is from the original composition. What little linguistic evidence there is, however, accords with the impression given by the content of this version, that it was composed not very long before the date of the manuscript. The lexical items *bread* and *seagnt*, mentioned above, support this impression. Particularly remarkable in the CCCC version is the occurrence of the Middle English indefinite pronouns *men* and *me* (from OE *man*) (chs. 6, 17 (twice), 19), though we cannot be sure that these reduced forms were what the original translator, as opposed to a later scribe, wrote.

More generally, the language of the CCCC version is characterized by a late Old English levelling of inflexions similar to that which we have observed in the Tiberius version. Thus among verbs we find infinitives in *-on* (*utlædon*, ch. 7 etc.) and *-en* (*finden*, ch. 4 etc.), pres. indic. pls. in *-eð* (*willeð*, ch. 10; *rædeð*, ch. 19) and *-æð* (*willæð*, ch. 19), subjunctive pls. in *-an* (*beswican*, ch. 5 etc.), pret. indic. pls. in *-an* (*noldan*, ch. 5 etc.) and *-en* (*ofercomen*, ch. 1 etc.), and strong past participles in *-on* (*gecwedon*, ch. 15 etc.) and *-an* (*befangan*, ch. 5 etc.). The following weak 3 sing. pret. indic. forms also occur: *gehersamedo* (ch. 4), *dydo* (ch. 5) and *seneda* (ch. 17).

In nominal groups, also, many of the traditional inflexional distinctions have been lost. Strong masc. nom. and acc. pls. occur in *-es* (e.g. *godes*, ch. 1; *cinges*, ch. 4) and neuters in *-a* (*deofla*, ch. 1) and *-e* (*deofle*, ch. 5). In the sequence 'weres ge wifes, ge cnihtes ge mægdenes' (ch. 4) the neuter nouns *wif* and *mægden* are assimilated to the masculine pattern, with *-es* in the nom. pl. Adjectival elements can have *-a* as well as *-e* in the nom. and acc. pl. (*gegrafena*, ch. 4 etc.). As well as *-um*, datives appear in *-an* (*gecorenan*, ch. 4 etc.), *-en* (*handen*, ch. 4 etc.) and *-on* (*wordon*, ch. 15). There is variation between *þære* and *þæra* in the gen./dat. fem. sing. and gen. pl. of the demonstrative *se* (e.g., *þæra micclan leofan lufan*, ch. 1; *ealra* *þære goda*, ch. 13); *þonu* appears as acc. sing. masc. of the demonstrative *se* (ch. 13).

As in Tiberius, there is confusion concerning the endings of oblique cases of weak nouns and adjectives, with much loss of the nasal. The dat. sing. of *heorte*, for example, appears as *heorta* (ch. 4), *heorte* (ch. 9), and *heortan* (ch. 17). In one short passage in ch. 18 the form *fæmne* appears as nom., acc. (twice), gen. and dat. Other lapses in traditional concord occur throughout the text, though less pervasively than in Tiberius. It is noticeable, for example, that the full inflexion of possessive adjectives is preserved more rigorously in CCCC: *mine sawle*, acc. (ch. 5; contrast *min sawle*, nom., ch. 5); *min gewitt and minne wisdom*, acc. (ch. 5); etc. Despite the solecisms in our text it is evident that CCCC reproduces with care conservative features of the late West Saxon language of its exemplar.

The Old English Life of St Margaret in
Cotton Tiberius A. iii (composite text)

Editorial Conventions

In the following Old English texts, punctuation, word-division and the capitalization of proper and sacred names are modernized.

Abbreviations have been expanded without notice. Note that we use the following sigla:

⟨ ⟩ used with a blank space indicates that something has been lost in the course of transmission

[[ ]] encloses letters or words that a scribe has deleted in the manuscript

[[. . .]] indicates indecipherable erased letters

[[⟨ ⟩]] indicates conjectured letters or words lost by erasure

` ´ indicates insertions by scribes

† indicates words judged corrupt

Words required for the sense in the English translation are supplied within single square brackets

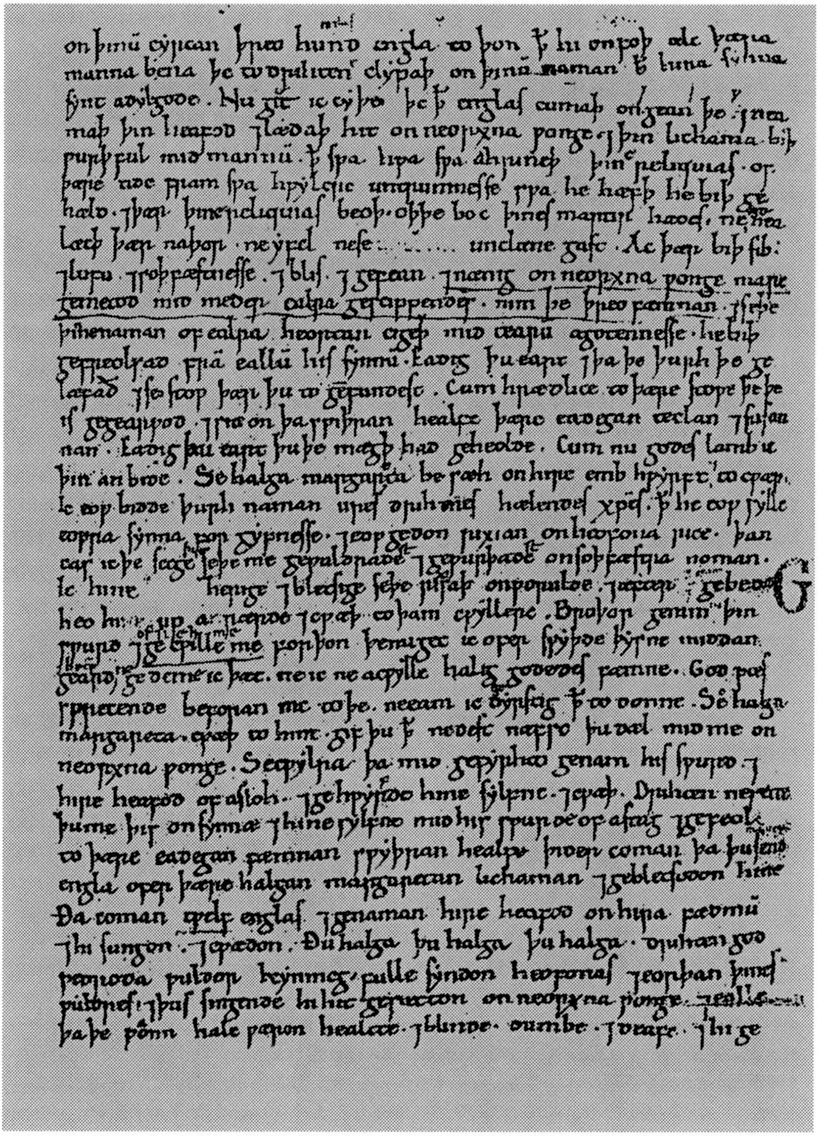

PLATE I London, British Library, Cotton Tiberius A. iii, 77r

1   Æfter[a] þære ðrowunge and þære æriste and þære wuldorfæstan
upastignesse ures Drihtnes, Hælendes Cristes, to Godfæder Ealmihtigum,
þa wæron[b] swiþe maniga martyres[c] þrowiende and þurh þa þrowunge to ece
reste becoman mid þære halgan Teclan and Susannan; and swiþe manega
eac þurh deofles lare beswicane[d] wæran, þæt hi beeodan[e] dumbe and deafe
deofolgeld, mannes handgeweorc, þe naþor ne heom ne him sylfum to[f]
nanre freme beon ne mihton.

2   Ic þa, Þeotimus,[a] þurh Godes gyfe hwæthwugo on bocum geleornode and geornfullice smeade and sohte ymb Cristes geleafan, and ne fand
ic næfre on bocum þæt ænig man mihte to ece reste becuman, butan he on
þa Halgan Þrynnysse rihtlice[b] gelifde, þæt is Fæder and Sunu and se Halga
Gast, and þæt se Sunu onfeng mennisc hiw and geþrowade deað for eall
mankin,[c] swa swa hit her bufan cwyþ. Blinde he onlihte, deafum he[d]
gesealde[e] gehernysse[f] and deade[g][1] he awæhte to life, and ealle þa þe on hine
trywlice gelæfaþ[h][2] he gehærþ. Ic þa, Ðeotimus, wilnode georne to witanne
hu seo[i] eadega Margareta wæs[j] wiþ þone deofol gefæht and hine oferswiþde
and þone[k] ece wuldorbeh[3] æt Gode onfengc. Geheraþ nu ealle and ongytaþ
hu seo[l] eadega Margareta geþrowade for Godes naman and þurh þæt
geswenc to ece reste becom mid þære halgan Teclan and Susannan.

3   Seo[a] eadiga Margareta wæs Ðeodosius dohter;[b] se wæs þære hæþenre
hehfæder. Deofolgeld he wurþode and fædde his dohter; seo[c] wæs mid
Halgum Gaste gefylled and þurh fulwiht heo wæs geedniwod. Heo wæs
geseald hire fostormoder to fædenne,[4] neh[d] Antiochia ðære ceastre, and
syþþan hire agen modor forþgefaren wæs of þisan life,[e] seo[f] fostormodor hi[g]

---

1   [a] *Æ three times bigger than other letters and in red. First four words filled in in red and partly
in majuscules.*   [b] þa wæron] *added by C above*   [c] martyres] *followed by erased word of about
five letters, probably* wæron   [d] beswicane] beswica[[.]]ne MS   [e] beeodan] -an *added by C
over A's* -e   [f] to] t- *added by B and* n *erased, changing A's on* to *to*
2   [a] Þeotimus] -t- *added by B on erasure*   [b] rihtlice] [[h]]riht'lice' MS, -lice *added by C
above*   [c] deað for eall mankin] *added by C above*   [d] he] h- *added by B on erasure, altering*
gesealde *to* he sealde   [e] gesealde] ge- *added by C above*   [f] gehernysse] ge- *added by C
above*   [g] deade] -e *altered from* u *by C*   [h] gelæfaþ] -a- *added by C above*   [i] seo] -o *added by A or
C*   [j] wæs] *added by C above*   [k] þone] *added by C above*   [l] seo] -o *added above, probably by B*
3   [a] seo] -o *added by A or C*   [b] dohter] -e *seems to have been altered from* -o   [c] seo] -o
added above, probably by C   [d] neh] e *altered from* i *by A or C*   [e] of þisan life] *added by C above*
[f] seo] -o *added above by A or C*   [g] hi] hi[[.e]] MS

1   After the Passion and the Resurrection and the glorious Ascension of Our Lord, the Saviour Christ, to God the Father Almighty, there were very many martyrs suffering and through their suffering they came to eternal rest with the holy Thecla and Susanna; and very many also were led astray through the devil's teaching, so that they worshipped dumb and deaf idols, the handiwork of men, which could be of no benefit either to those [who worshipped them] or to themselves.

2   Now I, Theotimus, have studied a certain amount in books through the grace of God and have zealously considered and inquired concerning the Christian faith, and I have never found in books that any man could come to eternal rest unless he believed rightly in the Holy Trinity, that is the Father and Son and Holy Spirit, and that the Son took on human form and suffered death for all mankind, just as it says here above. He made the blind to see and gave hearing to the deaf and he awakened the dead to life, and he hears all those who faithfully believe in him. I, Theotimus, then desired earnestly to know how the blessed Margaret fought against the devil and overcame him and received the eternal crown of glory from God. Listen now all and understand how the blessed Margaret suffered for God's name and through her tribulation came to eternal rest with the holy Thecla and Susanna.

3   The blessed Margaret was the daughter of Theodosius; he was the patriarch of the heathens. He worshipped idols and he brought up his daughter; she was filled with the Holy Ghost and she was renewed through baptism. She was given to her fostermother to be brought up, near the city of Antioch, and after her own mother had passed away from this life, her

miccle swyþor lufode þonne heo ær dyde. Heo wæs hire fæder swiþe laþ and Gode swyþe leof.

4   And mid þam[a] þe heo wæs fiftyne[b] wintra eald, heo lustfullode on hire fostormoder huse to beonne.[c] Heo gehyrde martyra geflitu, forþon þe mænig blod wæs agoten on þam tidum on eorþan for ures Dryhtnes naman, Hælendes Cristes, and heo wæs mid Halgan Gaste gefyld and hyre mægþhad Gode oðfæste.

5   Sume dæge, þa mid þam[a][5] þe heo geheold hyre fostormodor scæp[b] mid oþrum fæmnum, hire heafodgemacum,[c] ða ferde Olibrius[6] se gerefa fram Asia to Antiochia þære ceastre. Þa geseh he þa eadegan Margaretan be þam wege sittan[d] and hræddlice he hire þa[e] gyrnde and cwæþ to his þegnum: 'Gongaþ[f] ofostlice and geneomaþ þa fæmnan and axsiaþ hig[g] gif heo biþ freo, þæt ic hire onfo me to wife, and gif heo þeow biþ, ic sylle feoh[h] for hire, and heo byþ me for cyfese and hyre biþ weol on minum huse.'

Þa cempan þa eodan and hige[i] genoman. Seo[j] eadega Margareta þa ongan Criste clypian and þus cwæþ: 'Gemildsa me, Dryhten, and ne læt þu mine[k] sawle mid arleasum forwyrþan,[l] ac gedo me blissian and þe symble herian and ne læt þu næfre mine[m] sawle ne minna[n] lichoma wyrþan besmitan. Ac gesend me to minra[o] swiþran healfe and to þære winstran sibbe[7] englas to ontynenne mine sefan and to andswarienne[P] mid bylde þyssum arleasum and þissum unrihtum cwylleran.[q] Ic eom[r] nu, Drihten, swa swa nytenu onmiddan felde[s] and swa swa spærwe on nette and swa swa fisc on hoce. Gefylst[t] me, min Drihten, and geheald me and ne forlæt me on arleasra manna[u] handa.'

6   Ða cempan þa coman to þam gerefan and cwædon: 'Hlaford, ne miht þu hi[a] onfon, forþon to Gode heo hig[b] gebiddaþ, se þe wæs ahangan fram

4   [a] þam] -am *added by* C *over erasure of* -y   [b] fiftyne] *added by* C *over* A's .xv.   [c] to beonne] *added by* C *above*

5   [a] þam] -am *added by* C *above* A's -y   [b] scæp] scæp[[.]] MS   [c] heafodgemacum] -a- *and* -o- *added above by* C   [d] sittan] sittan[[.]] MS   [e] þa] *added above by* C   [f] gongaþ] *followed by erasure of two letters*   [g] hig] *added by* C   [h] feoh] *added by* C *instead of* A's fih   [i] hige] hi[[.e]] MS, -ge *added above by* C   [j] seo] -o *added by* A *or* C   [k] mine] -e *added by* B   [l] forwyrþan] *added by* C *above*   [m] mine] mi[[n]]ne MS   [n] minna] -na *added by* C *above*   [o] minra] min[[um]] MS, r *altered from* u *and* a *added on erasure by* B   [P] andswarienne] andswariende MS; *emendation suggested by Cockayne*   [q] cwylleran] -n *added by* C *over erased* s   [r] eom] [[b]]eo'm' MS, m *added by* B   [s] felde] *added by* C *over* A's feolde   [t] gefylst] *followed by* [[.y]]   [u] manna] *added by* C *above*

6   [a] hi] hi[[r.]] MS   [b] hig] *added by* C

fostermother loved her much more than she did before. She was very hateful to her father, but very dear to God.

4   And when she was fifteen years old she rejoiced to be in her fostermother's house. She heard of the struggles of martyrs, for much blood was shed in those times on earth in the name of Our Lord, the Saviour Christ, and she was filled with the Holy Ghost and she entrusted her virginity to God.

5   One day, when she was looking after her fostermother's sheep with other girls, who were her companions, the prefect Olibrius was travelling from Asia to the city of Antioch. He saw the blessed Margaret sitting by the road and at once he desired her and said to his attendants, 'Go quickly and seize that girl and ask her whether she is free, so that I may take her for my wife, and if she is a slave I will give money for her, and she will be my concubine, and she will be well [treated] in my house.'

The soldiers went then and seized her. Then the blessed Margaret began to call upon Christ and spoke as follows: 'Have mercy upon me, Lord, and do not abandon my soul among the wicked, but make me rejoice and praise you always and do not let my soul or my body ever be defiled. But send to my right side and to my left angels of peace to unlock my heart and to give answer with courage to these wicked and unrighteous executioners. I am now, Lord, like cattle in the midst of a field, like a sparrow in a net and like a fish on a hook. Help me, my Lord, and preserve me, and do not abandon me into the hands of wicked men.

6   The soldiers then came to the prefect and said, 'Lord, you cannot take her, for she prays to the God who was hanged by the Jews.' Olibrius the

Iudeum.' Olibrius se gerefa hi[c] het[d] to him gelædon and hire to cwæþ: 'Of hwylcum cynne eart þu? Sægæ me, eart[e] þu frig oðð þeow?' Seo[f] eadega Margareta him to cwæþ: 'Ic eom frig.' Se gerefa hire to cwæþ: 'Hwylces geleafan eart þu oþþe hwæt is þin nama?' Heo andswarode and cwæþ: 'In Dryhtne ic eom geciged.'[8] Se gerefa hire to cwæþ: 'Hwylcne god begæst þu?' Seo[g] halga Margareta him to cwæþ: 'Ic gebidde me[h] on Ealmihtigne God and on his Sunu, Hælend Crist, se þe minne magþhad[i9] unbesmiten geheold oþ þysne andweardan dæg.' Se gerefa hire to cwæþ: 'Clypest þu on þone Crist þe mine fæderas ahengon?' Seo[j] halga Margareta him[k] to cwæþ: 'Þine fæderas Crist ahengon and þy hi ealle[l] forwurdon, ac he þurhwunaþ on ecnysse and his rice is a butan ende.' Se gerefa wæs þa swiþe yrre and het þa halgan Margaretan on karcerne[m] betynan oþþæt he geþohte hu he hire mægþhad forspilde.[n10]

7 Se gerefa hire to cwæþ:[11] 'Gif þu ne gebiddest þe on minne[a] god, min swurd sceal fandian þines[b] lichaman[c] and ealle þine ban ic tobrysige. Gif þu me gehyrest and on minne god gelæfst, ætforan eallum þissum folce ic þe to cweþe þæt ic þe onfo me to wife and þe byþ swa wel swa me is.' Margareta him to cwæþ: 'Forþon ic sylle minne lichoman in tintrego, þæt min sawle mid soþfæstum[12] sawlum gereste.'[d13]

8 Se gerefa hi[a] het þa[b] ahon and mid smalum gyrdum swingan swyðe.[c] Seo[d] halga Margareta besæh up to[e] heofonum and cwæþ: 'On þe, Drihten, ic gelæfæ, þæt ic[f] ne si gescend. Loce on me and gemiltsa me of arleasra honda and of[g] honda þysses cwylleræs, þy læs min heorte her on ege sy. Send me hælo þæt syn onleohte[h] mine witu and þæt min sar[i] me cyme to gefean.'

---

[c] hi] hi[[r.]] MS   [d] het] [[. .]]het MS   [e] eart] *added by B on erasure*   [f] seo] -o *added above, probably by B*   [g] seo] -o *added above by C*   [h] me] *added by C*   [i] mægþhad] -had *added above by C*   [j] seo] -o *added above by C*   [k] him] hin[[.]] MS, m *altered from* n *by B*   [l] ealle] *added by C*   [m] karcerne] -e *added by B*   [n] forspilde] forswilde MS; *emendation suggested by Cockayne*
7   [a] minne] -ne *added above by C*   [b] þines] -es *added above by C*   [c] lichaman] -n *added by C*   [d] gereste] gereste[[þ]] MS
8   [a] hi] hi[[r. het]] MS   [b] het þa] *added by C,* het *on erasure,* þa *above*   [c] swyðe] *added above by C*   [d] seo] -o *added above by C*   [e] to] *added by B with* t *on erasure*   [f] ic] -c *added by A or B on erasure of* s   [g] and of] *added by B on erasure*   [h] on] *added by A or B*   [i] sar] sar [[me]] MS

prefect commanded her to be brought to him and said to her, 'What is your family? Tell me – are you free or a slave?' The blessed Margaret said to him, 'I am free.' The prefect said to her, 'Of what faith are you, and what is your name?' She answered and said, 'In the Lord I am called [Margaret].' The prefect said to her, 'Which god do you worship?' The holy Margaret said to him, 'I pray to Almighty God and to his Son, the Saviour Christ, who has preserved my virginity undefiled until this present day.' The prefect said to her, 'Do you call upon that Christ whom my ancestors hanged?' The holy Margaret said to him, 'Your ancestors hanged Christ and for that they all perished, but he will live on in eternity and his kingdom is for ever without end.' The prefect was very angry then and he ordered the holy Margaret to be shut up in prison while he considered how he might destroy her virginity.

7   The prefect said to her, 'If you do not pray to my god, my sword shall test your body and I will break all your bones. If you obey me and believe in my god, I say to you before all this crowd that I will take you as my wife, and it will be as well for you as it is for me.' Margaret said to him, 'I give my body to torments in order that my soul may rest with righteous souls.'

8   The prefect commanded her to be hung up then and to be beaten hard with thin rods. The holy Margaret looked up to the heavens and said, 'In you I trust, Lord, that I may not be confounded. Look upon me and deliver me from the hands of the wicked and from the hands of this executioner, lest my heart should be in terror here. Send me salvation that my torments may be light and that my sorrow may turn to joy.'

9 And mid þy þe heo þus hig^a gebæd, þa cwelleras swungon hire merwen lichaman þæt hyre^{b14} blod fleow on eorþan swa swa wæter deþ of þam clænestan wyllspringe. Se gerefa hire to cwæþ: 'Eala, Margareta, gelæf on me and þe byþ wel ofer oþre wif.' And ealle þa fæmnan^{15} þe þær stoden weopen bitterlice for þæm blode and cwædon: 'Eala, Margareta, soþlice we sariaþ ealle mid þe,^{c} forþon þe we geseoþ^d þe^e hnacode^f and^g þinne lichaman^h beon gecwylmed.^{i} Þes gerefa is swiþe hatheort man^j and he þe wile^k forspillan^l and þin gemynd of eorðan adiligian.^{m} Gelæf on hine and þu leofast.' Seo^n halga Margareta him to cwæþ: 'Eala, ge yfelan þehteras, gangaþ ge wif to eowrum husum and ge weras to eowrum weorcum! God me is fultumiende.^{o} Forþon nelle ic eow geheran, ne ic næfre me ne gebidde on eowerne^p god, se þe is dumb and deaf. Ac geleafaþ on minne^q God, se þe is strang on mægenne, and hrædlice he gehyrþ^r þa þe on hine gelæfaþ.'

10 And heo cwæþ þa^a to þam gerefan: 'Eala, þu ungeþunggena hund,^{b16} min God me is fultumiend and, þeah þu minnes^c lichaman^d geweald hæbbe, Crist genereþ mine^e sawle^f of þinre þare egeslican honda.' Seo^g halga Margareta besæh up to^h heofonum and cwæð: 'Gestrangie me, lifes Gast, þæt min gebed þurh heofonum gefare and þæt hit astige ætforan þinre^i gesihþe. And gesend me þinne þone Halgan Gast fram heofonum, se^j cyme me to^k fultume,^{l} þæt ic gehealde ungewæmedne^m minne mægþhad and þæt ic geseo minne^n wiþerweardan, se þe wiþ me gefihtaþ, ansyna^o to ansyna,^{17} and þæt sy bysen and blæd a eallum fæmnum þe on þe geleuat,^{p} forþon þin nama is^{q18} gebletsod on weorulde.' Þa cæmpan þa eodan and

---

9 ^{a} hig] *added by* C ^{b} hyre] *added above by* C *on erasure of* se ^{c} mid þe] *added above by* C
^{d} geseoþ] ge- *added above by* B ^{e} þe] *added by* B ^{f} hnacode] -e *added by* B ^{g} and] *added above by* C ^{h} lichaman] *contraction mark over final* -a *added by* A *or* C ^{i} gecwylmed] 'ge'cwylm[[i]]e[[n]]d MS, ge- *added by* B ^{j} man] *added above by* C ^{k} wile] wil[[l]]e MS
^{l} forspillan] forleosan MS, *with* -leosan *crossed out and* -spillan *added above by* C
^{m} adiligian] *third* -i- *added above by* B ^{n} seo] -o *added above, probably by* C ^{o} fultu-miende] *final* -e *added by* B ^{p} eowerne] -ne *added above by* C ^{q} minne] -ne *added above by* C ^{r} gehyrþ] gehyr[[a]]þ MS
10 ^{a} þa] *added above by* C ^{b} hund] *followed by* and þu ungefylledlican dracan, mannes ofen *crossed through* ^{c} minnes] -nes *added above by* B ^{d} lichaman] -n *added above by* B ^{e} mine] -e *added above by* C ^{f} sawle] -e *added by* C ^{g} seo] -o *added by* A *or* C ^{h} up to] up *added above by* C, to *by* B *on erasure, probably of* on ^{i} þinre] -re *added above by* C ^{j} se] s[[y m]]e MS ^{k} me to] 'me' 't'o[[n]] MS, me *added by* C, t *by* B ^{l} fultume] -e *added by* B ^{m} ungewæmedne] ungewæmd'medne' MS, *with* medne *added above by* C ^{n} minne] *first* n *added above by* C ^{o} ansyna] synna MS; *Herbst suggests* of ansyne ^{p} þe on þe geleuat] *added by* B *on erasure* ^{q} nama is] -ma is *added by* C

9   When she had thus prayed, the executioners beat her tender body so that her blood flowed on the ground as water does from the purest spring. The prefect said to her, 'O Margaret, believe in me and it will be well for you above other women.' And all the women who stood there wept bitterly because of the blood and said, 'O Margaret, truly we all feel sorry for you, for we see you naked and your body being tormented. This prefect is a very angry man and he wishes to destroy you and to blot out the memory of you from the earth. Believe in him and you will live.' The holy Margaret said to them, 'O, you evil counsellors! Go to your houses, women, and to your work, men! God is helping me. Therefore I will not listen to you, nor will I ever pray to your god, who is dumb and deaf. But believe in my God, who is strong in [his] might and who quickly hears those who believe in him.'

10   And then she said to the prefect, 'O, you base dog! My God is helping me and, though you have power over my body, Christ will save my soul from your terrible hands.' The holy Margaret looked to the heavens and said, 'Strengthen me, Spirit of life, so that my prayer may travel through the heavens and may ascend before your sight. And send me your Holy Spirit from the heavens, which may come to my aid, so that I may preserve my virginity undefiled and that I may see my enemy, who fights against me, face to face, and so that I may ever be an example and an inspiration to all women who believe in you, for your name is blessed in eternity.' The soldiers then came and tormented her body. Then the

cwylmdon hire lichaman. Ða bewrah se arleasa gerefa his ansyna mid his hacelan,[r] forþon þe he ne mihte on hire locian for þæm blode, and cwæþ to þære[s] fæmnan: 'Forhwon ne gehyrsumast þu minan[t] worde[u] ne þu[v] þines[w] sylfes ne eart[x] mildsigende? Efne, þin lichoma is gecwilmed[y] for minum þam egeslican dome. Geþafa me and gebide[z] þe on minne[a] god, þy læs þu deaþe swiltast. [19] Gif þu me ne gehyrast, min sweord sceal wealdan þines[b] lichoman.[c] Gif þu me[d] gehyræst,[e][20] atforan eallum þissum folce ic þe to cweþe þæt ic þe onfo me to wife.' Seo[f] halga Margareta him to cwæþ: 'Eala, þu unsnotra, forþon ic sylle minne[g] lichaman in tintrego, þæt min sawul sy gesygefæst on heofonum.'

11 Se gerefa hio[a] het on þystrum[b] carcerne[c] betynan and, mid þam[d] þe heo eode þærin, hio gebletsode ealle[e] hyre[f][21] lichaman mid Cristes rodetacne[g] and ongan hi[h] handan blesian[i][22] and þus cweþan: 'Loce on me and gemildsa me, Drihten, forþon þe ic ane eom[j] herinne,[k] and[l] min[m] fæder, [23] he me forlet. Ne forlæt[n] þu me, min Drihten, ac gemiltsa me, forþon þe ic ongete þæt þu eart[o] dema cwucra[p] and deadra.[q] Dem[r] nu betwux me and þyssum deoflum. Efne, ic sarige on minum witum. Ne yrsa þu wiþ me, min Drihten, forþon[s] þe þu wast þæt ic sylle mine[t] sawle for þe. Þu eart gebletsod on weorlde.'

---

impious prefect covered his face with his cloak, for he could not look upon her because of the blood, and he said to the virgin, 'Why do you not obey my word nor have pity on yourself? Look, your body is tortured because of my terrible judgement. Submit to me and pray to my god so that you will not perish in death. If you do not obey me, my sword shall have mastery over your body. If you obey me, I tell you before all this crowd that I will have you as my wife.' The holy Margaret said to him, 'O, you foolish one! For this reason I give my body over to torments, that my soul may be victorious in heaven.'

11   The prefect ordered her to be shut up in a dark prison, and when she went in there she blessed all her body with the sign of Christ's cross and began to bless herself with her hands and to say as follows: 'Look upon me and have mercy on me, Lord, for I am alone here and my father abandoned me. Do not you abandon me, my Lord, but have mercy on me, for I recognize that you are the judge of the living and the dead. Judge now between me and these devils. See, I grieve in my torments. Do not be angry with me, my Lord, for you know that I will give my soul for you. You are blessed in eternity.'

12   Ic þa, Þeotimus, hi[a] wæs fædende mid hlafe and mid wætre, and ic gesæh[b] þurh an[c] ehþyrl[d] eal hire geflit þe heo hæfde[e] wið ða[f] arleasan deofle; and ic awrat[g] ealle[h] hire gebedu.[i]

Þa eode ut of þæs karcernnes hwomme swiþe egeslic draca missenlices hiwes. His loccas and his beard wæron gylden geþuhte,[j] and his teþ wæron swilc swa asniden isen, and his egan scinan swa searagym, and ut æt his nosu eode micel[k] smoca,[l] and his tunga[m24] eþode, and micel fulnesse he dyde on þæm karcernne. And he hine[n] þa uparærde[o] and he hwystlode stranglicere[p] stemne. Ða wæs geworden micel leoht on þæm þystran karcerne[q] of ðæm fyre þe uteode of þæs dracan muþe. Seo[r] halgæ[s] fæmnæ[t] wæs þa geworden swiþe fyrht and gebigde hire cneowu on eorþan and aþenoda hire honda on gebede and þus cwæþ: 'God Ælmihti,[u] adwysc þises[v] miclan dracan mægen and gemildsa me þearfendra and earfoþra and ne læt ðu me næfre forwyrðan, ac gescyld me wiþ þys[w] wilddeor.'[x]

13   And mid þam[a] þe heo þus gebæd[b] hig to Crist,[c] se draca sette his muþ ofer þære halgan fæmnan heafod and hi[d] forswealh. Ac Cristes rodetacen, þe seo[e] halga Margareta worhte innan þæs[f] dracan innoþe,[g] seo[h] hine toslat on twæigen dælas, and seo[i] halgæ fæmna eode ut of þæs dracan innoþe[j] ungewæmmed. And on þære ilcan tide heo geseh[k] on hire wynstran

---

12   [a] hi] *added by C over MS* hire, *which is underlined*   [b] gesæh] ge- *added above by B*   [c] an] *added above by B*   [d] ehþyrl] ehþyrl[[e]] MS   [e] hæfde] *in right-hand margin after* hæfde *are two words by C of which the first is* þu *and the second is indecipherable*   [f] ða] ð[[.ne]] MS, a *added by B over erasure*   [g] awrat] *initial* a *added above, probably by C*   [h] ealle] *final* -e *added by B*   [i] gebedu] -u *added by C*   [j] geþuhte] -e *added, probably by C*   [k] micel] micel[[ne]] MS   [l] smoca] -a *altered from* -e   [m] tunga] tungla MS; *emendation suggested by Herbst*   [n] hine] hig MS, -g *added by A on erasure, probably of* -ne   [o] uparærde] 'up'a[[h]]rærde MS, up- *added by C and over* arærde *is an indecipherable word*   [p] stranglicere] -ere *added above by C*   [q] karcerne] *final* -e *added by B*   [r] seo] -o *added above, probably by C*   [s] halgæ] æ *altered from* a, *probably by C*   [t] fæmnæ] *second* æ *altered from* a, *probably by C*   [u] Ælmihti] *added above by C*   [v] þises] þæs *crossed out MS,* þises *added above by C*   [w] þys] þys[[ne]] MS   [x] wilddeor] wilddeor[[e]] MS

13   [a] þam] þy MS, *with* y *underlined and* -am *added above by C*   [b] gebæd] ge- *added by B*   [c] hig to Crist] *added by C*   [d] hi] hi[[re]] MS   [e] seo] -o *added by A or C*   [f] innan þæs] innan þæ MS, *added by C in right-hand margin to replace a word erased in the text after* worhte   [g] innoþe] -e *added above by C*   [h] seo] -o *added above, probably by C*   [i] seo] -o *added above by A or C*   [j] innoþe] -e *added, probably by C*   [k] heo geseh] gesæh heo 'geseh' MS, gesæh *crossed out,* geseh *added above by C*

12   I, Theotimus, was nourishing her then with bread and water, and I saw through a window all her struggles which she had with the wicked devil; and I wrote down all her prayers.

There came then out of the corner of the prison a most terrifying dragon of many different colours. His hair and his beard appeared golden, and his teeth were just like cut iron, and his eyes shone like strange gems, and from his nose there came a great amount of smoke, and his tongue breathed out and he caused a tremendous stench in the prison. Then he raised himself up and hissed with a loud sound. Then there was a great light in the dark prison from the fire which came out from the dragon's mouth. The holy maiden then became very afraid and she bent her knees to the ground and stretched out her hands in prayer and spoke as follows: 'God Almighty, extinguish the power of this huge dragon and have mercy on me in my need and hardship and never let me perish, but defend me against this wild beast.'

13   And as she prayed in this way to Christ, the dragon put his mouth over the holy maiden's head and swallowed her up. But the sign of Christ's cross, which the holy Margaret made in the dragon's belly, rent him into two parts, and the holy maiden came out from the dragon's belly uninjured. And at that same time she saw on her left side a devil sitting in the

healfe ænne deofol sittende^l swilcne^m anne^n sweartne man, and his honda to his cneowum gebundenne. And mid þy þe heo þinne^{25} gesæh, heo gebæd hi^o to Drihtene^p and þus cwæþ: 'Ic þe herige and wuldrige, þu undeadlica Kyning Crist.^{q} Þu eart geleafan trymnysse and ælcra snotra fruma^r and æghwylcre strengþo staþol. Nu ic geseo minne^s geleafan blowende^t and mine^u sawle anlyht^v and þysne dracan acwealdne licgean. Þancas ic þe secge, þu halga and þu undeadlica God. Þu eart ealra hælende Hælend. Si þin nama gebletsod on weorulde.'

14   And mid þy þe heo þus gebæd hi,^{a} se deofol uparas and genam þare^{b26} halgan fæmnan hond and cwæþ: 'Þæt genihtsumaþ þæt þu dydest. Gewit fram me, forþon þe ic geseo þe on forhæfdnesse þurhwunian. Ic sende to þe Hrufum, minne^c broþur, on dracan gelicnesse, to þam þæt he þe forswulge and þinne^d mægþhad and þinne^e wlite forlure and þin gemynd of eorþan adylige.^{f27} Þu hine þonne mid Cristes rodetacne^g acwealdest and nu þu wilt me acwyllan. Ac ic bidde þe for þinne^h mægþhad þæt þu me ne geswinge.' Seo^i halga Margareta gegrap þane^{j28} deofol þa^k be þæm locce and hine on eorþan awearp and his swyþran ege utastang and ealle^l his ban heo tobrysde^{29} and sette hire swiþran fott ofer his swyran^m and him to cwæþ: 'Gewit fram minum magþhade! Crist me is fultumiend, forþon his nama is scinende^n on weorulde.'

15   And mid þam^a þe heo þus cwæþ, þær scan swiþe micel leoht on þæm þystran quarterne and Cristes rode wæs gesewen fram eorþan up oþ^b heofen, and an hwit culfre stod ofer þære rode, and heo spræc and þus cwæþ:^{30} 'Secg

---

^{l} sittende] -e *added by* C ^{m} swilcne] -ne *added above by* C, *erasure of three letters follows, probably* swa ^{n} anne] -ne *added above by* B ^{o} hi] *added above by* C ^{p} Drihtene] -e *added, probably by* C ^{q} Crist] *added above by* C ^{r} fruma] fruma[[n]] MS ^{s} minne] -ne *added above by* C ^{t} blowende] blow[[i]]ende MS, w *and* en *underlined* ^{u} mine] -e *added above by* C ^{v} anlyht] *added by* C *over* A's gefeonde, *which is crossed out*

14   ^{a} hi] *added above by* C ^{b} þare] -r *added by* C, *followed by what is probably an* -e ^{c} minne] -ne *added above, probably by* B ^{d} þinne] -ne *added above by* C ^{e} þinne] -ne *added above by* C ^{f} adylige] adylg`i'an MS, -i- *added by* B; *emendation suggested by Cockayne*    $^g$ rodetacne] rodetac[[e]]ne`e' MS, *final* -e- *added by* A *or* B *and superscript* e *above it added by* B ^{h} þinne] -ne *added above by* C ^{i} seo] -o *added, probably by* A ^{j} þane] -ne *added by* C ^{k} þa] *added above by* C ^{l} his swyþran . . . ealle] *from* -s *in* his *to* ea *in* ealle *added by* A *on erasure* ^{m} swyran] swyre MS, *with* -an *added by* B *above* A's -e ^{n} scinende] -e *added above by* B

15   ^{a} þam] þy, *with* -am *added above by* C ^{b} oþ] oþ[[þe]] MS

appearance of a black man, with his hands fastened on his knees. When she saw him she prayed to the Lord and spoke as follows: 'I praise you and glorify you, immortal King, Christ. You are the support of faith and the origin of all wisdom and the foundation of all strength. Now I see my faith blossoming and my soul rejoicing and this dragon lying destroyed. I give thanks to you, holy and immortal God. You are the Saviour of all saviours. May your name be blessed in eternity!'

14   And as she prayed in this way, the devil rose up and grasped the holy maiden's hand and said, 'What you have done is sufficient. Depart from me, for I see that you persevere in your continence. I sent my brother Rufus to you in the appearance of a dragon, in order that he would swallow you up and destroy your chastity and your beauty and expunge the memory of you from the earth. You slew him then with the sign of Christ's cross and now you wish to slay me. But I ask you for the sake of your virginity that you do not beat me.' The holy Margaret then grabbed the devil by the hair and threw him to the ground and she put out his right eye and shattered all his bones and she set her right foot over his neck and said to him, 'Leave my virginity alone! Christ is helping me, for his name shines in eternity.'

15   And as she spoke thus, there shone a very great light in the dark prison and the cross of Christ could be seen stretching from earth to heaven, and there was a white dove on the cross, and it spoke and said as follows:

me, Margareta, þu þe þurh mægþhad gyrndest þæs^c eacan rices,^{d31} and
forþon hit^{e32} biþ þe geseald mid Abraham and mid Isaac and Iacob.³³ Eadig
eart þu þe þone feond oferswiþdest.' Seo^f halga Margareta þa cwæþ: 'Wuldor
þe sy, Crist, þu þe ane dest mænig wuldor. Ic þe wuldrige and herige,
forþon þu eart halig and micel on eallum þingum, þu þe gemedomast
gecyþan^g þinre þeowen³⁴ þæt þu eart ane hiht ealra gelifendra^h on þe.'

Seoⁱ culfra^j þa wæs eft sprecende and cwæþ: 'Margareta, axia^k þone þe þu
hæfst under þinum fotum be his dædum and he cyþ þe ealle^l his weorc,
and mid þy þe þu hine hæfst oferswiþd, þu cymst to me.' Seo^m halga
Margareta þa cwæþ to þæmⁿ deofle: 'Hwæt is þin nama, þu unclæne gast?'
Se^o deofol hire to cwæþ: 'Þu Cristes þeowwe,^p ahefe^q þinne^r fot of minan^s
swiran,^t þæt ic mine ban lithwan^u gereste and ic þe sægce ealle mine dæda.'
Seo^v halga fæmne þa ahof hire fot of his swiran.^w And se^x deofol þa cwæþ:
'On an^y manigne soþfæstna man^{z35} ic genam and ic gefæht wiþ him and ne
mihte me nan oferswiþan. Ac þu min ege utastunge and ealle mine ban
tobrisdest and minne^a broþor acwealdest. Nu ic geseo Crist wunian on þe
and þu dest ealle^b soþfæsnesse weorc.^c Ic hig^d ableonde fram geleafan^{e36} and
ic hi gedyde ofergeotan þa heofenlican gesælþe,^f and mid þy þe hy on slæpe
wæron, ic com ofer hi and þa þe ic ne mihte of þæm bedde adon, ic hi dyde
on þæm sylfan slæpe singian. Nu þonne fram anre gingre³⁷ fæmnan ic eam
oferswiþd. Hwæt do ic nu, forþon þe ealle^g mine wæpne synt tobrecenne?
And me ealra swiþost gedræfþ þæt þin fæder and þin modor mine
wæron.'^{h38}

---

^c þæs] þære MS   ^d rices] rice MS   ^e hit] h{[e]} MS, -i- *altered from* -e *and* -t *added on*
erasure by B   ^f seo] -o *added by* A *or* C   ^g gecyþan] gecyþ þonne; *emendation suggested by*
Cockayne   ^h gelifendra] 'ge'lif{[i]}endra MS, ge- *added above by* B   ⁱ seo] -o *added by* A
^j culfra] -a *altered from* æ *by* A   ^k axia] axie MS, *with* e *underlined and a added above by* A *or* C
^l ealle] *second* -e *added by* B   ^m seo] -o *added by* A *or* B   ⁿ þæm] *apostrophe after* æ *for* m
^o se] *added by* C *over erasure*   ^p þeowwe] -we *added above by* B   ^q ahefe] *second* -e *added by* B
^r þinne] -ne *added above by* B   ^s minan] -an *added above by* B   ^t swiran] a *altered from* e
and contraction mark added by C   ^u lithwan] t *added above by* C   ^v seo] -o *added by* A *or* C
^w swiran] swire MS, *with* -an *added above* -e *by* C   ^x and se] *added by* C *above* A's þæt
^y cwæþ: 'On an] cwæþan ongan MS, -an *and* onga *underlined*, on an *added above by* C
^z manigne soþfæstna man] manegra soþfæstra man{[. .]} MS, -egra *underlined*, -i- *and* -ne
added above by B; -tra *underlined*, -na *added above by* B   ^a minne] -ne *added above by* C
^b ealle] -e *added by* C   ^c weorc] *added above by* C   ^d hig] heo{[.]} MS, *with* hig *added*
above by C   ^e fram geleafan] hera sefan *underlined* MS, *with* fram geleafan *added above by* C
^f gesælþe] snyttro MS, *with* gesælþe *added above by* B   ^g ealle] *on erasure by* A   ^h wæron]
followed by underlined *and* þu ane wiþ me and wið eall hire cneo 'cing' rise. Cristes gefylgen-
dum, þurh þono deofla magen eall to nahte gebiþ. Cing *added above by* C *and* þone *corrected*
from þono *by* A *or* B

'Speak to me, Margaret, you who through virginity desired the eternal kingdom, and for this reason it will be granted to you with Abraham and with Isaac and Jacob. Blessed are you, who have overcome the enemy.' The holy Margaret then said, 'Glory be to you, Christ, who alone brings about many a glorious thing. I glorify and praise you, because you are holy and great in all things, you who condescend to reveal to your servant that you are the one hope of all who believe in you.'

The dove spoke again then and said, 'Margaret, ask him whom you have under your feet about his deeds and he will reveal to you all his works, and when you have defeated him you will come to me.' The holy Margaret then said to the devil, 'What is your name, you unclean spirit?' The devil said to her, 'Raise your foot from my neck, servant of Christ, so that I may rest my bones a little, and I will tell you all my deeds.' The holy maiden then raised her foot from his neck. And the devil then spoke: 'I have continually seized many a righteous man and fought with him and none could defeat me. But you have put out my eye and shattered all my bones and you have slain my brother. Now I see that Christ dwells in you and you perform all deeds of righteousness. I blinded them from their faith and caused them to forget heavenly wisdom and, when they were asleep, I came upon them and those whom I could not throw from their beds I caused to sin in their very sleep. Yet now I have been overcome by a young girl. What shall I do now, for all my weapons are destroyed? And it vexes me most that your father and your mother were mine.'

16   Seoᵃ halga fæmne him to cwæþ: 'Segeᵇ me nuᶜ þin cynn and hwa þe
gecende.'ᵈ³⁹ Seᵉ deofol hire to cwæþ: 'Sæcg me, Margareta, hwanon is þin
lif and þin lichama and hwanon is þin sawul and þin geleafa, oþþe hu wæs
Crist wuniend on þe? Sageᶠ me þis, þonne secge ic þe ealle mine dæde.' Seoᵍ
halga fæmne him answarode and cwæþ: 'Nys me alifed þæt ic þe to secgæʰ
forþon þu ne eart neⁱ wyrþe mine stefne to gehyrenne. Godes bebodu ic
wille gehyran and þæt gecyþan. And þu, deofol, adumbe nu, forþon þe ic
nelle nan word ma of þinum muþe gehyran.' And hrædlice seoʲ eorþe
forswalg þone wælhreowanᵏ deofol grimlice.

17   Ða, on oþran dæge, hetᵃ se gerefa þa halgan fæmnan to him
gelædan, and mid þy þe heo wæs utagangende, heo gebletsode eall hira
lichoma mid Cristes rodetacene.ᵇ Se gerefa hire to cwæþ: 'Eala, Margareta,
gelæf on me and gebid þe toᶜ minum gode.' Seoᵈ halga Margareta him to
cwæþ: 'Soþlice, þe gedafenaþ on mineᵉ God to gebiddane.' Se gerefa wearþ
þa swyþe yrre and het hiᶠ upahonᵍ and mid kandelum byrnan and hioʰ
dydan þaⁱ swa heom beboden wæs. Seoʲ halga Margareta þa cigde and cwæþ:
'Nelle ic næfre me gebiddan on eowerne god, se þe is dumb and deaf. Ne
magon ge oferswyþan clæne fæmnan. Crist sylf gebletsodeᵏ⁴⁰ minneˡ
lichaman,ᵐ and minreⁿ sawuleᵒ he sylleþ wuldres beh.'

18   Se arleasa gerefa het þider bringan anᵃ mycel leaden fæt and het hit
mid wætere afyllan and dyde hit ælanᵇ swyþe hat and het bindan fet and
honda þære halgan fæmnan and þæron don.⁴¹ Ða cwylras dyden þaᶜ swa
heom beboden wæs. Se eadega Margareta locade on heofonum and cwæþ:
'Drihten,ᵈ⁴² God Ealmihtig, þu þe eardest on heofonum, geunne me þæt
þisᵉ wæter sy me to hælo and to lihtnesse and to fulwihtes bæþe,ᶠ þæt hit me

16   ᵃ seo] -o *added above by* C   ᵇ sege] saga MS, -a- *and* -a *replaced above with* -e- *and* -e *by*
C   ᶜ nu] *added above by* C   ᵈ gecende] ge- *added above by* B   ᵉ se] [[þæt]] MS, se *added by*
C   ᶠ sage] saga MS, *with* e *altered from a by* B   ᵍ seo] -o *added above*   ʰ secgæ] secga[[.]]
MS, *with* æ *altered from a*   ⁱ ne] *added by* C   ʲ seo] -o *added, perhaps by* B   ᵏ wælhreo-
wan] *added above by* C

17   ᵃ het] [[ge]]het MS   ᵇ rodetacene] *final* -e *added by* B   ᶜ to] o[[.]] MS, t- *added by*
B   ᵈ seo] -o *added by* A *or* B   ᵉ mine] -e *added by* B   ᶠ hi] hi[[r.]] MS   ᵍ upahon] up-
added above by B   ʰ hio] syþþan *underlined* MS, *with* hio *added above by* B   ⁱ þa] *followed by*
nyxtan *underlined*   ʲ seo] -o *added by* A *or* C   ᵏ gebletsode] ge gebletsode MS   ˡ minne]
-ne *added above by* B   ᵐ lichaman] -n *added by* B   ⁿ minre] -re *added above by* C
o sawule] -e *added by* B

18   ᵃ bringan an] bringaˈaˈn MS, -a- *added by* C   ᵇ ælan] ælen MS, -a- *added by* C *over* -e-
c þa] *added above by* C   ᵈ Drihten] Ðrihten MS   ᵉ þis] þis[[ne]] MS   ᶠ bæþe] -e *added*
above by B, *followed by* *underlined* unaspringende

16   The holy maiden said to him, 'Tell me now your kindred and who begot you.' The devil said to her, 'Tell me, Margaret, whence comes your life and your body, and whence your soul and your faith, and how did Christ come to be dwelling in you? Tell me this, and then I will tell you all my works.' The holy maiden answered him and said, 'It is not permitted that I should speak to you, for you are not worthy to hear my voice. I wish to hear and to reveal God's commands. And you, devil, be silent now, for I do not want to hear one more word from your mouth.' And immediately in terrible fashion the earth swallowed up the cruel devil.

17   Then on the next day the prefect ordered the holy maiden to be brought to him, and, as she was coming out, she blessed all her body with the sign of Christ's cross. The prefect said to her, 'O, Margaret, believe in me and pray to my god.' The holy Margaret said to him, 'Truly, it befits you to pray to my God.' The prefect became very angry then and ordered his men to hang her up and burn her with torches and then they did as they were commanded. The holy Margaret then called out and said, 'I will never pray to your god, who is dumb and deaf. You cannot overcome a chaste virgin. Christ himself has blessed my body, and to my soul he will give a crown of glory.'

18   The impious prefect ordered a great leaden vessel to be brought there and he ordered it to be filled with water and [the water] to be made very hot and he commanded that the feet and hands of the holy maiden be bound and that she be put into it. Then the executioners did as they were commanded. The blessed Margaret looked to the heavens and said, 'Lord God Almighty, you who dwell in the heavens, grant to me that this water

aþwea to þam eacan life, and awyrp me from ealle^g43 mine synne and gehæl^h
me on þinum wuldre, forþon þe þu eart gebletsod on weorulde.' And mid þy
þe þæt gebed wæs gefyld, swa wearþ þær micel eorþhrærnesse geworden,
and on þære ylcan tid^i com an^j culfre of heofonum hæbbende beh on muþe
and raþe wæron alysde fet and honda þære halgan fæmnan and heo eode up
of þæm wætere, God herigende and wuldrigende, and þus cwæþ: 'Wuldor
ic þe secge, Drihten God, Hælend Crist, forþon þe^k þu me onlihtest^44 and
wuldradest and þu me wære mildsiend, þinre þeowene. Þu eart gebletsod^l
on weorlde.' And mid þy þe heo cwæþ 'Amen', stefn wæs þa^m geworden of
heofonum þus cweþende: 'Cum, Margareta, to heofonum. Eadig eart þu,^n
þu þe mægþhades^o45 gyrndest: for^p þon þingum þu eart eadig on ecnesse.'
And on þære ilcan tid gelæfde þas folces .xv. þusenda manna, butan wifan^q
and cildan.^r46

19   Olibrius se gerefa het acwyllan ealle þa þæ on Crist gelæfdon, and
hi wæron acwealde on Limes feolda,^a butan Ærmeniga þære ceastre. And
æfter heom he het^b acwyllan þa eadegan Margaretan and mid swurde
ofslean. Ða cwyllras læddon hi^c þa butan þara ceastre weallas^d47 and þa an of
heom cwæþ (his nama wæs Malchus gehaten): 'Aþene þinne^e sweora nu^f and
onfoh min swurd and gemildsa me, forþon þe ic her geseo Crist standand
mid his englum mid þe.'^g Margareta þa cwæþ: 'Ic bidde þe, broþor, gif þu
her Crist geseost, are^h me oþþæt ic me gebidde to him and minna^i gast him^j
oþfæste.' Se cwyllere hyre to cwæþ: 'Bide^k swa hwæt swa þu wille.'
    Se eadega Margareta þa ongan biddan and þus cweþan: 'God, þu þe
heofenan^l mid honda gemettest and eorþan on þinre fyst betyndest, geher
mine^m bena þæt swa hwilc man swa writeþ^48 mine^n þrowunga oþþe hi
geheraþ rædan,^o of þære tide syn adylgade heora^p synna; oþþe gif hwilc man

^g ealle] eall[[um]] MS, *second -e altered from* u *by* B   ^h gehæl] gehæl[[e]] MS   ^i tid]
followed by erasure of word, probably swa   ^j an] *added above by* C   ^k forþon þe] forþon þe
þe MS   ^l gebletsod] ge- *added above by* B   ^m þa] *added above by* C   ^n eart þu] [[þ.]] eart
'þu' MS, 'þu' *added by* C   ^o mægþhades] mægþhad MS   ^p for] þurh *underlined* MS, *with*
for *added above by* C   ^q wifan] -an *added above by* C   ^r cildan] -an *added above by* C
19   ^a feolda] -a *added by* A   ^b het] [[ge]]het MS   ^c hi] hi[[re]] MS   ^d weallas]
wealþas MS   ^e þinne] -ne *added above by* B   ^f nu] *added above by* C   ^g mid þe] *added by* C
^h are] ar[[ig]]e MS   ^i minna] -na *added above by* C   ^j him] *added above by* C   ^k bide]
-e *added by* C   ^l heofenan] -an *added above by* C   ^m mine] min[[.]]e MS   ^n mine] -e
added by A *or* B   ^o rædan] [[h]]rædan MS   ^p heora] hire MS, *with -e- altered from -i- and
-o- added by* C

may be for me a healing and an enlightening and a bath of baptism, so that it may cleanse me for the eternal life and may cast all my sins away from me and bring me to salvation in your glory, for you are blessed in eternity.' And when this prayer was completed, there occurred a great earthquake, and at that same moment a dove came from the heavens bearing a crown in its mouth and immediately the feet and hands of the holy maiden were freed and she came out of the water praising and glorifying God and saying as follows: 'I proclaim your glory, Lord God, Saviour Christ, for you have given me light and have glorified me and you have shown mercy to me, your servant. You are blessed in eternity.' And as she said 'Amen', there came a voice from the heavens, speaking thus: 'Come, Margaret, to the heavens. Blessed are you who have desired virginity: for this reason you are blessed in eternity.' And at the same time fifteen thousand men from the crowd believed, quite apart from women and children.

19   The prefect Olibrius ordered all those who believed in Christ to be executed, and they were put to death at the field of Lim, outside the city of Armenia. And after [their execution] he ordered that the blessed Margaret was to be executed and that she was to be killed with a sword. The executioners led her then outside the city walls and then one of them (his name was Malchus) spoke: 'Stretch out your neck now and receive my sword, and have mercy on me, for I see Christ standing here next to you with his angels.' Margaret then said, 'I ask you, brother, if you see Christ here, spare me until I pray to him and commit my soul to him.' The executioner said to her, 'Ask whatever you wish.'

The blessed Margaret then began to pray and to speak as follows: 'God, who measured the heavens with your hand and enclosed earth in your fist, hear my prayer that whoever writes out my passion or hears it read may

leoht deþ on minum cirican of his geswinge,^{q49} be swa hwylcan^r gylte swa
he bidde forgifenesse ne si him seo^s synna geteold. Ic bidde þe, Drihten,
þæt gif hwilc mon si gemetod on þinum þam egeslican dome and he si
gemindig minum naman and þines, gefreolsa hine, Drihten, of tintregan.^{t}
Get ic þe bidde, Drihten, þæt se þe macað^{u50} boc mines martirhades oþþe
on his huse hæbbe, sy his synna eal^v alætnesse, forþon þe we syndon flæsc
and blod æfre syngiende and næfre ablinnende. Get ic þe bidde, Drihten,^{w}
þæt se þe cyrcan timbrige on minum naman and þær awrite mine^x
þrowunge^y oþþe of his gewinne gebicge, send^{51} on hine, Drihten, þono
Halgan Gast. And þær boc sy mines martyrhades, ne sy þær geboren blind
cild ne healt, ne dumb, ne deaf, ne fram unclænum gaste geswenct, ac sy
þær sib and lufu and soþfæstnesse gast.^{52} And se þe þær biddeþ his synna
forgifnesse, gecyþe^z him,^{a} Drihten, his bene.'^{b53}

20   Ða wæs stefn geworden of heofonum mid þunre,^{a} and an^b culfre
com berende rode and cwæþ: 'Aris, Margareta, eadig wæs se innoþ se þe þe
gebær,^{54} forþon þe þu gemyndest^{c55} ealle þingc on þinum gebed. Ðurh
engla mægen ic þe swerige þæt swa hwæt swa þu bæde, eall hit biþ gehered
ætforan Godes gesyhþe,^{56} and swa hwæt swa þu wære gemyndig, þæt
forgifeþ þe God. God gesættet on þinum cyrcan þreo englas^{d57} to þon þæt hi
onfoþ^{58} ælc þæra manna bena, þe to Drihtene^e clypaþ on þinum naman þæt
hira synna synt adylgode. Nu get^f ic cyþe þe þæt englas cumaþ ongean þe
and neamaþ þin heafod and lædaþ hit on neorxnawonge;^{g} and þin lichama
biþ wurþful mid mannum, þæt swa hwa swa ahrineþ^h þine^i reliquias, of
þære tide fram swa hwylcre untrumnesse swa he hæfþ he biþ gehæld. And

---

^{q} geswinge] gewinne MS, -winne *underlined and* -swinge *added in margin by* C ^{r} hwylcan]
hwylc[[re]] MS, -an *added by* C ^{s} seo] -o *added* ^{t} tintregan] -a- *altered from* -o- *and* -n
added by C ^{u} macað] rærdeþ MS, *and above it* macað *by* C; *Cockayne proposed* maciaþ *and
Herbst could read only the* -a- *and the last letter, which she claims is also* -a-, *but* macað *is reasonably
clear with a magnifying glass* ^{v} eal] *added above by* C ^{w} Drihten] *added above by* C
^{x} mine] -e *added above by* C ^{y} þrowunge] -e *added by* C ^{z} gecyþe] -e *added above by* B
^{a} him] hi[[. .]] MS, m *altered from* n *by* B ^{b} his bene] *added above by* C
20   ^{a} þunre] þunr[[. . .]] MS, e *added by* B *on erasure* ^{b} an] *added above by* C
c gemyndest] gemano MS, *with* -ano *underlined and* -yndest *added above by* C ^{d} englas]
hund engla MS, *with* englas *added above* hund *by* C ^{e} Drihtene] -e *added above by* C
^{f} get] git MS, e *added probably by* B ^{g} neorxnawonge] -o- *in* -wonge *seems to have been
altered from* -a- ^{h} ahrineþ] a- *added by* B ^{i} þine] -e *added above by* B

from that time have his sins blotted out; and if anyone puts a light in my church [bought] from what he has earned, may the sin for which he asks forgiveness not be counted against him. I ask you, Lord, if anyone is found at the time of your terrible judgement and he is mindful of my name and of yours, deliver him, Lord, from punishment. I ask you further, Lord, that the person who makes a book of my martyrdom or has it in his house may have remission of all his sins, for we are flesh and blood and are always sinning and never ceasing. I ask you further, Lord, that to the person who builds a church in my name and writes out there [a copy of] my passion or buys one with what he has earned, you send, Lord, the Holy Spirit. And where the book of my martyrdom is [kept] may there not be born a child who is blind or lame or dumb or deaf or afflicted by an unclean spirit, but may peace be there and love and the spirit of truth. And to the person who asks there for forgiveness of his sins carry out, Lord, his prayer for him.'

20   Then there was a sound from the heavens, accompanied by thunder, and a dove came bearing a cross and said, 'Arise, Margaret, blessed was the womb that bore you, for you have been mindful of all things in your prayer. Through the power of angels I swear to you that whatever you have asked for shall all be heard in the sight of God and whatever you were mindful of God will grant to you. God will set in your church three angels so that they will receive all of the prayers of those who call upon the Lord in your name that their sins may be wiped out. I further reveal to you now that angels will come to you and take your head and bear it to paradise; and your body will be honoured among men, so that whoever touches your relics will be healed from that moment on of whatever

þær þine[j] reliquias beoþ oþþe boc þines martirhades, ne genealæcþ[k] þær naþor ne yfel ne se unclæne[l] gast. Ac þær biþ sib and lufu and soþfæstnesse and blis and gefea.[m59] And se þe þinne[n] naman of ealra heortan[60] cigeþ mid teara[o61] agotennesse, he biþ gefreolsad fram eallum his synnum. Eadig þu eart and þa þe þurh þe gelæfað and seo[p] stow þær þu to gefundest. Cum hrædlice to þære stowe þe þe is gegearwod and site[q] on þa swiþran healfe þære eadegan Teclan and Susannan. Eadig þu eart, þu þe mægþhad geheolde. Cum nu, Godes lamb, ic þin anbide.'

21 Se halga Margareta besæh on hire embhwyrft and[a] cwæþ:[62] 'Ic eow bidde þurh naman ures Drihtnes, Hælendes Cristes, þæt he eow sylle eowra synna forgyfnesse and eow gedo[b63] rixian on heofona rice.[64] Þancas ic þe secge þu[c] þe me gewuldradest[d] and gewurþadest[e] on soþfæstra noman. Ic hine[f] herige and bletsige se þe rixaþ[g65] on worulde.'

22 And æfter þam[a66] gebede heo hi[b] uparærde[c] and cwæþ to þam cwyllere: 'Broþor, genim nu[d] þin swurd and ofsleh me,[e] forþon þe nu get ic oferswyþde þysne middangeard.' He cwæþ: 'Ne[f67] gedeme[g] ic þæt, ne ic ne acwylle halig Godes[h68] fæmne. God wæs sprecende beforan me to þe. Ne eam ic gedyrstig[i] þæt to donne.' Seo[j] halga Margareta cwæþ to hine:[k] 'Gif þu þæt ne dest, næfst þu dæl mid me on neorxnawonge.' Se cwylra þa mid gefyrhto genam his swurd and hire heafod ofasloh and gehwyrfde[169] hine sylfne and cwæþ: 'Drihten, ne sette þu me þis on synnæ',[m] and hine

---

[j] þine] -e *added by* B   [k] genealæcþ] ge- *added above by* B   [l] unclæne] *preceded by erasure of* [[uncl . . .]]   [m] gefea] gefean MS, *followed by underlined and* nænig on neorxnawonge mare gemetod mid meder ealra Gescippendes nimþe þreo fæmnan.   [n] þinne] þi'n'ne MS, -n- *and* -e *added by* B   [o] teara] tearum MS   [p] seo] -o *added by* A *or* C   [q] site] -e *added by* C

21   [a] and] and to MS, and *added above by* C   [b] gedo] gedon MS   [c] þu] se *underlined* MS, þu *added above by* B   [d] gewuldradest] -st *added above by* B   [e] gewurþadest] -st *added above by* B   [f] hine] hine [[hine]] MS   [g] rixaþ] risaþ MS, -x- *added above* -s- *by* B

22   [a] þam] [[þæt]] MS, þam *added above by* C   [b] hi] hi[[re]] MS   [c] uparærde] upa[[h]]rærde MS   [d] nu] *added by* C   [e] ofsleh me] gecwille me *underlined* MS, *with* ofsleh me *added above by* B   [f] he cwæþ ne] *added by* B   [g] gedeme] -e *added by* B   [h] godes] godedes MS   [i] gedyrstig] ge- *added above by* B   [j] seo] -o *added above by* B   [k] hine] hi[[n.]] MS, *with* n *altered to* m *by* B *and* B's m *altered to* ne *by* C   [l] gehwyrfde] gehwy[[f]]de MS, *with* f *altered to* r *by* A *and* f *added by* B   [m] synnæ] -æ *probably altered from* -a *by* C

134

infirmity he has. Where your relics are {kept}, or a book of your martyrdom, neither evil nor the unclean spirit will approach there. But peace and love and truth and bliss and joy will be there. And the person who with shedding of tears wholeheartedly calls out your name will be released from all his sins. Blessed are you and those who believe through you and blessed is the place to which you are travelling. Come quickly to the place which is prepared for you and sit on the right side of the blessed Thecla and Susanna. Blessed are you who have preserved your virginity. Come now, lamb of God, I await you.'

21 The holy Margaret looked at the people who were standing around her and said, 'I ask you in the name of our Lord the Saviour Christ that he give you forgiveness of your sins and bring it about that you reign in the kingdom of heaven. I proclaim thanks to him who has glorified and honoured me among the names of the righteous. I praise and bless him who reigns in eternity.'

22 After this prayer she raised herself up and said to the executioner, 'Brother, take your sword and put me to death, for now indeed I have overcome this world.' He replied, 'I will not carry out the sentence nor will I put God's holy maiden to death. God spoke to you in front of me. I am not presumptuous enough to do this.' The holy Margaret said to him, 'If you do not do it, you will not share with me in paradise.' Then the executioner took hold of his sword with trepidation and he struck off her head and he turned and said, 'Lord do not reckon this against me as a sin.'

sylfne mid his swurde[n] ofastang[o70] and gefeol to þære eadegan fæmnan swyþran healfe. Þider coman þa manega[p] engla ofer þære halgan Margaretan lichaman and gebletsodon hine.

23 Ða coman englas[a71] and genaman hire heafod on hira fædmum, and hi sungon and cwædon: 'Ðu halga, þu halga, þu halga, Drihten God, weoroda Wuldorkynincg, fulle syndon heofonas and eorþan þines wuldres.' And þus singende hi hit gesætton on neorxnawonge. And ealle þa þe wannhale[b] wæron, healtte and blinde, dumbe and deafe, and hi onhri-non[c72] þære halgan fæmnan lichaman, ealle hi wurdon gehælde. And ængla stefn wæs gehered ofer hire lichaman, þus cweþende: 'Eadig eart þu[73] and þa þe þurh þe gelæfeþ, forþon þe þu gewunne[d] reste a oþ ende mid halgum fæmnum. And ne beo[e] þu sorhfull be þinum halgan lichaman, forþon þe he[f] is forlætan on eorþan to þon þæt swa hwylc mann swa hrineþ[g] þine reliquias oþþe þine ban, on þære tide syn adilgade heora[h] synna and hira naman[i] awritane[j] on lifes bocum.'

24 Ic, Þeotimus,[a] genam þa reliquias þære halgan fæmnan and ic hi[b] gesætte on niwe scrine[c] þe[d74] ic sylf ær of stane geworhte and mid swotum wyrtum gesweotte, and ic hio[e] geheold on sumes godes[f] wifes huse.[g] Hire nama wæs Sincletica. Ic, Þeotimus,[h] wæs þe hire geþenode mid hlafe and mid wætere and ic gesæh eall hire geflit þe heo hæfde wiþ þon[i] arleasan deoflum,[j] and hire gebed ic awrat and ic hit gesende to eallum Cristenum mannum. And seo[k] halga Margareta gefylde hire þrowung on Iulius monþe, on þone þreo and twentegþan dæge. Ealle þa þe þis gehyraþ on

---

[n] swurde] -e *added by* B   [o] ofastang] n *added above by* C   [p] manega] þusend MS, manega *added above by* C

23 [a] englas] *preceded by underlined* twelf   [b] wannhale] wonnhale MS, *with* a *added over* o, *probably by* A   [c] onhrinon] ge gehrinon MS, *with* on *for second* ge, *probably by* B   [d] gewunne] ge- *added above by* B   [e] beo] o *added, probably by* B   [f] he] hi[[.]] MS, e *altered from* i *by* B   [g] hrineþ] h *added, probably by* C   [h] heora] he'o'ra MS, *with* -e- *altered from* -i- *and* -o- *added by* C   [i] naman] *contraction mark over* -a *added, probably by* C   [j] awritane] a- *and* -e *added by* C

24 [a] Þeotimus] þeo[[þ]]imus MS, *with* o *altered from* þ *through erasure and* t *added over erasure by* B   [b] hi] hi[[t]] MS   [c] scrine] -e *added by* B   [d] þe] -e *added, probably by* B   [e] hio] hi[[t]] MS, o *added*   [f] godes] siþ *underlined* MS *and* godes *added above by* C   [g] huse] huse[[s]] MS   [h] Þeotimus] þeo[[þ]]imus MS, *with* t *added by* B *on erasure*   [i] þon] þone MS, *with* -ne *underlined and contraction mark over* o *added by* B   [j] deoflum] u *altered from* a *by* A, *contraction mark probably added by* C   [k] seo] -o *added, probably by* C

And he pierced himself with his sword and fell on the right side of the holy maiden. Then many angels came over the body of the holy Margaret and blessed it.

23   Then angels came and took her head in their embrace, and they sang, proclaiming, 'Holy, holy, holy, Lord God, glorious King of hosts, heaven and earth are full of your glory.' And thus singing they placed it in paradise. And all who were ill, the lame and the blind, the dumb and the deaf, when they touched the body of the holy maiden, they were all healed. And the voice of angels was heard over her body, proclaiming, 'Blessed are you and those who believe through you, for you have gained rest for ever with holy women. And do not be sorrowful concerning your holy body, for it is left on earth so that whoever touches your relics or your bones will have their sins wiped out at that moment and their name written in the book of life.'

24   I, Theotimus, took the relics of the holy maiden and placed them in a new shrine which I myself had fashioned from stone beforehand and had made fragrant with sweet plants, and I kept it at the house of a certain noble lady. Her name was Sincletica. I, Theotimus, was the person who served her with bread and water and saw all of the struggle which she had with the wicked devil, and I wrote down her prayer and sent it to all Christian people. And the holy Margaret completed her passion on the twenty-third day of the month of July. Be inspired in your hearts all who

heortan beon bliðe,[1] and þa þe Drihten Crist biddaþ and on hine[m][75] gelifaþ, and gemundyt[n][76] þære halgan Margaretan þæt heo mid hira benum us oþfæste on gesihþe[o] Hælendes Cristes. Þam sy wuldor and lof and wurðmynt and þrym and anweald and micelnys on ealra worulda woruld, soþlice a butan ænigum ende. Amen.

---

[1] beon bliðe] *added by* C *over underlined* wesaþ onbryrad   [m] hine] hire MS, *with* -re *underlined and* -ne *added by* B   [n] and gemundyt] and gemindoþ MS, *with* and gemundyt *added above by* B   [o] gesihþe] ge- *added above by* B

hear this, and all who pray to Christ the Lord and believe in him, and remember the holy Margaret so that she may with her prayers commend us in the sight of the Saviour Christ. To him let there be glory and praise and honour and majesty and power and greatness in all eternity, for ever indeed, world without end. Amen.

Commentary on Cotton Tiberius

[1] The original ungrammatical A-reading *deadum* probably resulted from association with the *deafum* of the previous clause, whose dative is governed by *gesealde*.

[2] The plural form is required here, as supplied by C's insertion of *a*. It is likely that the mistaken A-reading *gelæfþ* resulted from the proximity of the similar-looking verb *gehærþ*.

The manuscript reading *gehyraþ* (A, ch. 9), where a singular is required, appears to be the result of the reverse of the *gelæfþ* error. Here the plural form *gelæfaþ* occurs in proximity and may have distracted the scribe.

[3] On the unexpected occurrence of this characteristically 'Winchester' word in this version, see above, p. 98.

[4] The circumstance of Margaret's being entrusted to a fostermother is not very clear in this version of the legend, which is in this respect a faithful reproduction of the *BHL* nos. 5303–4 account. Theodosius's hostility towards his daughter is obviously a result of her conversion to Christianity but the circumstances of Margaret's conversion are obscure. The detail (in the previous sentence) that Margaret was renewed through baptism is not in any extant version of the Mombritius and pre-Mombritius tradition, although it probably was in the Old English translator's source (see above, p. 58).

[5] This alteration of the A-reading *mid þy þe* represents a favourite intervention of C: see also beginning of chs. 5, 12, 15 and, emending *mid þe* to *mid þam þe*, ch. 11. On the other hand a number of occurrences of *mid þy þe* is left unaltered: see beginning of chs. 9, 14 etc.

[6] Olibrius appears as a persecutor both in the passion of Margaret and in that of SS Justus and Abundius.

[7] *Sibbe* has generally been regarded as an error for *side* (see Cockayne and Herbst) but translates the Latin genitive *pacis* (Cas, p. 226).

[8] Margaret does not give her name in response to Olibrius's question: this could be due to the way in which the Old English translator abbreviates the source or

to scribal error either in the Old English version or in the Latin manuscript used as source.

9 A's mistaken reading *mægþ* is corrected by C.

10 A's mistaken reading *forswilde* is uncorrected in the manuscript.

11 Something has clearly been omitted here, as Margaret is locked in prison in one sentence and is before Olibrius in the next. In the Latin, Olibrius goes to Antioch and prays to his gods after Margaret has been locked up and then confronts her again the next day. The beginning of this scene of confrontation, as it appears in the Latin, is also omitted here.

12 This word has the sense 'just' in our text. Here it translates the Latin *iustis uirginibus* (Cas, p. 227). The sense 'just' for *soþfæst* is regarded as a characteristically Anglian lexical feature: see Jordan, *Eigentümlichkeiten des anglischen Wortschatzes*, p. 43; Wenisch, *Spezifisch anglisches Wortgut*, pp. 221–6; and Herbst, *Die altenglische Margaretenlegende*, p. 25. The word also translates Latin *iustus* in its other two occurrences in the *Legend* (chs. 15 and 21: for the latter of these occurrences compare M, p. 195, line 33 (P, ch. 21 and Cas, p. 233, have different wording at the corresponding point)).

13 The correction, by erasure of *þ*, of *geresteþ* avoids the irregular construction of *þæt* (purpose) taking an indicative verb. Note, however, the following uncorrected indicative constructions: *þy læs þu deaþe swiltast* (ch. 10) (contrast *þy læs min heorte her on ege sy*, ch. 7); *to þon þæt he onfoh* (ch. 20) (contrast to *to þam þæt he forswulge*, ch. 14). These latter two indicative clauses are either irregular purpose clauses or should be taken as expressing result.

14 A wrote *se* instead of *þæt*, giving the wrong gender to *blod*. The solecism is avoided by C's emendation to *hyre*.

15 Margaret is addressed here by women, although in the Latin there is no special mention of women at this point, but she replies, as in the Latin, to both men and women. Her reply indeed, 'gangaþ ge wif to eowrum husum and ge weras to eowrum weorcum!', distinguishes between men and women in a manner unparalleled in known Latin manuscripts.

16 The A reading *þu ungefylledlican dracan* (see Apparatus Criticus) follows Cas *insatiabilis draco* (p. 228). Grammatically, the phrase is either a mistake for the nominative forms *þu ungefylledlica draca* or the epithet is in the genitive case with the noun on which it is dependent having been lost. The former explanation is to be preferred as more closely reflecting Cas *insatiabilis draco* (vocative).

A goes on to refer to Olibrius as *mannes ofen*. The source of this strange epithet may lie in a confusion reflected in the Old English translation between the Latin words *fornax* 'furnace' and the more appropriate *fornix* 'fornicator'.

In Comp this whole problematic sequence, *þu ungefylledlican dracan mannes ofen*, is excised.

17 A's *synna to ansyna* (instead of *ansyne to ansyne*) is uncorrected in the manuscript but emendation is required. The corresponding Latin expression is *facie ad faciem* and Herbst emends the Old English to *of ansyne to ansyne*, but *ansyna to ansyna* is equally good Old English and avoids the difficulty of having to explain the loss of *of* (compare Deut. V. 4, 'Ansyne to ansyne he spræc to us').

18 A's reading *na* is clearly deficient, as recognized by C, who inserts *-ma is*.

19 Indicative mood in a purpose clause: see above, n. 13.

20 A writes *gehyræþ* instead of *gehyrast* (the latter form occurs in the immediately preceding sentence), with subsequent correction by B.

21 A writes *inre* instead of *hyre*, with subsequent correction by C.

22 Something is clearly missing after *handan* in the A reading, though it is unlikely to have been *blesian*, as C supplies. The Casinensis/Mombritius equivalent is simply *cepit orare* (Cas, p. 228; P, ch. 11) but the Old English translator may well, as Herbst suggests, have written something like 'stretched out her hands', as in the next section ('aþenode hire honda on gebede', ch. 12). In the present passage, the Old English exemplar followed by Tib may have read 'and ongan hire handa aþenian' and the A scribe may have added the *-n* to *handa* in anticipation of the *-n* of *aþenian*, which word was then omitted.

23 The Casinensis/Mombritius text has here, 'quia sola sum et unica terreni [this word is an addition unique to Cas] patris, et ipse me dereliquid' or variant (Cas, p. 228; P, ch. 11). A's version (*forþon þe ic ane beo and ange; mine fæder*) is very close to this, except that *mine* should probably read *mines* (*fæder* is a genitive form) and an *and* would also be syntactically desirable: 'forþon þe ic ane beo and ange mines fæder and he me forlet'. An *and* after *ange* could have been omitted because it followed so soon after the preceding *and*, which would have been separated from it only by the similar sounding *ange*. *Ange* may have been erased by B or C because it is a very unusual, largely poetic, word or because of the temptation to take it as referring to *fæder* rather than *ic* (Margaret), particularly since there is no distinctive genitive ending on *fæder*.

24 A's mistaken reading *tungla* is left uncorrected in the manuscript.

25 Cockayne says that this should read *hine*, while Herbst suggests that it is a form of *þisne*, with assimilation of *s* to *n*.

26 A's *þa* is corrected to *þare* by C. The original reading makes sense if we construe the demonstrative as referring to *hond*, from which it is separated by the genitive phrase *halgan fæmnan*, but the word order is unusual and has been found unsatisfactory by C.

27 The context requires a subjunctive verb, which is still not supplied by B's alteration of A's *adylgan* to *adylgian*. Our emendation of the Comp text follows Cockayne. Compare *gedon* (A)/*gedo* (Comp), ch. 21.

28 A's *þa* has been corrected by C. Either *þa* was a mistake for *þone*/*þane* or *þæt*

(*deofol* occurs as both a masculine and a neuter noun in this text) or the demonstrative had been omitted by the original scribe (in which case A's *þa* would be adverbial).

29 On the distinctive quality of Margaret's treatment of the black demon in this section, see above, p. 45. The Latin Casinensis version cannot be used for comparison here as it omits the entire sequence corresponding to our chs. 14–15.

30 Details of the following three speeches go back to the Latin original, though they are not reflected in known texts of the Mombritius and pre-Mombritius tradition (ch. 15 is omitted entirely in Casinensis): see above, pp. 45–7.

31 A's reading *þære eacan rice*, which has the wrong gender in *þære* and the wrong case in *rice*, is left uncorrected in the manuscript.

32 A's original reading *he* compounds the grammatical confusion noted in our comment on *þære eacan rice*: having been accompanied by a feminine demonstrative in the previous phrase, the neuter noun *rice* is here referred to by means of a masculine pronoun. B's correction removes at least some of the faulty grammar in this sequence.

33 There is a problem with the structure of this sentence, as the 'Secg me, Margaret, þu þe þurh mægþhad gyrndest þæs eacan rices' is never taken up later in the sentence, which instead has the syntactically discontinuous 'and forþon hit biþ þe geseald mid Abraham and mid Isaac and Iacob'. Possibly something is missing here (perhaps as a result of eyeskip from one *Margaret* to another) and 'Secg me' originally introduced an entirely different sentence. Variants of *BHL* no. 5303 are of no help here and, of course, this whole section is lacking in Casinensis.

34 The manuscript reading *gecyþ þonne þinre þeowen* requires emendation. *Gemedo-mast* in the meaning 'vouchsafe, condescend' demands an infinitive or a subordinate clause and *gecyþ* therefore needs to be completed to *gecyþan*. *þonne* does not make sense in the context, however, and Herbst suggests that a possible explanation for the incomplete *gecyþ* and the presence of *þonne* is that *gecyþan* was at one stage written *gecyþā* and that the abbreviation was then mistakenly detached from the stem and supplied with a *þ*, giving *gecyþ þanne*, which in turn was copied as *gecyþ þonne*.

35 *BHL* no. 5303, as Herbst points out, has at this point a genitive plural, which the Old English A text translates (*manegra soþfæstra manna ic genam*), but without retaining the noun on which the Latin genitive is dependent: 'multorum labores abstuli' (P, ch. 15; passage lacking in Cas). The Old English A reading is probably original, therefore, but is not good Old English, leaving the sentence without an accusative direct object. B has rewritten the phrase in order to remedy the grammatical deficiency.

36 There is a very abrupt transition in the devil's speech at the beginning of this

sentence, with a *non sequitur*: either something is missing from the source or there is a scribal lacuna. The deficiency is not remedied by C's rewriting of the phrase.

37 Dat. sing. fem of *geong*. The form appears to be Northumbrian: on this form, see above, p. 99.

38 The rest of this section, as it was written in Tib, is underlined for cancellation. The A-reading *and þu ane wiþ me and wið eall hire cneo< > rise* may be compared to *BHL* no. 5303 'modo tu surrexisti aduersus genus meum et me superasti. O quam mirandum est quia tenera puella superauit patrem et matrem et totam generationem suam . . .' (P, ch. 15 (emended); whole sequence lacking in Cas). In the Old English *cneo* appears to be a mistake for *cneorisse*, with the omission of *-risse* easily understandable in view of the very similar *rise* (from *surrexisti*), the next word. *Wið eall hire cneo* appears to reflect *totam generationem suam* but the beginning of this sentence in the Latin has been omitted in the Old English, perhaps because it adds nothing new to the previous sentence, or because of a textual corruption reflected in the Tiberius copy. The manuscript reading presents a jarring shift from second person pronoun (*þu*) to third (*hire*) in *þu ane wiþ me and wið eall hire cneo rise*. Logically, in the sentence as it appears here *hire* should instead read *þine*.

The remainder of the underlined passage, *Cristes gefylgendum, þurh þono deofla magen eall to nahte gebiþ*, may be compared to *BHL* no. 5303 'et Christum secuta est. Ligat demones, fugat diabolum, et aliquos occidit. Vere uirtus nostra nihil ualet quia <a> parua puella superati sumus' (P, ch. 15; passage lacking in Cas). The first phrase of the Old English clearly reflects the first clause of the Latin, though the Old English is grammatically confused, and the second phrase seems to be derived from 'Vere uirtus nostra nihil ualet', but again this is not what the Old English actually means. It is possible that instead of *gebiþ* the original could have read *biþ gebiged* (*gebiged* rendering *superati*), with the similarity of these two adjacent words leading to conflation: this would give 'þurh þono deofla magen eall to nahte biþ gebiged', which is close in meaning to the Latin. In this reconstruction, 'þurh þono' would refer to Christ, though the clause is hardly elegant.

The reading in *BHL* no. 5303 *et Christum secuta est* suggests that *Cristes gefylgendum* in the Old English is an epithet referring to Margaret. In this clearly corrupt reading, however, the case and gender are wrong. The whole passage is despairingly jettisoned in the Comp text.

39 There is no real reply to Margaret's question to the demon, which is answered at some length in Latin versions, including Casinensis (p. 230). In the Old English the question is simply left hanging. Again we have to assume a deficiency in the source of our text or attribute it to the characteristic abbreviation of the Old English writer, resulting here in the conflation of two speeches.

[40] The reading *ge gebletsode* is left uncorrected in the manuscript. This reading is an instance of straightforward dittography, with the first *ge* at the end of a line and the second at the beginning of the next line.

[41] Notable features of the account in the Tiberius version of Margaret's torture in a vessel of water are the description of the vessel as made of lead, found only in this version, and of the water as hot. On these features, see above, pp. 47–8.

[42] The A-reading *Ðrihten* is left uncorrected in the manuscript. This text does not otherwise confuse *d* and *ð*.

[43] A's *eallum* is corrected by B, making it accusative feminine agreeing with *synne* (*from* governs the preceding *me*).

[44] A's reading *þe þe þu me onlihtest* has dittography of *þe*, with the first *þe* occurring at the end of a line and the second at the beginning of the next line; left uncorrected in the manuscript.

[45] A's *mægþhad* is uncorrected in the manuscript, but *gyman* always takes the genitive.

[46] The number of people converted as a result of seeing Margaret's torture is specified as fifteen thousand, not counting women and children. On this figure, see above, p. 48.

[47] The A reading *wealþas*, already half corrected from *weaþþas*, has not been further modified in the manuscript.

[48] Margaret's prayer is notable syntactically for the vacillation between indicative and subjunctive verbs in subordinate indefinite clauses (relative and conditional). The corresponding Latin verbs (Cas, p. 232) are uniformly in the future perfect indicative, but the Old English has *writeþ*, *deþ* etc., interwoven with *si*, *timbrige* etc. The vacillation is particularly apparent in the following two parallel clauses later in the speech: 'se þe macað [A *rærdeþ*] boc mines martyrhades oþþe on his huse hæbbe'. See CCCC Commentary, nn. 44 and 50.

[49] The A text reads *gewinne*. Herbst points out (*Die altenglische Margaretenlegende*, pp. 25–6) that *gewin* in the sense 'gain', 'fruit of labour', suggested by the present context, is confined in Old English to the Tiberius *Margaret* legend and to the Anglian *Paris Psalter*. In *gewin* the denotation 'toil', as opposed to 'strife', is regarded as an Anglian feature (see Jordan, *Eigentümlichkeiten des anglischen Wortschatzes*, p. 43, n. 2; Herbst, *ibid.*; Wenisch, *Spezifisch anglisches Wortgut*, *passim*). In the present occurrence the word appears to be used to render the Latin *labor* (Cas, p. 232) but has been rejected by C and replaced by the West Saxon equivalent *geswing*. *Gewin* occurs again in the same sense a few lines later (ch. 19) but on this occasion is not corrected.

[50] C's insertion of this word replaces the meaningless A reading *rærdeþ*. If we take the latter as a mistake for *rædeþ* it reflects the Latin *legerit* (Cas, p. 232; P, ch. 19), whereas *macað* corresponds to *conparaverit* (Cas, *ibid.*; P, *ibid.*).

51 The Old English verb follows Casinensis *mitte* (p. 232) rather than *BHL* no. 5303 *reple* (P, ch. 19).

52 There is no equivalent in Latin versions (Casinensis is abbreviated at this point) to *ac sy þær sib and lufu and soþfæstnisse gast*, but the *Old English Martyrology* has 'blis and sib and soðlufu'. On this, see above, pp. 53–4.

53 The Latin texts read here 'digneris, Domine, dare ei indulgentiam' (Cas, p. 233) and 'indulge ei Domine' (M, p. 195, line 13; P deficient). In the Old English, scribal alterations to the A reading *gecyþ hine* testify to unease about the case of the pronoun and the lack of a satisfactory direct object for the verb: B changes *hine* to *him* and C adds *his bene*, with the clause now presumably meaning, 'perform, carry out his prayer for him'.

54 A reading corresponding to this is found in only one Latin variant, the copy of *BHL* no. 5303 printed by Mombritius (M, p. 195, line 17): on this reading, see above, p. 49. Casinensis omits the whole of our ch. 20 and is therefore of no assistance at this point.

55 A's *gemano*, written instead of *gemanst*, is corrected by C.

56 There is no equivalent in Latin versions (Casinensis omits the whole passage) to *eall hit biþ gehered ætforan Godes gesyhþe*, but the *Old English Martyrology* has 'þine bene syndon gehered ætforan Godes gesihðe.' On this, see above, p. 54.

57 The A text has *þreo hund engla*: the dove tells Margaret that God will appoint three hundred angels to receive the prayers of those who appeal to Christ in her name. This detail is paralleled in Usener's Greek but not in existing Latin versions (see above, p. 49). The C corrector here makes the first in a series of alterations which tone down the original translation. Where the A scribe wrote that God would place three hundred angels in Margaret's church to receive the prayers offered to God in her name, C replaces *þreo hund engla* with *þreo englas*; in ch. 22 the thousand angels who bless Margaret's body become *manega*; and in ch. 23 the twelve angels who take her head become simply *englas*, by the cancellation of *twelf*.

58 The conjunction *to þon þæt* is here followed by the indicative mood: see also above, n. 13.

59 The A-reading *gefean*, grammatically inconsistent with the rest of the list in which it occurs, remains uncorrected in the manuscript.

In A this word is immediately followed by *and nænig on neorxnawonge mare gemetod mid meder ealra Gescippendes nimþe þreo fæmnan*. This passage clearly caused difficulties to one of the revisers, as it is marked for cancellation. There is no known parallel to the passage in other versions of the legend (Casinensis, to which we might have hoped to look for enlightenment, omits all of ch. 20). In context, the clause must refer to the exaltation of Thecla, Susanna and Margaret above all other virgins, since the dove goes on to summon Margaret to her place on the right-hand side of Thecla and Susanna. It would seem, therefore, to mean that only Thecla and Susanna 'meet more' (i.e. 'spend more time in paradise'?) with the Virgin Mary. In this comparison, however, the number three is strictly illogical, as it includes Margaret with those to whom she is compared. The form *gemetod* is problematic too, in that it is either the past participle of the verb and in need of an auxiliary or a finite verb with a mistake in the ending.

60 The same phrase, *of ealre heortan*, occurs at the corresponding point in the *Old English Martyrology* but there is no equivalent in Latin versions (Casinensis omits this whole section): see above, p. 54.

61 The uncorrected manuscript reading *tearum* is presumably due to the influence of the adjacent word *mid*.

62 In A's reading, *to cwæþ* instead of *and cwæþ*, the *to* does not make sense in the context, while a conjunction is obviously missing. This is supplied by C. It would seem that the *to* is somehow an error for 7.

63 The manuscript reads *gedon*, but syntactically the clause is dependent and the infinitive should be a subjunctive. Compare *adylgan* (ch. 14), altered to *adylgian* by B (an emendation which still does not supply the required subjunctive form).

64 The principal and subordinate clauses in this sentence do not correspond: 'I ask you in the name of our Lord the Saviour Christ that he give you forgiveness of your sins and bring it about that you reign in the kingdom of heaven.' It is clear that Margaret is really asking the Lord, not the bystanders, for forgiveness of their sins. As Herbst points out, the discrepancy can be explained as due to the Old English translator's abbreviation of the source in such a way as to disrupt syntactic continuity. The Casinensis version has, 'Rogo uos per Dominum regem coelorum, memoriam facite animae meae, ut sine timore transeat principatus et potestates aeris huius. Sed obsecro uos ut Dominum deprecare dignemini pro me peccatricem, et commendate me Deo et sanctis eius. Et ego peccatrix obsecrabo pro omnibus uobis ad Dominum omnipotentem, ut det uobis Deus gratiam suam, et spem aeternam et heredes effici glorie eius' (p. 233). The inconsistency may be due to the translator jumping from the first part of the source, addressed to the bystanders, to the last part, which contains the prayer Margaret addressed to Christ on behalf of the people. Alternatively, this inconsistency may arise from scribal error in the transmission of the Old English text, involving haplography.

65 A's mistaken reading *risaþ* is corrected by B.

66 A's mistaken reading *þæt* is corrected by C.

67 In the A reading *middangeard gedem ic* an introduction to Malchus's speech is missing, as is a negative particle as the first word of the speech. The gap should be filled by something like B's *He cwæð ne*.

68 A's *Godedes*, instead of *Godes* (dittography), remains uncorrected in the manuscript.

69 A's *gehwyrde* (already altered from *gehwyfde*), is corrected by B.

[70] A mistakenly wrote *ofastag*, with subsequent correction by C.

[71] The A reading *twelf englas* goes back to the Greek and is reflected in part in the Latin Casinensis and Turin versions (see above, pp. 14–15 and 43). The Old English goes on to say that the angels brought the head to paradise: 'hi hit gesætton on neorxnawonge.' This corresponds to Casinensis 'et adduxerunt capud eius in paradiso' (p. 233); there is no mention of paradise in *BHL* no. 5303, in which the relevant phrase presents a less exact correspondence to the Old English: 'ascenderunt super nubem' (P, ch. 23).

[72] A's *ge gehrinon* is an instance of dittography, with the first *ge* at the end of one page and the second at the beginning of the next; changed in Comp to *onhrinon*.

[73] Among versions of the Margaret legend this speech is paralleled only, though not exactly, in Casinensis: see above, p. 44.

[74] A's *þ* is instead of *þæt* or *þe*; altered to *þe* in Comp.

[75] From the context, the pronoun must refer to Christ and should, therefore, as in the B-correction of A's *hire*, read *hine*.

[76] In the A-reading *and gemindoþ* the *and* disrupts the sense of the passage, in which, moreover, *gemindoþ* appears to parallel *wesaþ* as an imperative and should, therefore, read *gemindioþ*; B alters to *and gemundyt*.

The Old English Life of St Margaret in
Cambridge, Corpus Christi College 303

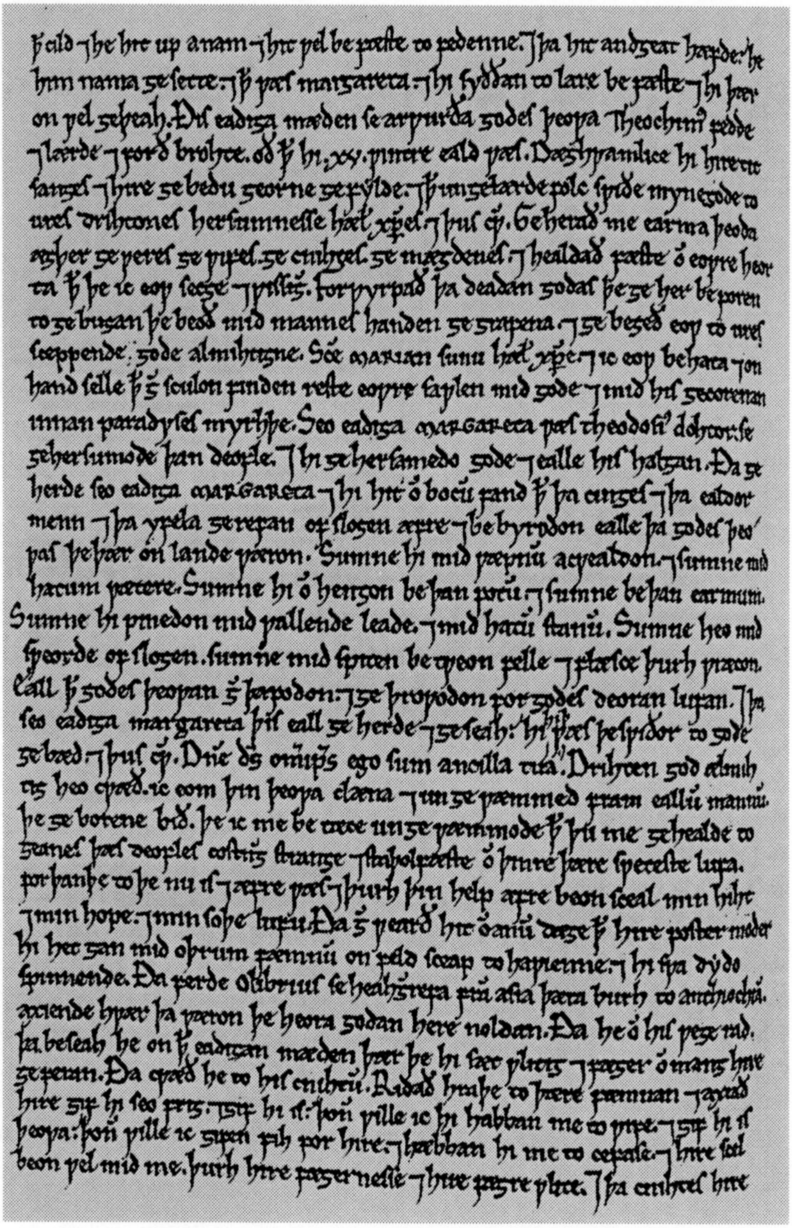

ꝥ eald ⁊ he hit up anam ⁊ hit ƿel befæste to fedenne. ⁊ þa hit andgeat hæfde: he
him nama gesette. ⁊ ꝥ ƿæs margareta. ⁊ hi syððan to lare befæste ⁊ hi þær
on ƿel geƿeah. Ðis eadiga mæden se arƿurða godes þeoƿa Theochimus fedde
⁊ lærde ⁊ forð brohte. oð ꝥ hi .xv. ƿintre eald ƿæs. Dæghƿamlice hi hire tit
sanges ⁊ hire gebedu georne gefylde. ⁊ ꝥ ungelærde folc sƿiðe myngode to
ures drihtenes hersumnesse hælendes cristes ⁊ þus cƿæð. Geherað me earma þeoda
ægðer ge ƿeres ge ƿifes. ge cnihtes. ge mægdenes. ⁊ healdað fæste on eoƿre heor
ta ꝥ þe ic eoƿ secge ⁊ ƿissige. Forƿyrpað þa deadan godas þe ge her beforen
to gebugan þe beoð mid mannes handen geƿorhta. ⁊ gebegeð eoƿ to ures
sceppende. gode almihtigne. Sancte marian sunu hælende criste. ⁊ ic eoƿ behata ⁊ on
hand selle ꝥ ge sculon finden reste eoƿre saƿlen mid gode ⁊ mid his gecorenan
innan paradyses myrhþe. Seo eadiga margareta ƿæs theodosius dohtor: se
gehersumode þan deofle. ⁊ hi gehersumedo gode ⁊ ealle his halgan. Ða ge
herde seo eadiga margareta ⁊ hi hit on bocum fand ꝥ þa cingces ⁊ þa ealdor
menn ⁊ þa ƿrecan gerefan ofslogen æfre ⁊ beƿyrpodon ealle þa godes þeo
ƿas þe ƿær on lande ƿæron. Summe hi mid ƿæpnum acƿealdon. ⁊ summe mid
hatum ƿætere. Summe hi on hengon be þan fotum. ⁊ summe be þan earmum.
Summe hi ƿinedon mid ƿallende leade. ⁊ mid hatum stanum. Summe heo mid
sƿeorde ofslogen. summe mid speren betƿeon ƿelle ⁊ flæsce þurh ƿræcon.
Eall ꝥ godes þeoƿan ge þoƿodon. ⁊ ge þrouodon for godes deoran lufan. ⁊ þa
seo eadiga margareta þis eall geherde ⁊ geseah: hi ƿæs þe sƿidor to gode
gebæd. ⁊ þus cƿæð. Domine deus omnipotens ego sum ancilla tua. Drihten god ælmih
tig heo cƿæð. ic eom þin þeoƿa clæna ⁊ ungeƿæmmed fram eallum mannum.
þe geborene beoð. þe ic me betæce ungeƿæmmode ꝥ þu me gehealde to
ganes þæs deofles costnunge strange ⁊ staþolfæste on þinre þære sƿetelste lufa.
forþanþe to þe nu is ⁊ æfre ƿæs ⁊ þurh þin help æfre beon sceal min hiht
⁊ min hope. ⁊ min soþe lufu. Ða geƿearð hit on anum dæge ꝥ hire foster moder
hi het gan mid oþrum fæmnum on feld sceap to hafienne. ⁊ hi sƿa dydo
spinnende. Ða ferde Olibrius se heahgerefa fram asia þæra burh to antiochia.
acsiende hƿær þa ƿæron þe heora godan hære noldan. Ða he on his ƿege rad.
þa beseah he on ꝥ eadigan mæden þær þe hi sæt ƿlitig ⁊ fæger on mang hire
geferan. Ða cƿæð he to his cnihtum. Radað hraþe to þære fæmnan ⁊ fraciað
hire gif hi seo freo. ⁊ gif hi is: þonne ƿille ic hi habban me to ƿife. ⁊ gif hi is
þeoƿa: þonne ƿille ic gifen fih for hire. ⁊ hæbban hi me to cefese. ⁊ hire sceal
beon ƿel mid me. þurh hire fægernesse ⁊ hire fægre ƿlite. ⁊ þa cnihtes hire

PLATE II Cambridge, Corpus Christi College 303, p. 100

Passio beate Margarete uirginis et martyris

1   Efter Drihtnes þrowunge[1] and his æriste þæt he of deaðe aras Hælend Crist, on þan dagum his halgan geþrowodon for his þæra micclan leofan lufan.[2] Eac þa gewearð hit, þæt þa halga seagntes ofercomen þa deofla þe wið heom gewunnon. And þa rican,[a3] þe on þan dagum wæron, hæfdon heom geworht godes of golde and of seolfre; þa wæron dumbe and deafe and blinde, and eal þæt hæþan folc swiðe gelefdon on þan godum.

2   Sum land is Anthiochia gehaten. On þam lande wæs an Godes þeowa, se wæs Theothimus gehaten. He wæs swiðe gelæred man.[4]

3   And þær on lande wæs sum hæþen cyningc, Theodosius gehaten, and his cwen mid him. Hit gewearð swa þæt heo bearn gestreonedon and þæt wearð geboren mædencild; and se hæþene cing his fæder hit het ut aweorpan and men swa dyde.[5] And se Godes þeowe Theothimus[b6] gefand þæt cild and he hit up anam and hit wel befæste to fedenne. And þa hit andgeat hæfde, he him nama gesette, and þæt was Margareta, and hi syððan to lare befæste, and hi þæron wel geþeah.

4   Ðis[7] eadiga mæden se arwurða Godes þeowa Theothimus[c] fedde and lærde and forðbrohte, oðþæt hi .xv. wintre eald wæs. Dæghwamlice hi hire utsanges and hire gebedu georne gefylde and þæt ungelærde folc swiðe mynegode to ures Drihtones hersumnesse, Hælendes Cristes, and þus cwæð: 'Geheraðe me, earma þeoda, ægþer ge weres ge wifes, ge cnihtes ge mægdenes, and healdað fæste on eowre heorta þæt þe ic eow secge and wissige. Forwyrpað þa deadan godas þe ge her beforen to gebugan, þe beoð mid mannes handen gegrafena, and gebegeð eow to ure[d] Sceppende Gode

---

[a] rican] ricem MS; *Assmann emends to* ricene   [b] Theothimus] Theochim' MS   [c] Theo-
thimus] Theochim' MS   [d] ure] ure[[s]] MS

152

1 In the days after the Lord's Passion and Resurrection, when Christ the Saviour arose from death, his saints suffered because of their great, dear love of him. It came about then also that the holy saints overcame the devils, who fought against them. And those who were in power in those days had made gods for themselves from gold and silver; these were dumb and deaf and blind and all the heathen people believed very much in these gods.

2 There is a certain country called Antioch. In that country there was a servant of God, who was called Theotimus. He was a very learned man.

3 And in that country there was a certain heathen king called Theodosius and his queen. It so happened that they begot a child and it was born a girl; and the heathen king its father commanded it to be cast out and this was done. And Theotimus, the servant of God, found the child and he took it up and entrusted it to where it would be nursed well. When it was capable of understanding, he gave it a name, which was Margaret, and afterwards he put her to learning and she excelled at it.

4 The pious servant of God Theotimus fostered this blessed maiden and taught her and trained her until she was fifteen years old. Daily she eagerly performed her matins and her prayers and ardently exhorted the unlearned people to obey our Lord, Christ the Saviour, and she spoke as follows: 'Hear me, wretched people, both men and women, boys and girls, and hold fast in your hearts that which I say and make known to you. Reject the dead gods to whom you have submitted up to now, who are carved by the hands of men, and subject yourselves to our creator, God Almighty, son of St

Ælmihtigne, Sancte Marian sunu, Halende Criste, and ic eow behata and on hand selle þæt ge sculon finden reste eowre sawlen mid Gode and mid his gecorenan innan paradyses myrhþe.' Seo eadiga Margareta wæs Theodosius dohtor: se gehersumode þan deofle and hi gehersamedo Gode and ealle his halgan. Ða geherde seo eadiga Margareta and hi hit on bocum fand, þæt þa cinges and þa ealdormenn and þa yfela gerefan ofslogen æfre and bebyrodon ealle þa Godes þeowas þe þær on lande wæron. Sumne hi mid wæpnum acwealdon and sumne mid hatum wætere. Sumne hi onhengon be þan fotum and sumne be þan earmum. Sumne hi pinedon mid wallende leade and mid hatum stanum. Sumne heo mid sweorde ofslogen; sumne mid spiten betweon felle and flæsce þurhwræcon. Eall þæt Godes þeowan geþafodon and geþrowodon for Godes deoran lufan. And þa seo eadiga Margareta þis eall geherde and geseah, hi hi þæs[e] þe swiðor to Gode gebæd and þus cwæð: 'Domine Deus omnipotens, ego sum ancilla tua. Drihten God Ælmihtig', heo cwæð, 'ic eom þin þeowa clæna and ungewæmmed fram eallum mannum, þe geborene bið. Þe ic me betæce ungewæmmode þæt þu me gehealde togeanes þæs deofles costung strange and staþolfæste on þinre þære sweteste lufa, forþan þe to þe nu is and æfre wæs and, þurh þin help, æfre beon sceal min hiht and min hope and min soþe lufu.'[8]

5 Ða gewearð hit on anum dæge þæt hire fostermoder hi het gan mid oþrum fæmnum on feld, sceap to hawienne, and hi swa dydo spinnende.[9] Ða ferde Olibrius se heahgerefa fram Asia þæra burh to Anthiochiam, axiende hwær þa wæron, þe heora godan here[10] noldan. Ða he on his wege rad, þa beseah he on þæt eadigan mæden þær þe hi sæt, wlitig and fæger, onmang hire geferan. Ða cwæð he to his cnihtum: 'Ridað hraþe to þære fæmnan and axiað hire gif hi seo frig, and gif hi is, þonne wille ic hi habban me to wife; and gif hi is þeowa, þonne wille ic gifen fih for hire and hæbban hi me to cefase and hire scel beon wel mid me þurh hire fægernesse and hire fægre wlite.' And þa cnihtes hire þa to comon and hire to spræcon, eall swa heom gehaten wæs. Ða Sancta Margareta heo to eorþan gestrehte and hi hire georne to Gode gebæd and þus cwæð: 'Miserere mei, Deus, miserere mei. Gemiltse me, Drihten, gemiltse me, þæt min sawle ne seo awæmmod þurh þisum hæþenum mannum. And ic þe wille biddan þæt deofle mine sawle ne beswican,[11] ne mine treowðe fram þe ahwerfan, ne minne clæne lichaman gefylan.[12] Drihten leof, æfre ic þe lufode, and, þu Wuldorcyn-

Mary, Christ the Saviour. And I promise and pledge you that you shall find rest for your souls with God and with his chosen ones in the joy of paradise.' The blessed Margaret was Theodosius's daughter: he obeyed the devil and she obeyed God and all his saints. Then the blessed Margaret heard and found it in books that the kings and noblemen and evil prefects were constantly putting to death and burying all the servants of God who were in that country. They killed one with weapons and another with hot water. They hung one by the feet and another by the arms. They tortured one with boiling lead and with hot stones. They slew one by the sword; they pierced through the skin and flesh of another with rods. The servants of God endured and suffered all this because of their dear love of God. And when the blessed Margaret heard and saw all this, she prayed all the more intensely to God and said as follows: 'Domine Deus omnipotens, ego sum ancilla tua. Lord God almighty', she said, 'I am your pure servant and unstained by any man ever born. I dedicate myself to you unstained so that you may keep me strong and steadfast in sweetest love of you against the temptation of the devil, because my trust and my hope and my true love is in you now and always was and, with your help, always will be.'

5   Then one day it came about that her fostermother directed her to go with other girls into the field to mind the sheep and she did so while spinning. Then Olibrius the high-prefect was going from the city of Asia to Antioch, inquiring where those people were, who did not wish to obey their gods. As he rode on his way, he saw the blessed maiden where she was sitting, beautiful and fair, among her companions. Then he said to his attendants, 'Ride quickly to that girl and ask her whether she is free; and if she is, then I will have her as my wife; and if she is a slave, then I will pay money for her and have her as my concubine and it will be well for her with me because of her fairness and her fair beauty.' And the attendants came to her and spoke to her just as they had been ordered. Then St Margaret prostrated herself on the ground and she prayed eagerly to God and spoke as follows: 'Miserere mei, Deus, miserere mei. Have mercy on me, Lord, have mercy on me, so that my soul may not be corrupted by these heathens. And I desire to entreat you that devils may not deceive my soul or turn my faith away from you or defile my pure body. Beloved Lord, I have always loved

155

ing, ne læt þu me naht beswican, ne næfre min gewit fram þe gehwerfan, ne min mægþhad afylan. Ac asænd me, leofa Drihten, þinne halga engel to fultume, þæt ic min gewitt and minne wisdom forðhealdan mote, forþon ic eom gesett betweonen þisum folce swa swa sceap betweonon wulfum, and ic eam befangan eal swa spearwe on nette, and eall swa fisc on hoce, and eal swa hra mid rape. Nu help[f] þu me, leofa Drihten, gehelp þu me.'

6   And þa cerdon þa cnihtas to heora hlaforde and cwædon: 'Nis þin mægn naht wið hire, forþon þe hi lufað þone God þe þine eldran aheongan on rode.' And þa wearð se gerefa swiðe yrre and het hi niman and him to gebringan. And he hire to cwæð and hire axode of hwilcere þeode hi wære and hwæder hi wære Cristen and frig oððe þeowa. And seo eadiga Margareta him andwyrde and cwæð: 'Ic eom frig and Cristen.' And se cniht hire to cwæð: 'On hwilcum godum is þin geleafa, þe þu on gelefst and forð wilt get gelefan?' Seo eadiga Margarete him þa geandswarede: 'Ic lufige God Ælmihtigne', cwæð hi, 'and on him ic gelefa, þe is Fæder and Sunu and Halig Gast, þone þe min mægþhad fægre and wel gehealdon hæfð: þæt is se þe þine yldran ahengan and þurh þære dæde hi losian sculon, forþon þe he is Cyning and his rice ne wurð næfre nan ænde.'[13] And þa wearð Olibrius swiðe yrre and het þa fægre fæmne genimen and innon his carcerne belucen, þær nan liht inne cumen ne mihte,[14] and men[15] swa dyde. Ða þis gedon wæs, þa for se gerefa Olibrius to Antiochia þære byrig, to his godan him to gebiddenne.

7   And he þanan to his gereorde eode and amang þan þe he æt, he to his þegnum spræc, and þus cwæð: 'On hwilca wisa ræde ge me hu ic muge þis mæden bismærian?'[16] And hi ealle þa swigedon. Ða se gerefa het hi utlædon of þan carcerne, and þæt wæs on þan oðre dæge, and het hi bringan beforen him, and he hire to cwæð: 'Ðu earma fæmna, læt beon þin mycela mod, þe þu to me hæfst, and gemiltse þinum fægran[g] lichaman and gebide þe to minum gode and ic þe gife ælc god genoh and þu scealt eal mines godes wealden mid me selfum.' Sancta Margareta him andswerode and þus cwæð: 'Drihten hit wat, þæt ic min mægþhad wel þurh him gehealdan habbe, and ne miht þu me beswican, ne þu ne miht me becyrran of minum rihtan geleafan, ne fram minum rihte hlaforde. And ic eom geara', cwæð hi, 'on Drihten to gelefanne, þe gesceop heofonas and eorðan, and he sæ

---

[f] help] 'h'elp MS   [g] fægran] fægreran MS

you and, King of Glory, do not allow me to be deceived in any way or my understanding to be turned away from you or my virginity to be defiled. But, beloved Lord, send your holy angel to help me, that I may preserve my understanding and my wisdom henceforth, because I am placed among these people like a sheep among wolves and I am ensnared like a sparrow in a net and like a fish on a hook and like a roe by a rope. Now help me, beloved Lord, help me.'

6   Then the attendants returned to their master and said, 'You have no power over her because she loves the God whom your ancestors hanged on a cross.' And then the prefect was very angry and commanded that she be seized and brought to him. And he spoke to her and asked what people she came from and whether she was a Christian and whether she was free or a slave. And the blessed Margaret answered him and said, 'I am free and a Christian.' And the attendant said to her, 'In what gods do you have faith, in whom you believe and will go on believing?' The blessed Margaret answered him then: 'I love Almighty God,' she said, 'and I believe in him, who is the Father and the Son and the Holy Spirit, who has graciously preserved my virginity intact: it is he whom your ancestors hanged and because of that deed they must perish, because he is king and his kingdom will have no end.' And then Olibrius became very angry and commanded that the beautiful girl be taken and locked in his prison, into which no light could come, and this was done. When this had been done, then the prefect Olibrius went to the city of Antioch, in order to pray to his gods.

7   And from there he went to his meal and while he ate, he spoke to his servants and said as follows: 'How would you advise me to put this maiden to shame?' And they were all silent. Then the prefect commanded that she be led out of the prison and on the second day he commanded that she be brought before him and he said to her, 'You wretched girl, abandon the great arrogance which you feel towards me, and have mercy on your fair body and pray to my god, and I shall give you enough of every good thing and you shall possess all my goods with me.' St Margaret answered him and said as follows: 'The Lord knows that through him I have preserved my virginity intact and you cannot deceive me nor can you seduce me from my right belief or from my rightful Lord. And I am ready', she said, 'to believe in the Lord who created the heavens and the earth and he compelled the sea,

bedraf, þær þe heo frohtað[h][17] dæges and nihtes.' Olibrius þa cwæð: 'Gif þu nylt to minum gode þe gebiddan, min swyrd sceal þinne[i] þone fægran lichaman eall to styccan forcyrfan and þine lieman ealle tosindrian, and þine ban ic sceal ealle forbærnan. And gif þu woldest me lufian and to minum godum þe gebiddan, þe sceolde beon eall swa wel eall swa me selfan.' And seo eadiga Margareta him andswerode and cwæð: 'Ic habbe minne licchaman and mine sawla Gode bebodan, for he is min hlaford and min help and min werigend and min fultum wið þe and wið eallum þinum leasum gewitum. Crist hine selfne to þan geeadmedde þæt he for mancynne micele þrowunge geþrowode and na for his gewyrhtum, ac for ure alesednesse. And ic wille', cwæð hi, 'for his leofan wille bliðelice þrowian.'

8   Ða het se gerefa hi niman and het hi be þan fotan uppahon and mid greatum roddum beaton. And seo eadiga Margareta hire handan uppahof and hi to Gode gebæd and þus cwæð: 'On þe ic gelefa, leofa Drihten, and þæt ic þe bidde, þæt þu ne þole þæt ic næfre forwurþe, ne þæt me mine feond næfre oferswiðan ne moten, forþan min hiht is to þe, leofe Drihten.' And hi þa get hire clæne gebedu forðhild and þus cwæð: 'Æfre wunu þu mid me, leofa drihten, heofonlice Cyng. Miltse me and genere me of deofles anwealde.'

9   Ealle þa men, þe hire abutan stodon, to hire cleopoden and þus cwædon:[18] 'Hwi nelt þu, earme fæmne, gelefan on ure gode and to ure hlaforde þe gebugan and lutan? Æle, fægre fæmne, ealle we þe bemænað sarlice, forþon þe we geseoð þe swa nacode sittan and þinne fægra lichaman to wundre macian, and us þæt þincþ, þæt he ah þines gewald, hwæþer swa he wille to deaðe oððe to life. Gelef on ure gode, þonne most þu mid us lif habben.' Seo eadiga Margareta heom andswerode: 'Æle, ge geleasan witan, gað hraðe to eowrum weorce, forþan ðe min God is mid me on fultume. Hwæt, wene ge þæt me þæt ofþynce, þæt min lichame þrowige? Ic wat þæt min sawle is þæs þe clænre mid Gode. Ac, earme þeode, gelefað get on minum Gode, and for he is strang and mihtful and ealle þan mannen gefultumað, þe mid rihte farað and mid clænre heorte him to gebiddað, and he heom geofð in paradise eardingstowe. Ne þurfe ge næfre þæs wenan, þæt ic æfre eowrum godum me to gebidde, forþon þe hi syndon dumbe and deafe and blinde and mid drycræfte geworhte.'

[h] frohtað] wrohtað MS   [i] þinne] þ'i'nne MS

where it fears day and night.' Olibrius then said, 'If you will not pray to my god, my sword will have to cut your beautiful body into pieces and sunder all your limbs and I will have to burn all your bones. And if you would love me and pray to my gods, then it would be quite as well for you as for me.' And the blessed Margaret answered him and said, 'I have offered up my body and my soul to God, because he is my Lord and my help and my defender and my aid against you and against all your false advisers. Christ humbled himself to such an extent that he endured great suffering for mankind and it was not at all because of his own deeds, but in order to redeem us. And I wish', she said, 'to suffer joyously for his dear sake.'

8   Then the prefect commanded that she be taken and he commanded that she be hung up by the feet and beaten with thick sticks. And blessed Margaret raised up her hands and prayed to God and spoke as follows: 'I believe in you, beloved Lord, and I entreat you never to allow me to perish nor my enemies ever to overcome me, because my hope is in you, beloved Lord.' And she still kept up her pure prayers and spoke thus: 'Remain with me always, beloved Lord, heavenly King. Have mercy on me and rescue me from the devil's power.'

9   All the people standing about her called to her and spoke thus: 'Why, wretched girl, will you not believe in our god and submit and bow down to our lord? O fair girl, we all lament for you grievously because we see you sitting naked like this and your fair body made into a spectacle and it seems to us that he has power over you, as to whether he wishes you to die or live. Believe in our god, then you will be able to have life among us.' Blessed Margaret answered them, 'O you false advisers, go quickly about your work because my God is with me helping me. What, do you think that it grieves me that my body should suffer? I know that my soul is all the purer in the sight of God. But, wretched people, even now believe in my God because he is powerful and mighty and helps all those who act rightly and pray to him with a pure heart and he will grant them a dwelling in paradise. You must never think that I will ever pray to your gods, because they are dumb and deaf and blind and created by sorcery.'

10   Ða wearð se gerefa eorre geworþan and cwæð to hire: 'Ðu wyrcest
þines fæðeres weorc,[19] þæt is se deofol self.' And seo fæmne andswaro geaf:
'Hwæt, þu nu, earming, mid leasunge færst and me is min Drihten on
fultume.' Ða cwæð se gerefa: 'Hwær is se God, þe mæg þe gebeorgan of
mine handan?' Seo eadiga Margareta him to cwæð: 'Geswiga þu earmingc,
ne hæfst[j] þu nan þingc on me to donne, ac eall þu eart full and þu scealt
faran into þære nigenda niþhelle[20] and þu scealt þær onfon þa yfelan
geweorc, þe þu her gefremest and gefremed hæst.'[21] Ða het se gerefa hio
nimon and be þan fexe upahon and bæd wyrcan scearpa piles and het wrecen
betweon flæsce and bane. And seo eadiga Margareta hire handa upahof and
hi georne to Drihtne gebæd and þus cwæð: 'Ðu, Drihten leof, beo þu me on
fultume, for me beoð abuton hundes swa manega and heo willeð minne
lichamen to sticcan gebringan. Drihten leof, deme mine sawla and ðu
genere minne lichome, for ic ne recce þise leasere þrowunge. Gehelp þu me,
Drihten, and sænd me fultum,[22] þæt ic wið minum feondum fihtan muge,
þæt ic mid minum eagne twam þe geseon mote on þine rice.' Ða þa leasan
gewiten hi swiðe gepinedon and se gerefa hire to cwæð: 'Gecer, earme
fæmne, to me and to minum gode, and gif þu nelt, þu scealt to wundre
gewurðan.' Seo eadiga Margareta him andswerode: 'Gif ic minne lichaman
to þe geeadmede, þonne scealt þu inne þæt wallende pic into hellewite, þær
þu scealt wunian æfre.[23] Þonne miht þu habban minne lichaman þe to
gæmene, and God hæfð mine sawle fram þe generod.'

11   Ða wearð se gerefa swiðe yrre and het hi innan þan carcerne belucen.
And hi ineode into þan carcerne and mid Cristes rodetacne hi hi gebletsode;
and hi seofon tide þæs dæges[24] þærinne gesæt and hi to Gode gebæd and
þus cwæð: 'Drihten leof, þe ic þancige þeoses domes þe þu[k] me insændest,
for þu eart ælces mannes fultum, þe on þe gelefað, and þu eart fæder ealra
þære þe fæderlease syndon. And ne geswic þu me næfre, Drihten leof, ac
help þu me, þæt ic me bewerige wið minum feondum, and ne læt þu me
næfre mine sawle beswican, for þu eart ealre demena dema and dem nu[l][25]
betweon me and heom.'

12   Ða com hire fosterfæder gan to hire and þurh an eahþyrl he hire to
spræc and he hire brohte bread and wæter. Þæs wæteres hi gebreac and
nanes breades.[26] And he hire þrowunge fægre sette on Godes bocum. And

---

[j] hæfst] hæfh MS   [k] þe þu] þe þ[[e]]ʻuʼ MS   [l] and dem nu] and nu MS

10   By now the prefect had become angry and he said to her, 'You do your father's work, who is the devil himself.' And the girl replied, 'Indeed, miserable man, you continue with your deceit and my Lord is helping me.' Then the prefect said, 'Where is the God who can deliver you from my hands?' Blessed Margaret said to him, 'Be silent, you miserable man, you have nothing to do with me but you are completely vile and you will have to go into the ninth hell of malice and you will have to undergo there the evil afflictions which you are perpetrating here and have perpetrated.' Then the prefect commanded that she be taken and hung up by the hair and he commanded sharp pointed sticks to be made and ordered that they be driven between flesh and bone. And blessed Margaret raised up her hands and prayed eagerly to the Lord and said as follows: 'Beloved Lord, help me, because there are so many dogs around me and they want to reduce my body to pieces. Beloved Lord, judge my soul and protect my body, because I do not care about this false suffering. Help me, Lord, and send me aid so that I can fight against my enemies and so that I may see you with my two eyes in your kingdom.' Then the false advisers tormented her terribly and the prefect said to her, 'Submit to me, wretched girl, and to my god, and, if you will not, you must become a spectacle.' Blessed Margaret answered him, 'If I submit my body to you, then you will have to go in boiling pitch into the torment of hell, where you will have to remain forever. Then you will have been able to have my body as your plaything but God will have rescued my soul from you.'

11   Then the prefect was very angry and commanded that she be locked in the prison. And she went into the prison and blessed herself with the sign of Christ's cross; and she remained in there for seven hours of the day and she prayed to God and spoke as follows, 'Beloved Lord, I thank you for this ordeal into which you have sent me, because you are the help of every person who believes in you and you are the father of all who are fatherless. And do not ever desert me, beloved Lord, but help me so that I may defend myself against my enemies and never allow me to betray my soul, because you are the judge of judges: judge now between me and them.'

12   Then her fosterfather came to her and he spoke to her through a window and he brought her bread and water. She partook of the water and not of the bread. And he wrote down her suffering elegantly in God's

hit þa færunge gewearð sona æfter þan, þæt þær inneode an grislic deofol.[27] His nama wæs Ruffus and he wæs swiðe mycel on dracan heowe and eall he wæs nædderfah. And of his toþan leome ofstod, ealswa of hwiten swurde, and of his eagan swilces fyres lyg, and of his nasþyrlum smec and fyr ormæte mycel, and his tunge þreowe his sweore belygde.[28] Sancta Margareta hi to eorðan gestrehte and hire rihtwise gebedu to Gode gesænte and þus cwæð: 'Drihten, God Ælmihtig, georne ic þe bæd, þæt ic hine geseage, and nu ic þe eft gebidde, þæt ic hine ofercumen mote.' And hi þa upparas and hire earmes eastweard aðeonode and þus cwæð: 'Drihten God Ælmihtig, þu þe gesceope heofona and eorþa and eal mancyn and heora lif, þe on heom syndon, and þa þu on rode wære gehangen and þu to helle astige and þu þine halgan utgedydost and þone mycele deofol Sathan fæste gebunde, gehelp þu me, leofe Drihten, þæt ic þisne deofol fæste mote gebinden.'

13 And se deofol him þa abalhc and þa fæmne forswelgan wolde.[29] And seo eadiga fæmne sona mid hire swiðre hand wið þonu sceocca wel gebletsode and on hire forhæfde rodetacna mærcode and swa wið þone draca wel generode. And seo eadiga fæmne hal and gesund fram him gewænte. And eall sticmælum toðwan se draca ut of þan carcerne, and hi nan yfel on hire ne gefelde. Ac hi sona to eorðan gestrehte and hi geornlice to Gode gebæd and þus cwæð: 'Drihten leof, lof sy þe selfum and wuldor ealra þære goda þe þu me dest and gedon hæfst, and get is min hopa, þæt þu don wille aa in ealra worulda woruld.'

14 And þa hi hire gebedu gefyld hæfde, þa beseah hio hio on þære wynstre healfe þæs carcernes and hi oþerne deofol sittan geseah, sweart and unfæger, swa him gecynde[m] wæs, and he þa uparas and to hire weard eode. Þa seo fæmne on him beseah, þa cwæð hi to þan deofle: 'Ic wat hwæt þu þæncst, ac geswic þu þæs geþohtes, forþon ic wat eall þin yfel geþanc.'[30] And se deofol hire andswerode and cwæð: 'Ic minne broþor Rufonem to þe gesænde on dracan gelice, þæt he sceolde þe fordon, and nu hæfst þu hine mid Cristes rodentacn ofslagen, and ic wat, þæt þu me mid þinum gebedum ofslean wilt.' Seo eadiga Margareta upparas and þone deofol be þan fexe gefeng and hine niþer to eorðan gewearp, and hi hire[n][31] swiðre fot uppon his swire gesette and him to cwæð: 'Geswic þu earming, ne miht þu

---

[m] gecynde] gecynd'e' MS   [n] hire] hirne MS

books. And immediately after that it suddenly happened that a horrible devil entered. His name was Rufus and he was very large, with the appearance of a dragon, and he was all spotted like a snake. And a glare emanated from his teeth, as if from a bright sword, and it was as if a flame of fire came from his eyes and smoke and an immense great fire from his nostrils, and his three tongues lay around his neck. Margaret prostrated herself on the ground and uttered her righteous prayers to God and spoke thus: 'Lord God Almighty, I prayed to you fervently that I might see him and now I pray to you again, that I may overcome him.' And she rose up and stretched out her hands eastwards and spoke as follows: 'Lord God Almighty, you who created the heavens and earth and all mankind and the life which is in them and then you were hanged on the cross and you descended to hell and you rescued your saints and bound fast the great devil Satan, help me, beloved Lord, that I may bind fast this devil.'

13   Then the devil was angry and wanted to devour the girl. And the blessed maiden immediately blessed herself against the demon with her right hand and made the sign of the cross on her forehead and so protected herself thoroughly against the dragon. And the blessed maiden turned away from him, safe and uninjured. And, having burst all in pieces, the dragon vanished from the prison and she felt no hurt. But she immediately prostrated herself on the ground and eagerly prayed to God and spoke as follows: 'Beloved Lord, praise and glory be to you for all the good things which you do and have done for me and it is still my hope that you will continue to do them for ever and ever.'

14   And when she had completed her prayers, she looked into the left-hand side of the prison and saw another devil sitting there, black and ugly, as was his nature, and he got up and came towards her. When the maiden saw him, she said to the devil, 'I know what you are intending, but banish that idea because I know all your evil purpose.' And the devil answered her and said: 'I sent my brother Rufus to you in the likeness of a dragon in order that he should destroy you and now you have slain him with the sign of Christ's cross and I know that you wish to slay me with your prayers.' The blessed Margaret rose up and seized the devil by the hair and hurled him to the ground and she put her right foot on his neck and said to him, 'Stop, you wretch, you cannot at all seduce my virginity because I have my Lord

to nahte minne mægþhad me to beswicenne, for ic hæbbe minne Drihten me to fultume, and ic eam his þeowa and he is min hlaford and ic eom him beweddod, þe gehalgod is aa in ealra worulda woruld.'

15   Đa hi þis gecwedon hæfde, þa þærinne com Drihtnes engel and þær wearð inne swa mycel leoht, swa hit beoð on middæg, and he hæfde Cristes rodentacen on hande. Đa wearð Sancta Margareta swiðe bliðe and hio þancode Gode eall, þæt hi ær and sioððan þurh Gode ofte and gelome gesegon hæfde. And hi þa seo fæmne wið þone deofol wordum dælde and þus cwæð: 'Sege me earmingc, hwanan eart þu oððe hwanon come þu?' Se deofol hire to cwæð: 'Ic þe gebidde, forþon þe þu eart gehalgod fæmne, þæt þu þinne fot of minum sweorum alihte, and ic þe secgan wille eall, þæt ic gedon hæbbe.' And hio þa seo eadiga Margareta hire fot upahof and he hire sæde eall þæt he wiste and cwæð: 'Siððan Sathan gebunden wearð, siððan ic mid mannum æfre gewunode and manega Godes þeowas ic gehwearf fram Gode and næfre ne mihte me nan man ofercuman buton þu ane. Minne broþor þu ofsloge and þu mines eall geweald ahst, forþan ic geseo þæt God is mid þe. And get ic þe mare secge of minum dædum ealle syndrige. For ic nam ealle wæstmes fram mancynne þe on Gode gelefdon: sume ic spræce benam and sume heora hlyste;[32] sumen heora fet and sume heora handa, and heo þurh þæt creopeles wurðon; sumum ic eagen benam and sumum his gewittes; sume ic slæpende beswac and sume eac wacigende; sume mid winde and sume mid wætere; sume mid mæte°[33] and sume mid drænce, ofte þonne hio ungebletsodon wæren; sume mid slehte and sume on some; sume on morðdædum; and sume mid oðres mannes wife gehæmdon; sume mid feowerfoted nytene for minum willen gefremedon;[34] and sume heora eldran mid wordon gegræmedon. Eal þis ic me ane wat and þæt me nu hearde hreowð. Þin fæder and þin modor mine wæron and þu ane fram fæder and fram modor and fram eallum þine cynne to Gode þu gehwurfe.'

16   And seo eadiga fæmna him to cwæð: 'Hwanan wearð eow,[35] þæt ge mihton ahan Godes þeowes to beswicenne?' And þa se deofol hire to cwæð: 'Sege me, hwanen is þin lif, Margareta, and hwanan beoð þine liman, and hwu and on hwilce wise is Crist mid þe, and ic þe secge eall þæt ic wat.' And þa seo fæmne to þan deofle cwæð: 'Nelle ic hit þe secgan, forþon þe þu ne

° mæte] miste MS

to help me and I am his servant and he is my Lord and I am betrothed to him, who is sanctified for ever and ever.'

15 When she had said this, the Lord's angel entered and there was a great light within just as there is at mid-day, and he had Christ's crucifix in his hand. Then St Margaret was very happy and she thanked God for everything which she had seen and continued to see, again and again, through God. And then the girl uttered words to the devil and spoke thus: 'Tell me, wretch, where are you from and where have you come from?' The devil said to her, 'I entreat you, because you are a sanctified maiden, to take your foot from my neck and I will tell you everything that I have done.' And blessed Margaret raised up her foot and he told her everything that he knew and said, 'Ever since Satan was bound I have dwelt among people and I have turned many of God's servants away from God, and no-one was ever able to overcome me except you alone. You slew my brother and you have total control over me, because I see that God is with you. And I will tell you yet more about my deeds, one by one. For I deprived mankind, those who believed in God, of all prosperity: I deprived some of speech and some of their hearing; some of their feet and some of their hands, and because of that they became cripples; I deprived one of his eyes and one of his senses; I led some astray while they were sleeping and some also while they were awake; some by means of wind and some by means of water; some by means of food and some by drink, often when they were not blessed; some with slaughter and some in reconciliation; some in murders; and some when they had sexual intercourse with another man's wife; some on my account had relations with fourfooted beasts; and some enraged their parents by their words. I alone know all this and this grieves me very much now. Your father and your mother were mine and you alone, of your father and your mother and all your family, turned to God.' (or: you alone turned from your father and your mother . . . to God)

16 And the blessed maiden said to him, 'Where do you come from, that you are able to have control over God's servants in order to deceive them?' And then the devil said to her, 'Tell me where your life comes from, Margaret, and where your limbs come from and how and in what way Christ is with you, and I will tell you everything that I know.' And the

165

eart þæs wurþe, þæt ic wið þe wordum dæle, for God is swiðe god and him
sy geþancod, for ic eam his nu and æfre ma beon wille.' Se deofol hire to
cwæð: 'Sathana urne cyning, hine gewræc Drihten of paradises myrhþe and
him þa twa land agæf: an is Gamne and oðer is Mambre,[36] and þider he
gebrincð ealle þa þe he begeton mæig of mancynne. Nu ic soðlice þe to
sprece and for þi ne mæig ic na læng beon, forþon ic geseo þæt God is mid
þe. Ac ic þe bidde, eadige fæmne, þæt ic wið þe an word dælan mote, and ic
þe hælsige þurh þinne God and þurh his Sunu and his þone Halgan Gast, þe
þu on belefst, þæt þu me na mare yfel ne do and ic þe behate, and þæt þe
gelæste, þæt ic næfre ma nænne mon on þisum life ne beswice and þæt ic
þin bebod fæste[P] gehealdan wille.' And seo eadiga fæmne him andswarode:
'Gewit þe heonan on weig and sea eorðe þe forswelge and þu þær wunige to
Domesdæge!'[37]

17   And þa þæs oðres dæges se gerefa het þæt me[38] him þæt mæden
toforen brohte. And þa seo fæmne ut of þan carcerne gelæd wæs, hio hy
sona seneda, þa hio ut eode, and me þær forworhte men of Antiochia þære
burh gesamnoden, þæt hi þa fæmne geseon woldan. And þa se gerefa to
þære fæmne cwæð: 'Wilt þu me get geheran and to minum gode þe
gebiddan?' And hi þa andswera ageaf: 'Ne þe, ne þinum godum ic næfre ne
lufige, ac þe wel gerisde, þæt þu minnen Gode wel geherdest and lufodest,
þane þe lufað ælc þære manna þe hine mid inwearde heortan lufiað.' Ða het
se gerefa hio genimon and bead heom hire claðes ofniman and hi upahon bi
þan fotum, and he het wallende stanes on hire fægre lichaman geworpan.
And heo þa leasan gewitan eac swa dydon. And þa cwæð se gerefa to þære
fæmne: 'And nylt þu me get lufian, ne to minum gode þe gebugan, ne þe to
him gebiddan?' And seo eadiga fæmne nolde him andswarigen nan word.[39]

18   Ða wærð se gerefa swiðe eorre and het mycel fyr[40] onælan and ænne
cytel þærofer gesettan and bæd þære fæmne fet and handan tosomne gebindon
and innen þone weallende cetel gesetton. And seo eadiga Margareta heo
georne to Gode gebæd and þus cwæð: 'Ic þe wille biddan, leofa Drihten
Cyning, þæt þæt wæter gewurðe me to fulluhtes bæðe and to clænsunge
ealra minum synnum.' And þa þær com fleogan Drihtnes ængel and he þa
gehalgode þæt wallende wæter to fonte and þa halga fæmne genam be þære
swiðre hand and of þan wætere þa fæmne gesette and hire on þan wætere na

P fæste] fæste[[n]] MS

166

maiden said to the devil, 'I will not tell you, because you are not worthy that I should utter words to you, because God is very good and thanks be to him that I am now his and will be his for evermore.' The devil said to her, 'The Lord expelled Satan our king from the joy of paradise and gave him two lands: one is Jamnes and the other is Mambres, and he brings there all the people whom he can seize. Now I am speaking truly to you and therefore I cannot remain longer, because I see that God is with you. But I entreat you, blessed maiden, that I may utter one word to you and I implore you through your God and through his Son and his Holy Spirit, in whom you believe, that you do no more harm to me, and I promise you, and I will fulfil it [the promise] for you, that I will never again deceive a man in this life and that I will keep your command strictly.' And the blessed maiden answered him, 'Depart from here and may the earth swallow you and may you remain there until Doomsday!'

17   Then the next day the prefect ordered that the maiden be brought before him. And when the girl was led out of the prison she immediately blessed herself as she went out, and sinful men from the city of Antioch gathered there in order that they would see the girl. And then the prefect spoke to the girl: 'Will you listen to me even now and pray to my god?' And she replied, 'I will never love either you or your gods; but it would be fitting for you to praise and love my God who loves each person who loves him with a sincere heart.' Then the prefect ordered that she be taken and commanded them to take off her clothes and to hang her up by the feet and he ordered red-hot stones to be thrown at her beautiful body. And the false advisers did that too. And then the prefect said to the girl, 'Will you still not love me or submit to my god or pray to him?' And the blessed maiden would not answer him one word.

18   Then the prefect was very angry and ordered that a large fire be lit and a cauldron be set above it and that the girl's feet and hands be tied together and that she be put inside the boiling cauldron. And the blessed Margaret prayed eagerly to God and spoke thus: 'I wish to entreat you, beloved Lord and King, that this water be for me the bath of baptism and the purification of all my sins.' And the Lord's angel came flying there and consecrated the boiling water as a font, and he took the blessed maiden by her right hand and he led the girl from the water and she was not harmed in

lað ne gewearð. Ða þæt geherdon and geseagon þe hire ymbstodan, wundor heom þuhte. Hio geherdon stefne of heofone clypion to þære fæmne þus: 'Ic eom þin godfæder and þu min goddohtor and ic eallum gearige, þe on þe gelefað.[41] Eadig eart þu, halig fæmne Sancta Margareta, forþon þe þu þine hande and þinne hige clæne gehylde and for minre lufu mycel geþrowodest.' And embe lytle fece, næs hit lang to þan, eac hit sona gewearð þurh þære fæmne þrowunge, þæt þær to Gode gebugan fif þusend manna.

19   Þa wearð se gerefa swiðe eorra and he het ealle ofslean, þa þe on Gode gelefdon. And se gerefa[q] cwæð to his þeowum Malcum (se ilca dernunga Gode geþenode):[42] 'Gedrah þu þin swurd', cwæð se gerefa, 'and þa fæmne þu ofsleah.' And þa Godes wiðerwinnan þa fæmnan genamon, ut of þære byrig ungerædelice hi togoden, and þa hi þær becomon þær me[43] hio slean scolde and þa leasan witan to Malcum spræcan and cwæðon: 'Drah hraþa þin swurd and þa fæmna þu ofsleah.' And hire þa to leat Malcus swa dreohlice and hire georne bæd and þus cwæð: 'Gemune þu me, earminge, on þinum gebedum.' And seo eadige fæmne him to cwæð: 'Ic wille þe fore biddan.' And hio hio to eorþan gestrehte and þus cwæð: 'Drihten God Ælmihtig, þu þe heofones gescope and eorþe and eall þæt men bilibbað, geher þu mine bene, þæt ælc þære manna synne sy forgiofene þe mine þrowunge rædeð,[44] and ælcum þære mannu, þe hi for Godes lufu geheran willæð. And get ic þe, leofa Drihten, biddan wille, þæt þu ælc þæra manna,[45] þe on minum naman cirice arære, and þan þe me mid heora lihte gesecan willað,[46] and mid oðrum ælmessan, and þan þe mine þrowunge gewritað, oððe mid heora figa gebicgað,[47] þæt innan heora husum nan unhal cild sy geboren, ne crypol, ne dumb, ne deaf, ne blind, ne ungewittes, ac forgif þu, leofa Drihten, ealle heora synna for þinra þære mycele ara and for þinum godcundum wuldre and for þinre þære mycelen mildheortnesse.'

20   And hio hi eft niðer gestrehte and heore hleor wið þæra eorþan gelegde and þa ealle þe hire ymbstodan feollan heom on cneowgebedum.[r] And þa ure Drihten him self com[48] of heofonum to eorþan astigan and hire sona to cwæð: 'Ic þe geofa and behate, swa hwæt swa þu[s49] bidst and gebeden hæfst. Eal hit is þe getyðed.' And eft cwæð ure Drihten: 'Ælc þæra þe on þinre lufa me to gebiddað[50] and ælmessan bringað oððe mid leohte secað[51] oððe þine þrowunge rædað oððe write oððe mid his fige gebycge[52] oððe inne

---

[q] gerefa] ge're'fa MS   [r] cneowgebedum] cweowgebedum MS   [s] þu] þe MS

the water. When those who were standing near her heard and saw this, it seemed a miracle to them. They heard a voice from heaven speaking thus to the maiden: 'I am your godfather and you are my goddaughter and I will have mercy on all who believe in you. Blessed are you, holy maiden St Margaret, because you have kept your hands and your spirit pure and you have suffered much for love of me.' And after a little while – it was not long – it happened also within a short time that five thousand people converted to God because of the virgin's suffering.

19   Then the prefect was very angry and he ordered all those who believed in God to be slain. And the prefect said to his servant Malchus (the same man secretly served God): 'Draw your sword', said the prefect, 'and kill the girl.' And the enemies of God seized the girl [and] dragged her roughly out of the city, and then they arrived at where she was to be slain, and the false advisers spoke to Malchus and said, 'Draw your sword quickly and kill the girl.' And Malchus humbly bowed down to her and eagerly entreated her and spoke thus: 'Remember me, a wretched man, in your prayers.' And the blessed maiden said to him, 'I will pray for you.' And she prostrated herself on the ground and spoke thus: 'Lord God Almighty, you who created heaven and earth and everything by which men live, hear my prayer that all of the sins of those people who read my passion be forgiven and of those people who wish to listen to it for love of God. And furthermore, beloved Lord, I wish to entreat you that in the houses of each of those people who build a church in my name and of those who wish to come to me with candles and with other alms and of those who write down my passion or buy it with their money no unhealthy child be born and no cripple or dumb or deaf or blind or mad child but, beloved Lord, forgive all their sins for your great mercy and for your divine glory and for your great loving-kindness.'

20   And she prostrated herself again and laid her face on the ground and all those who stood about her fell on their knees in prayer. And then our Lord himself descended from the heavens to earth and immediately said to her, 'I grant you and promise you whatever you ask for and have asked for. It is all granted to you.' And again our Lord said, 'No harm will ever befall any of those who for love of you prays to me and brings alms or comes with a light or reads your passion or writes it or buys it with his money or

his huse hæbbe, ne sceal nan yfel næfre on him becuman. And ælc þære þe his synne forgifennesse habban wille on þinre lufan, eall hit sio forgifen. Eadig eart þu, Margareta, and ealle þa þurh þe on me gelefdon and gelefan willað.'

21 And þa seo eadiga Margareta uparas of hire gebedum, feagre gefrefred, and cwæð to eallum þan þe hire ymbstodan: 'Geherað me, mine gebroðra and swustra, ealda and geunga, ealle gemænelice! Ic eow bidde þæt ge gelefan on Drihten God Ælmihtigne and on his Sunu and on his Halgan Gaste and ic eow bidde þæt ge me on eowrum bedum gemunnen, forþan ic eam swiðe synfull.'

22 Þa þa hi hire gebedu gefylled hæfde, þa cleopode hi swiðe hlude þone þe hi slean sceolde and cwæð: 'Malche,ᵗ nim nu þin swurd and do þæt þe gehaten is, for nu is min time gecuman.'⁵³ Malcus hire to cwæð: 'Nylle ic þe ofslean, forþon ic geseo þæt Crist is mid þe, and ic geherde hu he spræc to þe and cwæð þæt þu his fæmne wære.' And seo fæmne him to cwæð: 'Gif þu nylt me ofslean, nafa þu nan hlot mid me on heofene rice.' And he þa Malcus to hire fotum gefyll and þus cwæð: 'Ic þe bidde, leofa eadige fæmne, þæt þu gebidde for me and forgif þu me þas wite, for min Drihten hit wat, þæt ic hit unwillende do, þæt ic æfre þas dæda gefremme.' And þa seo fæmne hi to Gode gebæd and þus cwæð: 'Drihten leof, forgif þu him ealle þa synne þe he gefremeð hæfð.'⁵⁴ And he þa Malcus his swurd adroh and þæra eadigra fæmne þæt heafod ofasloh. And seo eadiga fæmne Margareta hire sawle Gode agef and Malcus on hire swiðran uppan his swurda feol, and his sawle Godes ængles underfeongan and þurh þæra eadigra fæmne bene Gode betæhton.ᵘ

23 Ða hit geherdon ealle þa untruman þe wæron þær on lande, ealle hi hire lic gesohton and heora hæle þear gefetton: sume hi wæron blinde and deafa and sume crypeles and sume dumbe and sume ungewitfulle. Ealle hi heora hæle æt þære halgan fæmnan onfenge, and mycel mancyn, ealle þa þe unhale wære,ᵛ þære fæmnen lic gesohton; ealle hi hale and gesunde on heora wege ham gewænton. And ures Drihtnes ænglæs þider comon and þa sawla underfengon and heo on heofone rice gebrohton. And nu hi is mid Gode and mid eallum his halgum, and þær hi wunað nu and æfre wunian sceal in ealra worulda woruld a butan ænde. AMEN.

ᵗ Malche] Ma'l'che MS   ᵘ betæhton] 7 betæhton MS   ᵛ wære] wære '7' MS: *ampersand inserted above line*

has it in his house. And each of those who desires forgiveness for his sins out of love for you will be entirely forgiven. Blessed are you, Margaret, and all who have believed and will believe in me through you.'

21 And then the blessed Margaret rose up from her prayers well consoled and said to all those who stood around her, 'Hear me, my brothers and sisters, old and young, all together: I entreat you to believe in the Lord God Almighty and in his Son and in his Holy Spirit and I entreat you that you remember me in your prayers, because I am very sinful.'

22 When she had completed her prayers, then she called out very loudly to him who had to kill her and said, 'Malchus, take your sword and do what you have been commanded to, because now my time has come.' Malchus said to her, 'I do not wish to kill you, because I see that Christ is with you and I heard how he spoke to you and he said that you are his maiden.' And the maiden said to him, 'If you will not kill me, you will have no part with me in the kingdom of heaven.' And then Malchus fell to her feet and said thus: 'I entreat you, beloved blessed maiden, that you pray for me and forgive me for these torments, for my Lord knows that I am unwilling ever to do these deeds.' And the maiden prayed to God and said thus: 'Beloved Lord, forgive him for all the sins that he has committed.' And then Malchus drew his sword and struck off the head of the blessed maiden. And the blessed maiden Margaret delivered up her soul to God and on her right side Malchus fell upon his sword, and God's angel received his soul and gave it up to God because of the prayer of the blessed maiden.

23 When all the infirm people who were in the country heard this, they all sought out her corpse and obtained their health there: some were blind and deaf and some cripples and some dumb and some mad. They all received their health from the holy maiden and many people, all those who were sick, sought out the maiden's corpse; and they all went on their way home, well and healthy. And our Lord's angels came there and received the soul and brought it to the kingdom of heaven. And now she is with God and with all his saints and she dwells there now and will dwell world without end for ever and ever. Amen.

Commentary on CCCC

[1] The opening section bases itself fairly closely on an original in the *BHL* no. 5303 tradition, but one which, like P, would have had the mention of Christ's passion – *prowunge* – in its opening words. It shows slight simplification of the Latin. The only distinctive details are the references to *þæra micclan leofan lufan* displayed by Christ's martyrs, a phrase which introduces what will be a major theme in this version of the legend, and to the *rican* 'powerful ones' of those days (other aspects of *þæra micclan leofan* and *rican* are discussed below in nn. 2 and 3).

[2] The construction represented in *his þæra micclan leofan lufan*, in which the possessive is followed by the demonstrative and the weak form of an adjective, is repeated later in the text: *on þinre þære sweteste lufa* (ch. 4). Vleeskruyer suggests that the use of a possessive pronoun along with a demonstrative is archaic (*The Life of St Chad*, p. 140) and originated in literary Mercian (p. 48), but Mitchell (*OES* §§104–12) points out that our construction is widely found in Old English, including in Ælfric, and considers that it would seem to be a normal Old English construction (§112). The inclusion of the demonstrative is not obligatory in such phrases in CCCC, as is seen by the occurrence of the phrase *min soþe lufu* (ch. 4), in the same sentence as the second example quoted above. The construction is perhaps a reflection of the formality of the prose style cultivated by the Old English translator.

[3] The manuscript reading *ricem* is perhaps an error for *rican* 'powerful ones'. Assmann emends to the otherwise unattested *ricene*. This detail appears to be the translator's addition, as there is no equivalent word in the analogues.

[4] The *BHL* no. 5303 chapter of approximately 130 words is virtually ignored in the Old English: only the name *Theothimus* and the description of him as *swiðe gelæred man* have equivalents in the Latin. The *BHL* no. 5303 chapter is replaced by twenty-one words giving the location of the story as a 'land' called Antioch (Antioch is first mentioned in the Latin in ch. 3) and introducing, in the third person, Theotimus.

5 There are different versions of the story of Margaret's infancy and of why she is brought up by a fostermother. The Old English is distinctive in implying that Margaret is rejected because she is a girl and in making Theotimus her fosterfather (on Theotimus, see below, n. 6). In this it explains far more than most other versions, in which the details of Margaret's infancy are often unclear, particularly on the question of why she is rejected by her father. CCCC is also unlike other analogues in having Margaret's father a king rather than chief priest.

6 The role of Theotimus fluctuates in the Margaret tradition and is significantly different in this version from that in other versions. In the Mombritius and pre-Mombritius tradition, Theotimus is generally a devout, recently baptized and learned Christian, who wished to know how St Margaret 'pugnauit . . . contra demonem et uicit hunc mundum' (P, ch. 2). He has therefore read everything written about her by her contemporaries, 'et scripsi in libris cartaneis omnia quae passa sit beatissima Margareta' (P, *ibid.*). With apparent inconsistency, however, considering his professed lack of knowledge concerning the saint, Theotimus is also presented as an eyewitness to all that happens to her.

In CCCC, perhaps in response to this apparent inconsistency, the role of Theotimus appears changed and clarified. Here he is Margaret's fosterfather, who finds her when she is cast out by her natural father, entrusts her to a fostermother, and educates her when she is old enough. When Margaret is in prison, he speaks to her through the window, and brings her bread and water, and he afterwards writes down her passion. Although the Old English says that Theotimus 'hire þrowunge fægre sette on Godes bocum' (ch. 12), he is not, as is normal in the Mombritius texts, the first-person narrator of Margaret's passion. There is no mention of him at the end of the story, where he is usually described as taking relics of Margaret and placing them in a shrine which he himself has made.

7 Much of this long Old English section has no equivalent in other versions. Margaret preaches the faith to the people; then there is an extended emotive account of the persecution of the Christians, leading up to a powerful prayer by Margaret. None of this has a known source. As we noted in the Introduction, however (above p. 64), the prayer is unlikely to have been the Old English writer's creation: it follows a translation strategy seen again in ch. 5. The prayer in ch. 4 is notable for its striking development of the imagery of love: *on þinre þære sweteste lufa* and *min soþe lufu.*

8 On the self-conscious rhetorical patterning apparent in this sentence and throughout ch. 4 of the OE, see above, p. 68, n. 155.

9 In presenting the picture of Margaret and the other girls looking after her fostermother's sheep (this is the first mention of the fostermother in CCCC)

the Old English has the unusual detail that they passed the time spinning.

[10] *here*. Instead of *herian*.

[11] This verb and the accompanying *ahwerfan* and *gefyllan* are subjunctive plurals. Their late Old English endings serve to highlight the parallelism between these verbs and their repeated forms (infinitives) later in the sentence.

[12] It is at this point that the important theme of deception and falseness is first introduced. The speech in which it occurs recasts Margaret's prayer as it appears in *BHL* no. 5303 (cf. P, ch. 5) into a new rhetorical structure which succeeds in re-creating in quite different terms something of the incantatory style of the Latin. Thematic preoccupations of the speech are emphasized in particular by the repetition (as referred to above, n. 11) of the verbs *beswican, ahwerfan/ gehwerfan* and *gefylan/afylan*.

[13] This speech of Margaret corresponds to two separate utterances in most copies of the Latin, divided by a speech by Olibrius which is absent in the Old English (see M, p. 191, line 12). The intervention by Olibrius does not appear in P (see ch. 6).

[14] The emotively descriptive phrase *þær nan liht inne cumen ne mihte* is not paralleled in the analogues.

[15] This word is a reduced form of the indefinite pronoun *man*, as widely found in Middle English. See above, p. 106, as well as below, n. 38.

[16] Olibrius's consultation with his advisers has no equivalent in the Mombritius and pre-Mombritius tradition, though curiously there is an analogous passage in the Rebdorf version (see above, pp. 63–4). The unexpected correspondence with the Rebdorf version is further underlined in Olibrius's immediately subsequent exclamation to Margaret, 'læt beon þin mycela mod, þe þu to me hæfst'. There is nothing like this in *BHL* nos. 5303–4, but at this point in the Rebdorf version Olibrius refers to Margaret's 'pertinacia et superbia mentis' (*ASS*, Iul. V, 36D).

[17] The manuscript reading *wrohtað*, a word which does not occur elsewhere, causes difficulties, and BT suggests that it is a mistake for *frohtað*, a form of *forhtian* 'to fear' (presumably due to confusion of *wyn* with *f*). This would indeed correspond to the Latin *formidat* (P, ch. 7), although the Old English passage as a whole is not very close to the Latin here. Assmann offers the meaning 'Schaden tun' for *wrohtað*, from *wroht* in the sense of 'cause of complaint, injury, hurt' (BT), but since this does not fit the context very well we have accepted the BT emendation.

[18] The speech of the bystanders is cast in much more direct and urgent terms than in the manneredly rhetorical Latin. A particularly seductive detail in their appeal to Margaret that she should give in is the socially inclusive phrase *mid us*, in the last sentence of the speech: 'Gelef on ure gode, þonne most þu mid us lif habban.'

[19] On the change of speaker in this speech, as compared to the Latin, see above, p. 62.

[20] The concept of nine hells also occurs in an Old English homily, *In uigilia ascensionis*, in the same manuscript as our text (CCCC 303, pp. 223–6). This homily enumerates nine different hells, each devoted to a different vice, and the ninth is reserved for those who bear malice in their hearts towards others: 'Ðonne is þær seo nigoðe atelic stow, seo is eall mid niðum and mid næddrum afylled; þær sceal ælc þære manne inne beon beseanct mid sawle and mid lichamen þe nið bereð wið his broðer oððe wið nyttan freond' (lines 72–5, ed. Bazire and Cross, *Eleven Old English Rogationtide Homilies*, p. 63). The concept of different hells or of different compartments of hell is relatively widespread, but the number varies and Bazire and Cross suggest that the number nine (reflected also in Dante's nine circles of hell) 'may have been derived ultimately from the nine meanderings of the river Styx in Virgil's description' (*ibid.*, p. 58).

BHL no. 5303 has no mention of hell at the point corresponding to the present reference and the Old English writer may therefore have been composing relatively freely here. It is possible that the translator's knowledge of the nine hells motif may have been derived from the very homily which is also preserved in this same manuscript, as it does not appear to occur elsewhere in Anglo-Saxon texts. The reference in the Margaret text preserves not only the number of hells, but also the detail that the punishment will be fitted to the crime committed in this world: 'þu scealt faran into þære nigenda niþhelle and þu scealt þær onfon þa yfelan geweorc, þe þu her gefremest and gefremed hæst.'

On the idea of nine pains of hell, see E. J. Becker, *A Contribution to the Comparative Study of the Medieval Visions of Heaven and Hell, with Special Reference to the Middle English Versions* (Baltimore, MD, 1889): Becker states that the pains of hell are 'usually eleven, sometimes nine' (p. 30) and refers (*ibid.*, n. 5) to the *Cursor Mundi*, which describes the nine pains in detail (*Cursor Mundi*, ed. R. Morris, EETS os 66 (London, 1877) IV, 1327–31). Nine torments of hell are catalogued by the twelfth-century writer Honorius Augustodunensis in his *Elucidarium* (III. 13; PL 172, 1159–60): fire, cold, worms, stench, scourging, darkness, confusion, sight of devils and dragons, fetters of fire. Such divisions of torments are based, however, on types of suffering rather than, as in the CCCC homily, on categories of sin. The Latin *Visio Tnugdali* (text dated 1149), in a list based on categories of sin (murder, treachery, pride, etc.), speaks of the eight torments of superior hell combined with inferior hell, making nine in all (*The Vision of Tnugdal*, trans. J.-M. Picard, with an introduction by Y. de Pontfarcy (Dublin, 1989), p. 49).

[21] The phrase *gefremest and gefremed hæst* is an instance of the rhetorical figure of *adnominatio*, involving repetition of the same stem with different inflexions. It

is found several times in CCCC: note also *dest and gedon hæfst* (ch. 13), *bidst and gebeden hæfst* (ch. 20), *gelefst and forð wilt get gelefan* (ch. 6), *gelefdon and gelefan willað* (ch. 20) and, in a nominal group, *þurh hire fægernesse and hire fægre wlite* (ch. 5).

[22] Margaret asks the Lord to send help to her. CCCC nowhere has the image of the miraculous heavenly dove which brings comfort to Margaret in other versions: it consistently substitutes a different image where *BHL* no. 5303 has *columba* (see also chs. 15, 18 and 20).

[23] There is a misunderstanding here. In the Latin Margaret tells Olibrius that, if she saves her body from tortures, her soul, like his soul, will go to hell (P, ch. 10); in the Old English this has, oddly, become a concern for Olibrius's soul: the original sense has become lost in the course of transmission.

[24] On the apparent misunderstanding in *seofon tide þæs dæge*, see above, p. 62.

[25] We supply the verb *dem*. *BHL* no. 5303 reads here, 'tu iudica inter me et illum' (P, ch. 11), indicating that the imperative may be missing in the Old English, as the syntax of the Old English would also suggest. Our emendation inserts the 'regular' form *dem*, but note that the imperative sing. of this verb appears earlier as *deme* (ch. 10).

[26] Unlike *BHL* no. 5303, CCCC has Theotimus speak to Margaret at the beginning of this scene, as well as bringing her bread and water in prison. The Old English also contrasts with the Latin in saying that Margaret took the water but not the bread.

[27] The description of the dragon is slightly abbreviated as compared with that of *BHL* no. 5303 and there is no mention of the saint's fear. The major departure from the regular *BHL* no. 5303 account, however, is that, as in many other versions of the legend, it is specified here at the very beginning of the description that Margaret's assailant is a devil (the Old English even gives his name at this point): we learn that he is a devil even before being told that he comes in the shape of a dragon. In identifying the nature of the apparition at the beginning of the description the Old English avoids the sense of crisis of confidence on the part of the saint in the face of the unknown, which is present in the Latin at this point. The CCCC treatment lessens the dramatic and visual impact of the scene, and removes the element of uncertainty (both on the part of the saint and of the audience).

[28] This apparent mention of the dragon's three tongues is not paralleled in any of the analogues and may be due to a corruption in the transmission of the Old English text (as is also suggested by the irregular word order). *Preowe* is perhaps a metathesized and corrupted form of the preposition *þurh* 'over', corresponding to the Latin *super collum* (P, ch. 12).

The Latin versions have varying accounts of the tongue. Most copies of *BHL* no. 5303 have 'lingua eius anhelabat; super collum eius erat serpens' (M,

p. 192, line 34). CCCC may reflect a variant which, like P (ch. 12), omitted *erat serpens*. The variant printed by Gerould speaks of 'lingua eius niger' ('A New Text of the *Passio S. Margaritae*', p. 532), while the Turin version has 'lingua eius uelut sanguis' (Vr, 167r). The Middle English *Seinte Marherete* has a reading which is quite like the CCCC one, apart from the number of tongues: 'ant lahte ut his tunge, se long þet he swong hire abuten his swire' (ed. Mack, p. 20, lines 29–30).

29 In the Old English the dragon does not actually swallow Margaret, although he wishes to do so. In this respect, the OE contrasts with P, ch. 13, *degluttiuit*.

30 Margaret's speech which instigates the debate with the black demon has no equivalent in most variants of the Latin: the debate begins in *BHL* no. 5303 with the demon's speech (corresponding to the next speech in CCCC (cf. M, p. 193, line 12)). P is corrupt at this point, allocating the beginning of the demon's speech to Margaret (ch. 12). CCCC clearly follows a reading of this kind.

31 The manuscript reading *hirne* looks like an inflected form of the feminine possessive pronoun (ostensibly agreeing with *fot*, acc. sing. masc.), but such a form is quite unparalleled in Old English and *hirne* must be taken as a mistake for *hire*.

32 This part of the black demon's speech of confession is recast in the form of a *sum . . . sum* passage, containing particular details unique to CCCC. As in other rhetorically heightened passages in the *Legend*, the translator makes sustained use of parallelism, repetition and alliteration. On this passage see above, p. 67.

33 The manuscript reading *miste* seems very odd in the context and may have been influenced by the wind and water image of the previous clause. *Mæte and drænce*, on the other hand, already go together as a set phrase in Old English and this phrase fits the present context better than the peculiar pairing of mist and drink.

34 The context, immediately after 'sume mid oðres mannes wife gehæmdon', suggests a meaning like 'had sexual intercourse with' for *gefremedon*, but the word does not otherwise have this meaning and needs to be combined with something like *unrihthæmed*. The sin is one which is frequently legislated against in the penitentials, e.g. 'on oðre stowe hit cwið þe he sceolo reowe don, swa se ðe mid nytenum hæmð' (*Poenitentiale Theodori*, ed. F. J. Mone, 'Zur Geschichte und Kritik der angelsächsischen Gesetze', *Quellen und Forschungen zur Geschichte der teutschen Literatur und Sprach* 1 (1830), 501–28 (§197, p. 526)); 'yfelra geligera mid wifum and mid nytenum' (*ibid.*, §168, p. 523); '. . . yfela . . . in unrihthæmede mid neatenum' (*Confessionale Pseudo-Egberti*, ed. R. Spindler, *Das altenglische Bussbuch* (Leipzig, 1934), pp. 176–94 (line 123)). It is possible that a word is missing in the text and that it should read

'sume mid feowerfoted nytene unrihthæmed [*or* geliger] for minum willen gefremedon'.

[35] The word *eow* and the closely following *ge* are not startlingly early occurrences of the formal second person pronoun, which appears in English from the thirteenth century. Margaret has no desire to express respect for the demon. The use of the plural reflects the Latin *uobis* (P, ch. 16).

[36] This passage is based on a misunderstanding of the Latin source, where the mention of Jamnes and Mambres is an allusion to the apocryphal book in which, it is said, the lineage of the devils is recorded, while in the Old English they are the two lands given by God to Satan when the latter is expelled from paradise. Jamnes and Mambres are identified in apocryphal tradition as the two magicians who fought against Moses and Aaron in Exodus VIII and they are first attested in the Damascus Document of *c.* 100 B.C. The Book of Jamnes and Mambres, first mentioned by Origen in the third century A.D., was known in Anglo-Saxon England and an extract from it is contained in Cotton Tiberius B. v. It records how Mambres raised his dead brother Jamnes from hell by necromancy, and Jamnes, among other things, describes hell to him. This may be what lies behind the allusion in the Latin Margaret text, but the Old English translator has instead made the two magicians into countries. Price suggests that the source of the confusion could lie in Mamre, Abraham's dwelling-place, and that 'the mistake in CCCC 303 may have been a bold and yet quite sensible attempt to make sense of a corrupt or confusing version of the Latin legend' ('The Virgin and the Dragon', p. 356, n. 28). See further T. N. Hall, 'Jamnes and Mambres', in *Sources of Anglo-Saxon Literary Culture: A Trial Version*, ed. F. M. Biggs, T. D. Hill and P. E. Szarmach, Medieval and Renaissance Texts and Studies 74 (Binghamton, NY, 1990), 27–9.

On Jamnes and Mambres, Usener's Greek has the following: οἱ δὲ πρῶτοι ἀρχιδαίμονες λέγονται ἐν Αἰγύπτῳ καὶ Αἰθιοπίᾳ γεγονέναι, καθὼς εἰς τὴν Ἔξοδον Μωυσέως περὶ Ἰαννὴ καὶ Ἰαμβρὴ περιέχει (138r, lines 13–15): 'The first archdemons are said to have arisen in Egypt and Ethiopia, as it is held concerning Janne and Jambre in the Exodus of Moses.'

[37] In *BHL* no. 5303 the earth receives the demon, while in the Old English Margaret expresses a wish that it may do so. This transfer of the material from narrative to direct speech could be the result of a different Latin textual tradition or it could be a purposeful change in the Old English to heighten Margaret's authority.

[38] A feature of the transition from Old English to Middle English is the reduction of the indefinite pronoun *man* to *men* and then its further reduction to *me*. Both these forms appear in our text (for *men*, see above, n. 15), though the earliest occurrences of *men* and *me* in this sense cited by the *Oxford English Dictionary* are in the later twelfth-century *Lambeth Homilies*.

The indefinite pronoun *me* occurs again in the sentence immediately following the present instance. In this next occurrence it is used with a plural verb (*gesamnoden*) but elsewhere it has a singular (chs. 17 and 19), as the variant *men* also does (ch. 6). The verb *gesamnoden* has perhaps been attracted into the plural because of the confusing intervention of *men* 'men' in the clause: 'me þær forworhte men of Antiochia þære burh gesamnoden'. On *man* with a plural verb Mitchell comments, 'The few sentences in which *man* is immediately followed by a plural verb are to be regarded with suspicion as possible scribal errors' (*OES* §367).

39 Margaret's speech of defiance in the Latin at the end of this section (P, ch. 17) is replaced in the Old English by an eloquent silence.

40 CCCC agrees with Tiberius in having the water in which Margaret is tortured hot, a detail which is in no known Latin version (see above, pp. 47–8).

41 The opening sentence of the speech of the heavenly voice has no parallel in other versions of the legend.

42 The sequence of dialogue which the persecutor Olibrius and his followers engage in with the executioner Malchus is unparalleled in other versions of the legend (on this, see above, p. 65).

43 See above, n. 38.

44 The verb is present indicative plural, with *-eð* instead of *-að*. Note the switch in this passage from indicative plural (*rædeð, willæð*) to subjunctive singular (*arære*). The subjects of these verbs have identical antecedents, *ælc þære/þæra manna*. The subjunctive *arære* reflects the indefinite quality of the relative clause. After *arære*, however, the remaining verbs in the sequence revert to the indicative plural (*willað, geuritað, gebicgað*). A similar inconsistency of mood is noted below (n. 50). See also Commentary on Tib, n. 48.

45 The Old English translator appears to lose the thread of the structure of this sentence, going from *þæt þu ælc þæra manna* to *þæt innan heora husum*, without a verb to go with *ælc*. The length of the intervening passage has evidently caused this anacoluthon. Compare the change in direction in the second last sentence of ch. 12.

46 There is no precise equivalent in texts of *BHL* no. 5303 to the supplication on behalf of *þan þe me heora lihte gesecan willað*. The Old English is perhaps based on a corruption of the Latin 'quisquis lumen fecerit in basilica mea de suo labore' (M, p. 195, line 5; P deficient); compare the Middle English *Seinte Marherete* reading, 'Hwa-se . . . findeð in ham liht oðer lampe' (ed. Mack, p. 46, lines 31–3).

47 There is no precise equivalent in texts of *BHL* no. 5303 to Margaret's supplication on behalf of *þan þe mine þrowunge . . . mid heora figa gebicgað*. The Latin has 'qui tulerit in manu sua' (P, ch. 19).

48 Instead of the dove (see P, ch. 20), it is stated that in response to Margaret's

prayer 'Our Lord himself descended'. The excision in CCCC of references to the heavenly dove is noted above, n. 22.

[49] The manuscript reading *þe* is a simple scribal error.

[50] As in the passage discussed above, n. 44, the indefinite relative clauses (with antecedent *ælc þæra*) in this sequence vary between having plural indicative verbs (*gebiddað, bringað, secað, rædað*) and singular subjunctive verbs (*write, gebycge, hæbbe, wille*). The alternation is particularly evident in the pair *rædað oððe write*.

[51] This is a recapitulation of the distinctive detail of Margaret's prayer of intercession mentioned above in n. 46.

[52] This is a recapitulation of the distinctive detail of Margaret's prayer of intercession mentioned above in n. 47.

[53] The biblically inspired phrase (cf. Ezech. VII. 7; Matth. XXVI. 18; Mark XII. 33; John II. 4; etc.) *for nu is min time gecuman* is not paralleled elsewhere in the tradition of *BHL* no. 5303.

[54] On the different allocation of speeches between Margaret and Malchus in the Old English as compared to the Latin, see above, p. 63.

APPENDIX 1

The A-text of Cotton Tiberius A. iii

This semi-diplomatic edition of the A scribe's text presents, insofar as the state of the manuscript allows, what the A scribe wrote. See above, pp. 87–92 for a discussion of editorial principles and p. 110 for a list of editorial conventions.

1 Æfter[a] þære ðrowunge and þære æriste and þære wuldorfæstan upastignesse ures Drihtnes, Hælendes Cristes, to Godfæder Ealmihtigum, swiþe maniga martyres [[⟨wæron⟩]] þrowiende and þurh þa þrowunge to ece reste becoman mid þære halgan Teclan and Susannan; and swiþe manega eac þurh deofles lare beswican[[⟨n⟩]]e wæran þæt hi beeode dumbe and deafe deofolgeld, mannes handgeweorc, þe naþor ne heom ne him sylfum o[[n]] nanre freme beon ne mihton.

2 Ic þa, Þeo[[⟨þ⟩]]imus, þurh Godes gyfe hwæthwugo on bocum geleornode and geornfullice smeade and sohte ymb Cristes[a] geleafan and ne fand ic næfre on bocum þæt ænig man mihte to ece reste becuman, butan he on þa halgan Þrynnysse [[h]]riht gelifde, þæt is Fæder and Sunu and se Halga Gast, and þæt se Sunu onfeng mennisc hiw and geþrowade swa swa hit her bufan cwyþ. Blinde he onlihte, deafum [[⟨g⟩]]esealde hernysse and †dead[[um]] he awæhte to life, and ealle þa þe on hine trywlice gelæfþ he gehærþ. Ic þa, Đeotimus, wilnode georne to witanne hu se[b] eadega Margareta wiþ þone deofol gefæht and hine oferswiþde and ece wuldorbeh æt Gode onfengc. Geheraþ nu ealle and ongytaþ hu se eadega Margareta geþrowade for Godes naman and þurh þæt geswenc to ece reste becom mid þære halgan Teclan and Susannan.

1 [a] Æfter] *Æ three times as large as other letters and in red. First four words filled in in red and partly in majuscules.*

2 [a] Cristes] cri- *on erasure* [b] se] -o *added by* A *or* C

3   Se[a] eadiga Margareta wæs Ðeodosius dohtor;[b] se wæs þære hæþenre hehfæder. Deofolgeld he wurþode and fædde his dohter; se wæs mid Halgum Gaste gefylled and þurh fulwiht heo wæs geedniwod. Heo wæs geseald hire fostormoder to fædenne, n[[i]]h[c] Antiochia ðære ceastre, and syþþan[d] hire agen modor[e] forþgefaren wæs, se[f] fostormodor hi[[⟨r⟩e]] miccle swyþor lufode þonne heo ær dyde. Heo wæs hire fæder swiþe laþ and Gode swyþe leof.

4   And mid þ[[y]] þe heo wæs .xv. wintra eald, heo lustfullode on hire fostormoder huse. Heo gehyrde martyra geflitu, forþon þe mænig blod wæs agoten on þam tidum on eorþan for ures Dryhtnes naman,[a] Hælendes Cristes, and heo wæs mid Halgan Gaste gefyld and hyre mægþhad Gode oðfæste.

5   Sume dæge, þa mid þy þe heo geheold hyre fostormodor scæp[[.]] mid oþrum fæmnum, hire hefdgemacum, ða ferde Olibrius se gerefa fram Asia to Antiochia þære ceastre. Þa geseh he[a] þa eadegan |[74r] Margaretan be þam wege sittan[[.]][b] and hræddlice he hire gyrnde and cwæþ to his þegnum: 'Gongaþ [[⟨ge⟩]] ofostlice and geneomaþ þa fæmnan and axsiaþ gif heo biþ freo, þæt ic hire onfo me to wife, and gif heo þeow biþ, ic sylle fih for hire, and heo byþ me for cyfese and hyre biþ weol on minum huse.'

Þa cempan þa eodan and hi[[⟨r⟩e]] genoman. Se[c] eadega Margareta þa ongan Criste clypian and þus cwæþ: 'Gemildsa me, Dryhten, and ne læt þu min sawle mid arleasum, ac gedo me blissian and þe symble herian and ne læt þu næfre mi[[⟨n⟩]]ne sawle ne min lichoma wyrþan besmitan. Ac gesend me to min[[um]] swiþran healfe and to þære winstran sibbe englas to ontynenne mine sefan and to †andswariende mid bylde þyssum arleasum and þissum unrihtum cwyllera[[s]]. Ic [[b]]eo nu, Drihten, swa swa nytenu onmiddan feolde and swa swa spærwe on nette and swa swa fisc on hoce. Gefylst [[.y]] me, min Drihten, and geheald me and ne forlæt me on arleasra handa.'

6   Ða cempan þa coman to þam gerefan and cwædon: 'Hlaford, ne miht þu hi[[r⟨e⟩]] onfon, forþon to Gode heo gebiddaþ, se þe wæs ahangan fram Iudeum.' Olibrius se gerefa hi[[r⟨e⟩]] [[⟨ge⟩]]het to him gelædon and hire

---

3   [a] se] -o *added by* A *or* C   [b] dohtor] *second o seems to have been altered to* e   [c] nih] i *altered to* e *by* A *or* C   [d] syþþan] *downstroke between first and second* þ   [e] modor] m *altered from* a *or* o *by* A   [f] se] -o *added by* A *or* C

4   [a] naman] -an *on erasure*

5   [a] he] *on erasure*   [b] sittan] *perhaps followed by erased* -u   [c] se] -o *added by* A *or* C

to cwæþ: 'Of hwylcum cynne eart þu? Sægæ me, [[⟨bist⟩]] þu frig oðð þeow?'
Se eadega Margareta him to cwæþ: 'Ic eom frig.' Se gerefa hire to cwæþ:
'Hwylces geleafan eart þu oþþe hwæt is þin nama?'ª Heo andswarode and
cwæþ: 'In Dryhtne ic eom geciged.' Se gerefa hire to cwæþ: 'Hwylcne god
begæst þu?' Se halga Margareta him to cwæþ: 'Ic gebidde on Ealmihtigne
God and on his Sunu, Hælend Crist, se þe minne †mægþ unbesmiten
geheold oþ þysne andweardan dæg.' Se gerefa hire to cwæþ: 'Clypest þu on
þone Crist þe mine fæderas ahengon?' Se halga Margareta hi[[ne]] to cwæþ:
'Þine fæderas Crist ahengon and þy hi forwurdon, ac he þurhwunaþ on
ecnysse and his rice is a butan ende.' Se gerefa wæs þa swiþe yrre and het þa
halgan Margaretan on karcern betynan oþþæt he geþohte hu he hire
mæþhad †forswilde.

7   Se gerefa hire to cwæþ: 'Gif þu ne gebiddest þe on min god, min
swurd sceal fandian þin lichama and ealle þine ban ic tobrysige. Gif þu me
gehyrest and on minne god gelæfst, ætforan eallum þissum folce ic þe to
cweþe þæt ic þe onfo me to wife and þe byþ swa wel swa me is.' Margareta
him to cwæþ: 'Forþon ic sylle minne lichoman in tintrego, þæt min sawle
mid soþfæstum sawlum gereste[[þ]].'

8   Se gerefa hi[[r⟨e⟩]] [[het]] ahon and mid smalum gyrdum swingan.
Se halga Margareta besæh up [[⟨on⟩]] heofonum and cwæþ: 'On þe,
Drihten, ic gelæfæ, þæt icª ne si gescend. Loce on me and gemiltsa me of
arleasra honda [[⟨and⟩]] honda þysses |⁷⁴ᵛ cwylleræs,ᵇ þy læs min heorte her
on ege sy. Send me hælo þæt syn leohteᶜ mine witu and þæt min sar [[me]]
me cyme to gefean.'

9   And mid þy þe heo þus gebæd, þa cwelleras swungon hire merwen
lichaman þæt †[[se]] blod fleow on eorþan swa swa wæter deþ of þam
clænestan wyllspringe. Se gerefa hire to cwæþ: 'Eala, Margareta, gelæf on
me and þe byþ wel ofer oþre wif.' And ealle þa fæmnan þe þær stoden
weopen bitterlice for þæm blode and cwædon: 'Eala, Margareta, soþlice we
sariaþ ealle, forþon þe we seoþ hnacod þinne lichamaª beon cwylm-
[[i]]e[[n]]d. Þes gerefa is swiþe hatheort and he þe wil[[⟨l⟩]]le forleosan and
þin gemynd of eorðan adiligan. Gelæf on hine and þu leofast.' Se halga
Margareta him to cwæþ: 'Eala, ge yfelan þehteras, gangaþ ge wif to eowrum

6   ª nama] m *altered from* n *by* A
8   ª ic] -c *on erased* -s *by* A *or* B   ᵇ cwylleræs] -s *altered from* -f *by* A   ᶜ leohte] 'on' leohte
MS: on *added by* A *or* B
9   ª lichama] *contraction mark over final* -a *added by* A *or* C

husum and ge weras to eowrum weorcum! God me is fultumiend. Forþon nelle ic eow geheran, ne ic næfre me ne gebidde on eower god, se þe is dumb and deaf. Ac geleafaþ on min God, se þe is strang on mægenne, and hrædlice he gehyr[[a]]þ þa þe on hine gelæfaþ.'

10   And heo cwæþ to þam gerefan: 'Eala, þu ungeþunggena hund and þu †ungefylledlican †dracan, mannes ofen, min God me is fultumiend and, þeah þu min lichama geweald hæbbe, Crist genereþ min sawl of þinre þare egeslican honda.' Se[a] halga Margareta besæh [[o⟨n⟩]] heofonum and cwæð: 'Gestrangie me, lifes Gast, þæt min gebed þurh heofonum gefare and þæt hit astige ætforan þin gesihþe. And gesend me þinne þone Halgan Gast fram heofonum s[[y]] [[m]]e cyme o[[n]] fultum, þæt ic gehealde ungewæmd minne mægþhad and þæt ic geseo mine wiþerweardan, se þe wiþ me gefihtaþ, †synna to ansyna, and þæt sy bysen and blæd a eallum fæmnum [[⟨þe⟩ g⟨elæfa⟩þ on þe]], forþon þin na⟨ ⟩ gebletsod on weorulde.' Þa cæmpan þa eodan and cwylmdon hire lichaman. Ða bewrah se arleasa gerefa his ansyna mid his hacela, forþon þe he ne mihte on hire locian for þæm blode, and cwæþ to †þam fæmnan: 'Forhwon ne gehyrsumast þu min word ne þu [[ne]] þin sylf[[. .]] mildsigende? Efne, þin lichoma is cwilmd for minum þam egeslican dome. Geþafa me and gebid þe on min god, þy læs þu deaþe swiltast. Gif þu me ne gehyrast, min sweord sceal wealdan þin li'c'homa. Gif þu me [[⟨ne⟩]] †gehyræ[[þ]], ætforan eallum þissum folce ic þe to cweþe þæt ic þe onfo me to wife.' Se halga Margareta him to cwæþ: 'Eala, þu unsnotra, forþon ic sylle mine lichaman in tintrego, þæt min sawul sy gesygefæst on heofonum.'

11   Se gerefa hio[[.]][a] het on þystru carcern |[75r] betynan and mid þe heo eode þærin hio gebletsode eall †inre lichaman mid Cristes rodetac[[m]][b] and ongan hi[[re]] handan ⟨ ⟩ and þus cweþan: 'Loce on me and gemildsa me, Drihten, forþon þe ic ane [[b]]eo and [[ange]] †mine fæder ⟨ ⟩ he me forlet. Ne læt þu me, min Drihten, ac gemiltsa me, forþon þe ic ongete þæt þu bist dema cwuca and deaþe. De[[a]]m[[a]] nu betwux me and þyssum deoflum. Efne, ic sarige on minum witum. Ne yrsa þu wiþ me, min Drihten, f[[e]]orþon þe þu wast þæt ic sylle min sawle for þe. Þu eart gebletsod on weorlde.'

---

10   [a] se] -o *added by* A *or* C
11   [a] hio] -o *by* A *on erasure of two letters*   [b] rodetacm] -m *partly erased to form* -n

12 Ic þa, Peotimus, hire wæs fædende mid hlafe and mid wætre, and ic sæh þurh ehþyrl[[e]] eal hire geflit þe heo hæfde wið ð[[⟨o⟩ne]] arleasan deofle; and ic wrat eall hire gebed.

Þa eode ut of þæs karcernnes hwomme swiþe egeslic draca missenlices hiwes. His loccas and his beard wæron gylden geþuht, and his teþ wæron swilc swa asniden isen, and his egan scinan swa searagym, and ut æt his nosu eode micel[[ne]] smoce,[a] and his †tungla eþode, and micel fulnesse he dyde on þæm karcernne and he hi[[⟨n⟩e]][b] þa a[[h]]rærde and he hwystlode stranglic stemne. Ða wæs geworden micel leoht on þæm þystran karcern of ðæm fyre þe uteode of þæs dracan muþe. Se halg[[a]] fæmn[[a]][c] wæs þa geworden swiþe fyrht and gebigde hire cneowu on eorþan and aþenoda hire honda on gebede and þus cwæþ: 'God, adwysc þæs miclan dracan mægen and gemildsa me þearfendra[d] and earfoþra and ne læt ðu me næfre forwyrðan, ac gescyld me wiþ þys[[ne]] wilddeor[[e]].'

13 And mid þy þe heo þus bæd, se draca sette his muþ ofer þære halgan fæmnan heafod and hi[[re]] forswealh. Ac Cristes rodetacen, þe se[a] halga Margareta worhte [[...]] dracan innoþ, se hine toslat on twæigen dælas, and se[b] halgæ fæmna eode ut of þæs dracan innoþ ungewæmmed. And on þære ilcan tide gesæh heo on hire wynstran healfe ænne deofol sittend swilc [[s⟨wa⟩]] an sweartne man, and his honda to his cneowum gebundenne. And mid þy þe heo þinne gesæh, heo gebæd to Drihten and þus cwæþ: 'Ic þe herige and wuldrige, þu undeadlica Kyning. Þu eart geleafan trymnysse and ælcra snotra fruma[[n]] and æghwylcre strengþo staþol. Nu ic geseo min geleafan blow[[i]]ende and min sawle gefeonde and þysne dracan acwealdne licgean. Þancas ic þe secge, þu halga and þu undeadlica God. Þu eart ealra hælende Hælend. Si þin nama gebletsod on weorulde.'

14 And mid þy þe heo þus gebæd, se deofol uparas and genam †þa halgan fæmnan hond and cwæþ: 'Þæt genihtsumaþ þæt þu dydest. Gewit fram me, forþon |[75v] þe ic geseo þe on forhæfdnesse þurhwunian. Ic sende to þe Hrufum, min broþur, on dracan gelicnesse, to þam þæt he þe forswulge and þin mægþhad and þin wlite forlure and þin gemynd of[a] eorþan †adylgan. Þu hine þonne mid Cristes rodetac[[e]]ne[b] acwealdest and nu þu wilt me acwyllan. Ac ic bidde þe for þin mægþhad þæt þu me ne geswinge.'

12 [a] smoce] -e *altered to* -a   [b] hine] hig MS: -g *on erasure by* A   [c] halga fæmna] *final* -a *on both words altered to* æ *by* A *or* C   [d] þearfendra] d *altered from* ð *by* A
13 [a] se] -o *added by* A *or* C   [b] se] -o *added by* A *or* C
14 [a] of] -r *altered to* -f *by* A   [b] rodetac[[e]]n] *followed by* -e *and* 'e' *above it; first* e *possibly by* A

185

Se[c] halga Margareta gegrap þa ⟨ ⟩ deofol be þæm locce and hine on eorþan awearp and his swyþran ege utastang and ealle[d] his ban heo tobrysde and sette hire swiþran fott ofer his swyre and him to cwæþ: 'Gewit fram minum mægþhade! Crist me is fultumiend, forþon his nama is scinend on weorulde.'

15 And mid þy þe heo þus cwæþ, þær scan swiþe micel leoht on þæm þystran quarterne and Cristes rode wæs gesewen fram eorþan up oþ[[þe]] heofen, and an hwit culfre stod ofer þære rode, and heo spræc and þus cwæþ: 'Secg me, Margareta, þu þe þurh mægþhad gyrndest †þære eacan †rice, and forþon †th[[e]] biþ þe geseald mid Abraham and mid Isaac and Iacob. Eadig eart þu þe þone feond oferswiþdest.' Se[a] halga Margareta þa cwæþ: 'Wuldor þe sy, Crist, þu þe ane dest mænig wuldor. Ic þe wuldrige and herige, forþon þu eart halig and micel on eallum þingum, þu þe gemedomast †gecyþ †þonne þinre þeowen þæt þu eart ane hiht ealra lif[[i]]endra on þe.'

Se[b] culfræ[c] þa wæs eft sprecende and cwæþ: 'Margareta, axie[d] þone þe þu hæfst under þinum fotum be his dædum and he cyþ þe eall his weorc, and mid þy þe þu hine hæfst oferswiþd, þu cymst to me.' Se[e] halga Margareta þa cwæþ to þæm[f] deofle: 'Hwæt is þin nama, þu unclæne gast?' [[. .]] deofol hire to cwæþ: 'Þu Cristes þeow, ahef þin fot of min swir[[e]], þæt ic mine ban †lihwan gereste and ic þe sægce ealle mine dæda.' Se[g] halga fæmne þa ahof hire fot of his swire. Þæt deofol þa cwæþan ongan: '†Manegra †soþfæstra †man[[n⟨a⟩]] ic genam and ic gefæht wiþ him and ne mihte me nan oferswiþan. Ac þu min ege utastunge and ealle mine ban tobrisdest and min broþor acwealdest. Nu ic geseo Crist wunian on þe and þu dest eall soþfæsnesse. Ic heo[[⟨m⟩]] ableonde hera sefan and ic hi gedyde ofergeotan þa heofenlican snyttro and, mid þy þe hy on slæpe wæron, ic com ofer hi and þa þe ic ne mihte of þæm bedde adon, ic hi dyde on þæm sylfan slæpe singian. Nu þonne fram anre gingre fæmnan ic eam oferswiþd. Hwæt do ic nu, forþon þe ealle[h] mine wæpne synt tobrecenne? And me ealra swiþost |[76r] gedræfþ þæt þin fæder and þin modor mine wæron and þu ane wiþ me and wið eall hire cneo⟨ ⟩ rise, Cristes gefylgendum, †þurh þono[i] deofla magen eall to nahte gebiþ.'[j]

---

[c] se] -o *added, probably by* A   [d] his swyþran ege utastang and ea] *from* s *in* his *to* ea *in* ealle *added on erasure by* A 15   [a] se] -o *added by* A *or* C   [b] se] -o *added by* A   [c] culfræ] -æ *altered to* -a *by* A   [d] axie] -e *underlined:* 'a' *by* A *or* C   [e] se] -o *added by* A *or* B   [f] þæm] *apostrophe rather than contraction mark for nasal*   [g] se] -o *added by* A *or* C   [h] ealle] *on erasure by* A   [i] þono] -o *altered to* -e *by* A *or* B   [j] and þu ane . . . to nahte gebiþ] *underlined for omission*

16   Se halga fæmne him to cwæþ: 'Saga me þin cynn and hwa þe cende.'
[[Þæt]] deofol hire to cwæþ: 'Sæcg me, Margareta, hwanon is þin lif and þin
lichama and hwanon is þin sawul and þin geleafa, oþþe hu wæs Crist
wuniend on þe. Sag[[a]] me þis, þonne secge ic þe ealle mine dæde.' Se[a]
halga fæmne him answarode and cwæþ: 'Nys me alifed þæt ic þe to
secga[[.]][b] forþon þu ne eart wyrþe mine stefne to gehyrenne. Godes
bebodu ic wille gehyran and þæt gecyþan. And þu, deofol, adumbe nu
forþon þe ic nelle nan word ma of þinum muþe gehyran.' And hrædlice se
eorþe forswalg þone deofol grimlice.

17   Ða, on oþran dæge, [[g]]het se gerefa þa halgan fæmnan to him
gelædan and, mid þy þe heo wæs utagangende, heo gebletsode eall hira
lichoma mid Cristes rodetacen. Se gerefa hire to cwæþ: 'Eala, Margareta,
gelæf on me and gebid þe o[[n]] minum gode.' Se[a] halga Margareta him to
cwæþ: 'Soþlice þe gedafenaþ on min God to gebiddanne.' Se gerefa wearþ þa
swyþe yrre and het hi[[r⟨e⟩]] ahon and mid kandelum byrnan and syþþan
dydan þa nyxtan swa heom beboden wæs. Se[b] halga Margareta þa cigde and
cwæþ: 'Nelle ic næfre me gebiddan on eowerne god, se þe is dumb and deaf.
Ne magon ge oferswyþan clæne fæmnan. Crist sylf †ge gebletsode min
lichama and min sawul he sylleþ wuldres beh.'

18   Se arleasa gerefa het þider bringan mycel leaden fæt and het hit mid
wætere afyllan and dyde hit ælen swyþe hat and het bindan fet and honda
þære halgan fæmnan and þæron don. Ða cwylras dyden swa heom beboden
wæs. Se eadega Margareta locade on heofonum and cwæþ: '†Drihten, God
Ealmihtig, þu þe eardest on heofonum, geunne me þæt þis[[ne]] wæter sy
me to hælo and to lihtnesse and to fulwihtes bæþ unaspringende[a] þæt hit
me aþwea to þam eacan life and awyrp me from †eall[[um]] mine synne and
gehæl[[e]] me on þinum wuldre, forþon þe þu eart gebletsod on weorulde.'
And mid þy þe[b] þæt gebed wæs gefyld, swa wearþ þær micel eorþhrærnesse
geworden, and on þære ylcan tid [[s⟨wa⟩]] com culfre of heofonum
hæbbende beh on muþe and raþe wæron alysde fet and honda þære halgan
fæmnan and heo eode up of þæm wætere, God herigende and wuldrigende,
and þus cwæþ: 'Wuldor ic þe secge, Drihten God, Hælend Crist, forþon þe
†þe þu me onlihtest and wuldradest and þu me wære mildsiend, þinre
þeowene. Þu eart bletsod on weorlde.' And mid þy þe heo cwæþ 'Amen',

16   [a] se} -o *added by* A, B *or* C   [b] secga} -a *altered to* æ
17   [a] se} -o *added by* A *or* B   [b] se} -o *added by* A *or* C
18   [a] unaspringende} *underlined*   [b] þe} þ *altered from* ꝥ *by erasure*

|^{76v} stefn wæs geworden of heofonum þus cweþende: 'Cum, Margareta, to heofonum. Eadig [[þ⟨u⟩]] eart, þu þe †mægþhad gyrndest: þurh þon þingum þu eart eadig on ecnesse.' And on þære ilcan tid gelæfde þæs folces .xv. þusenda manna, butan wif and cild.

19   Olibrius se gerefa het acwyllan ealle þa þæ on Crist gelæfdon and hi wæron acwealde on Limes feold,[a] butan Ærmeniga þære ceastre. And æfter heom he [[ge]]het acwyllan þa eadegan Margaretan and mid swurde ofslean. Ða cwyllras læddon hi[[re]] þa butan þara ceastre †wealþas[b] and þa an of heom cwæþ (his nama wæs Malchus gehaten): 'Aþene þin sweora and onfoh min swurd and gemildsa me, forþon þe ic her geseo Crist standand mid his englum.' Margareta þa cwæþ: 'Ic bidde þe, broþor, gif þu her Crist geseost, ar[[ig]]e me oþþæt ic me gebidde to him and min gast oþfæste.' Se cwyllere hyre to cwæþ: 'Bid swa hwæt swa þu wille.'

Se eadega Margareta þa ongan biddan and þus cweþan: 'God, þu þe heofen mid honda gemettest and eorþan on þinre fyst betyndest, geher min[[⟨n⟩]]e bena þæt swa hwilc man swa writeþ min[c] þrowunga, oþþe hi geheraþ [[h]]rædan, of þære tide syn adylgade hira synna; oþþe gif hwilc man leoht deþ on minum cirican of his gewinne, be swa hwylc[[re]] gylte swa he bidde forgifenesse, ne si him se[d] synna geteold. Ic bidde þe, Drihten, þæt gif hwilc mon si gemetod on þinum þam egeslican dome and he si gemindig minum naman and þines, gefreolsa hine, Drihten, of tintrego. Get ic þe bidde, Drihten, þæt se þe †rærdeþ boc mines martirhades oþþe on his huse hæbbe, sy his synna alætnesse, forþon þe we syndon flæsc and blod æfre syngiende and næfre ablinnende. Get ic þe bidde þæt se þe cyrcan timbrige on minum naman and þær awrite min þrowung oþþe of his gewinne gebicge, send on hine, Drihten, þono Halgan Gast. And þær boc sy mines martyrhades, ne sy þær geboren blind cild ne healt, ne dumb, ne deaf, ne fram unclænum gaste geswenct, ac sy þær sib and lufu and soþfæstnesse gast. And se þe þær biddeþ his synna forgifnesse, gecyþ hi[[n⟨e⟩]], Drihten.'

20   Ða wæs stefn geworden of heofonum mid þunr[[. . .]][a] and culfre com berende rode and cwæþ: 'Aris, Margareta, eadig wæs se innoþ se þe þe gebær, forþon þe þu †gemano ealle þingc on þinum gebed. Ðurh engla

---

19 [a] feold] -a *added by* A   [b] wealþas] þ *altered to* l *by erasure*   [c] min] -e *added by* A *or* B
[d] se] -o *added by* A, B *or* C
20 [a] þunr[[. . .]]] *Cockayne suggests* þunrode: 'þunre in rasura, ubi, ni fallor, steterat þunrode'.

mægen ic þe swerige þæt swa hwæt swa þu bæde, eall hit biþ gehered
ætforan Godes gesyhþe, and swa hwæt swa þu wære gemyndig, þæt forgifeþ
þe God. God gesættet |[77r] on þinum cyrcan þreo hund engla to þon þæt hi
onfoþ ælc þæra manna bena þe to Drihten clypaþ on þinum naman þæt hira
synna synt adylgode. Nu git ic cyþe þe þæt englas cumaþ ongean þe and
neamaþ þin heafod and lædaþ hit on neorxnawonge;[b] and þin lichama biþ
wurþful mid mannum, þæt swa hwa swa hrineþ þin reliquias, of þære tide
fram swa hwylcre untrumnesse swa he hæfþ he biþ gehæld. And þær þin
reliquias beoþ oþþe boc þines martirhades, ne nealæcþ þær naþor ne yfel ne
se [[unclᐸæneᐳ]] unclæne gast. Ac þær biþ sib and lufu and soþfæstnesse
and blis and †gefean and nænig on neorxnawonge mare gemetod mid
meder ealra Gescippendes nimþe þreo fæmnan.[c] And se þe þin naman of
ealra heortan cigeþ mid †tearum agotennesse, he biþ gefreolsad fram
eallum his synnum. Eadig þu eart and þa þe þurh þe gelæfað and se[d] stow
þær þu to gefundest. Cum hrædlice to þære stowe þe þe is gegearwod and sit
on þa swiþran healfe þære eadegan Teclan and Susannan. Eadig þu[e] eart, þu
þe mægþhad geheolde. Cum nu, Godes lamb, ic þin anbide.'

21   Se halga Margar`e'ta besæh on hire embhwyrft †to cwæþ: 'Ic eow
bidde þurh naman ures Drihtnes, Hælendes Cristes, þæt he eow sylle eowra
synna forgyfnesse and eow †gedon rixian on heofona rice. Þancas ic þe secge
se þe me gewuldrade and gewurþade on soþfæstra noman. Ic hine [[hine]]
herige and bletsige se þe †risaþ on worulde.'

22   And æfter †[[þæt]] gebede heo hi[[re]] upa[[h]]rærde and cwæþ to
þam cwyllere: 'Broþor, genim þin swurd and gecwille me, forþon þe nu get
ic oferswyþde þysne middangeard.' ᐸ ᐳ 'Gedem ic þæt, ne ic ne acwylle
halig †Godedes fæmne. God wæs sprecende beforan me to þe. Ne eam ic
dyrstig þæt to donne.' Se halga Margareta cwæþ to hi[[nᐸeᐳ]]: 'Gif þu þæt
ne dest, næfst þu dæl mid me on neorxnawonge.' Se cwylra þa mid
gefyrhto genam his swurd and hire heafod ofasloh and †gehwy[[r]]de[a]
hine sylfne and cwæþ: 'Drihten, ne sette þu me þis on synn[[a]]', and hine
sylfne mid his swurd †tofastag and gefeol to þære eadegan fæmnan swyþran
healfe. Þider coman þa þusend engla ofer þære halgan Margaretan lichaman
and gebletsodon hine.

[b] neorxnawonge] *second o probably altered to* a   [c] *and* nænig . . . þreo fæmnan] *underlined*
[d] se] -o *added by* A *or* C   [e] þu] *altered from* ea *by* A
22   [a] gehwyrde] r *altered from* f *by* A

189

23   Ða coman twelf englas and genaman hire heafod on hire fædmum
and hi sungon and cwædon: 'Ðu halga, þu halga, þu halga, Drihten God,
weoroda Wuldorkynincg,[a] fulle syndon heofonas and eorþan þines
wuldres.' And þus singende hi hit gesætton on neorxnawonge. And ealle þa
þe wonnhale[b] wæron, healtte and blinde, dumbe and deafe, and hi †ge |77v
gehrinon þære halgan fæmnan lichaman, ealle hi wurdon gehælde. And
ængla stefn wæs gehered ofer hire lichaman, þus cweþende: 'Eadig eart þu
and þa þe þurh þe gelæfeþ, forþon þe þu wunne reste a oþ ende mid halgum
fæmnum. And ne be þu sorhfull be þinum halgan lichaman, forþon þe
hi[[⟨t⟩]] is forlætan on eorþan to þon þæt swa hwylc mann swa rineþ þine
reliquias oþþe þine ban, on þære tide syn adilgade hira synna and hira nama
writan on lifes bocum.'

24   Ic, Þeo[[þ]]imus,[a] genam þa reliquias þære halgan fæmnan and ic
hi[[t]] gesætte on niwe scrin †þ ic sylf ær of stane geworhte and mid
swotum wyrtum gesweotte, and ic hi[[t]] geheold on sumes siþwifes
huse[[s]]. Hire nama wæs Sincletica. Ic, Þeo[[þ]]imus, wæs þe hire
geþenode mid hlafe and mid wætere and ic gesæh eall hire geflit þe heo
hæfde wiþ þone arleasan deofla[b] and hire gebed ic awrat and ic hit gesende
to eallum Cristenum mannum. And se halga Margareta gefylde hire
þrowung on Iulius monþe, on þone þreo and twentegþan dæge. Ealle þa þe
þis gehyraþ on heortan wesaþ onbryrdad and þa þe Drihten Crist biddaþ and
on †hire gelifaþ and †gemindoþ þære halgan Margaretan þæt hi mid hira
benum us oþfæste on sihþe Hælendes Cristes, þam sy wuldor and lof and
wurðmynt and þrym and anweald and micelnys on ealra worulda woruld,
soþlice a butan ænigum ende. Amen.

---

23   [a] Wuldorkynincg] k *altered from* c *by* A   [b] wonnhale] a *over* o, *probably by* A
24   [a] Þeoþimus] o *altered from* þ *by* A   [b] deofla] -a *altered to* -u *by* A

The Latin *Passio S. Margaretae* in Paris, BN, lat. 5574

The presentation of a text of *BHL* no. 5303 is an essential accessory to that of the Old English versions edited above. In supplying this accessory we have not, however, attempted to produce a full critical edition of the Latin, as such an edition would be beyond the scope of the present work and would be of limited relevance to the Anglo-Saxon material. Instead, it has been thought worthwhile to print a reasonably good early copy of *BHL* no. 5303, chosen from among those which have not yet been published. The copy of the *passio* in the tenth-century Paris manuscript, BN, lat. 5574 (P), is particularly appropriate in this regard, as this manuscript was written in Anglo-Saxon England. The St Margaret text it contains is by no means an exact representation of the variant of *BHL* no. 5303 used by the CCCC translator, though it does present a number of significant correspondences to the Old English. These are identified below in the Commentary on the Latin text (see also Commentary on CCCC), as are places where CCCC appears to depart markedly from P. Words and phrases treated in the Commentary are signalled with a sequence of superscript numbers (in one sequence throughout the whole text).

The text of P is set out here in accordance with the conventions of modern punctuation, and abbreviations have been silently expanded. Evident omissions have been supplied, indicated in the edited text by angle brackets, ⟨ ⟩. The Latinity of P is poor and so we present here a corrected text, in which obvious lapses have been rectified. Such editorial interventions are noted in the apparatus criticus, which also highlights discrepancies between P and other Latin witnesses, though minor textual variants are not exhaustively recorded. In identifying characteristic features of P, we make particular reference to the texts of *BHL* no. 5303 printed by Mombritius (M) and Assmann (As). Lemmata for which there are textual

191

variants are keyed to the apparatus criticus by a sequence of superscript letters in alphabetical order (beginning again with *a* once z is reached). The major deficiency of P is a substantial lacuna near the end (amounting, we estimate, to some 420 words). To remedy this lacuna we have supplied the text from another early copy of the *passio*, that in the ninth-century manuscript Saint-Omer, Bibl. mun., 202 (O). The latter manuscript preserves a generally reliable text of the Latin and can be regarded as of interest in an Anglo-Saxon context, as it is known to have been in England in the eleventh century.

The Latin 'Passio S. Margaretae'

Appendix 2

PASSIO SANCTE MARGARETAE MARTYRIS[a] QUOD EST
.XIII. KALENDAS AUGUSTI

1 Post passionem et[b][1] resurrectionem Domini nostri Iesu Christi et gloriosae ⟨tempus⟩[c][2] ascensionis eius in caelum ad Deum Patrem omnipotentem, in illius nomine multi passi sunt apud Deum,[3] et uicerunt hunc mundum[4] et superauerunt carnifices in nomine Domini nostri Iesu Christi. Adhuc tamen obtinebat insaniae diaboli ⟨rabies⟩[d] homines ut idola surda et muta ac ceca manu hominum[e] facta[5] adhorabant, quae nec illis nec sibi proderunt.

2 Ego autem in nomine Christi credens, Theotimus nomine uocatus[f] a Domino et doctus profunditate litterarum, posui me omnes cartas legere et non inueni neminem in quem oportet credere nisi in nomine Christi, qui caelos inluminat,[6] surdos audire fecit,[7] mortuos suscitauit,[8] martyres coronauit, et omnes in se credentes saluos fecit.[9] Ego enim baptizatus in nomine Patris et Filii et Spiritus Sancti, posui[g] me caute cognoscere quomodo pugnauit beatissima Margareta contra demonem[h] et uicit hunc mundum.[10] Ego secundum meam uirtutem dedi pretium et cartas comparaui hab eis qui in illo tempore scriptores[i] erant et scripsi in libris cartaneis omnia quae passa sit beatissima Margareta. Omnes aures habentes audite[j] corde, et intelligite[11] uiri; mulieres, uirgines, ⟨uelut⟩[k] tenere puelle proponite[l] ⟨uos⟩[m] in cordibus uestris, et ita laborate, ut accipiatis salutem anime uestrae et requiem sempiternam cum iustis a Domino coronatis.[n][12]

3 Beatissima autem Margareta erat Theodosi filia, qui[o] erat gentilium patriarcha et idola adorabat. Illam unicam filiam insensatam habebat. Ipsa uero Spiritu Sancto repleta, mox autem ut de sua[p] matre nata est, data est ad nutriendum in quendam ciuitatem habentem ab Antiochia stadia .xv. Suscepta est etiam a sua[q] nutrice diligenter. Quando uero mortua est mater beata Margareta[r] ampliori desiderio tenebatur a sua nutrice, quia formosa erat et Christum inuocabat Deumque adhorabat. Odiosa erat a patre suo, dilecta namque a Domino Iesu Christo.

---

[a] martyris] martyrae P   [b] passionem et] *om.* MAs   [c] tempus] M: *om.* P   [d] rabies] MAs: *om.* P   [e] hominum] hominem P   [f] uocatus] uocatur P   [g] posui] et posui P   [h] demonem] demonum P   [i] scriptores] scriptares P   [j] audite] MAs: audire P   [k] uelut] MAs: *om.* P   [l] proponite] MAs: ponite P   [m] uos] MAs: *om.* P   [n] coronatis] coronatus P   [o] qui] que P   [p] sua] suo P   [q] sua] suo P   [r] Margareta] Margarete P

194

THE PASSION OF ST MARGARET, MARTYR, WHICH IS ON 20 JULY

1   After the Passion and Resurrection of Our Lord Jesus Christ and the time of his glorious Ascension into heaven to God the Father Almighty, in his name many people suffered in the presence of God, and they overcame this world and conquered their tormentors in the name of Our Lord Jesus Christ. As yet, however, the raging of the madness of the devil held people in its grip, so that they worshipped deaf, dumb and blind idols, fashioned by human hand, which were of benefit neither to them nor to themselves.

2   I am a believer in Christ called Theotimus by name, and having been trained in the deep study of literature I set myself to read all books, and I found no one in whom it was right to believe except in the name of Christ, who gives light to the skies, who made the deaf hear, raised the dead, crowned martyrs and brought salvation to all who believed in him. I was baptized, then, in the name of the Father and of the Son and of the Holy Spirit, and I set myself carefully to learn how the most blessed Margaret fought the demon and overcame this world. According to my capacity, I gave money and obtained written accounts by those who were writers at that time, and I wrote in the pages of my books all that the most blessed Margaret underwent. All who have ears to hear, listen with your heart, and understand, men; women and maidens, imagine yourselves as tender girls in your hearts, and so strive that you may receive the salvation of your soul and eternal rest with the just who have been crowned by the Lord.

3   The most blessed Margaret, then, was the daughter of Theodosius, who was chief priest of the pagans and worshipped idols. This only daughter he regarded as irrational. She, however, filled with the Holy Spirit, as soon as she was born from her mother, was given to be fostered in a certain city fifteen stades from Antioch. She was attentively received into the care of her fostermother. Indeed when her mother died the blessed Margaret was held in even greater affection by her fostermother, because she was beautiful and she prayed to Christ and worshipped God. She was hateful to her father, for she was beloved by the Lord Jesus Christ.

4   Erat autem annorum .xv. et delectabatur in domo nutricis sue. Audiuit autem beata Margareta omnia certamina martyrum et effusionem sanguinis iustorum in illis temporibus pro nomine Iesu Christi saluatoris. Ipsa uero spiritu sancto repleta totam se tradidit Deo qui eam saluam fecit et uirginitatem eius inmaculatam custodiuit.

5   Pascebatque beata Margareta oues nutricis suae cum ceteris puellis coetaneis suis. Factum est autem illis ⟨diebus⟩[s] dum transiret Olibrius prefectus de Asia in Antiochiam ciuitatem persequere Christianos et deos suos uanos adorare suaderet; et ubi audierat aliquos Christum nominare, statimque eos ferreis nexibus constringebat. Vidit autem beatam Margaretam pascentem oues nutricis suae; statim concupiuit eam. Dixit ministris suis, 'Ite festinanter,[t] conprehendite hanc puellam. Si est libera, accipiam eam[u] mihi uxorem. Si ancilla est, dabo pretium pro ea[v] et erit mihi concubina. Bene erit ei[13] in domo mea propter pulchritudinem eius.' Cum autem conprehenderunt eam milites qui missi fuerant a prefecto, coepit beata Margareta inuocare Christum ac dicere, 'Miserere mei, Domine, miserere mei.[14] Ne perdas cum impiis animam meam et cum uiris[w] sanguinum uitam meam.[15] Fac ex ore[x] meo, Domine Iesu Christe, semper laudationem tibi proferre,[16] et ne permittas animam meam contaminari nec polluatur fides mea. Non inquinetur corpus meum, non inmutetur scientia mea,[17] non proiciatur[y] margareta mea in lutum, non immutetur sensus meus a turpitudine iniqua et ab insipientia diaboli, sed transmitte angelum tuum sanctum doctorem ad aperiendum sensus faucis meae et ⟨ad⟩[z] respondendum[a] cum fiducia impium et iniquum prefectum.[b] Video enim me sicut ouem in medio luporum,[18] et facta sum sicut passer[19] ab aucupe conprehensa in retia et sicut piscis in amo;[20] ecce conprehensa sum uelut capra in laqueo.[21] Adiuua me,[22] Domine, et sana me.[23] Ne derelinquas me in manus impiorum.'[24]

6   Venerunt milites et dixerunt ei, 'Domine, potestas tua non potest ei esse communis, quia non est seruiens diis nostris sed Deum inuocabat, et Christum quem Iudei crucifixerunt adorabat. Tunc Olibrius immutauit faciem suam et iussit uenire eam ante se et dixit ei, 'Ex qua genere es tu?

---

[s] diebus] MAs: *om.* P   [t] festinanter] festinantem P   [u] eam] meam P   [v] ea] eo P
[w] uiris] uiri P   [x] ore] oro P   [y] proiciatur] proicatur P   [z] ad] MAs: *om.* P
[a] respondendum] respuendum P   [b] prefectum] prefectu P

4 She was fifteen years old and she took delight in the home of her fostermother. The blessed Margaret heard of all the struggles of the martyrs and of the pouring out of the blood of the just in those times in the name of Jesus Christ the Saviour. In fact, filled with the Holy Spirit, she committed her whole self to God, who brought her salvation and preserved her chastity undefiled.

5 The blessed Margaret was looking after the sheep of her fostermother with other girls of the same age. This occurred, however, in the days when the prefect Olibrius was travelling from Asia to the city of Antioch to persecute Christians and in order to urge them to worship his worthless gods; and when he heard of any people mentioning the name of Christ, at once he had them fettered in iron bonds. However, he saw the blessed Margaret looking after the sheep of her fostermother; at once he lusted after her. He said to his attendants, 'Go quickly, lay hold of that girl. If she is free-born, I will take her as my wife. If she is a slave I will give money for her and she will be my concubine. She will prosper greatly in my household because of her beauty.' When the soldiers who had been sent by the prefect laid hold of her, the blessed Margaret began to call upon Christ and to say, 'Have mercy on me, Lord, have mercy on me. Do not destroy my soul among the wicked nor my life among men of blood. From my mouth, Lord Jesus Christ, make me always render praise to you, and do not let my soul be defiled nor my faith polluted. Let not my body be contaminated, let not my mind be changed, let not my pearl be cast forth into the mud, let not my understanding be changed by unjust wickedness and by the folly of the devil, but send me your holy angel as a guide to open the channels of my understanding, so that I may reply with confidence to the wicked and unjust prefect. For I see myself as a sheep in the midst of wolves, and I am become as a sparrow caught by a fowler in a net, and as a fish on a hook; behold, I am caught like a she-goat in a snare. Help me, Lord, and heal me. Do not abandon me into the hands of the wicked.'

6 The soldiers came and said to him, 'Lord, your power cannot associate with her, because she does not serve our gods but calls upon God, and she worships Christ, whom the Jews crucified. Then Olibrius changed his countenance and ordered her to come before him, and he said to her,

Enarra mihi. Es libera an ancilla?' Beata Margareta respondit, 'Libera sum
et Christiana.' Prefectus dixit, 'Cui fidem credis, uel quomodo nuncupa-
ris?' Sancta Margareta respondit, 'Nomen meum Margareta est.' Prefectus
dixit, 'Quem deum colis uel quem adoras?' Sancta Margareta respondit,
'Ego inuoco Deum omnipotentem et Filium eius Dominum Iesum Christum, qui meam uirginitatem usque in presentem diem inlesam atque
inuiolatam custodiuit. Ego inuoco nomen Christi, quem patres[c] tui
crucifixerunt et propter hoc perierunt. Ipse autem permanet in aeternum[25]
et regni eius non erit finis.' Tunc iratus prefectus iussit beatam Margaretam
in carcerem recludi donec inueniret per qualem machinationem uirginitatem eius perderet. Introiuit uero iniquus prefectus in Antiochiam
ciuitatem et adorauit deos suos surdos et mutos secundum suam fidem.

7   Secundo autem die uenit et sedit pro tribunali iniquus prefectus et
iussit adducere puellam et dixit ad eam, 'Vana[d] puella, miserere corporis[e]
tui pulchritudini[f] et teneritati tuae. Magis autem consente mihi et adhora[g]
deos meos, et multam[h] tibi dabo pecuniam et bene tibi erit[26] super omnem
familiam meam.' Sancta Margareta respondit, 'Cognoscit Deus, qui meam
uirginitatem consignauit, quia non me suadebis[i] nec poteris me mouere de
uia ueritatis[27] quam ego inchoaui. Nam ego illum adhoro quem terra
contremescit,[28] mare formidat, quem[j] tu metuere[k] debes et omnis crea-
tura, cui regnum permanet in secula seculorum.'[29] Praefectus dixit, 'Si non
adoraueris deos meos, gladius meus deuorabit carnem tuam[l] et ossa tua
disperdam[m][30] super ignem ardentem. Nam etsi obedieris mihi et adoraueris deos meos et corpus tuum copularis mihi in amorem, ecce ante
omnes tibi dico, ego accipiam te ad coniugium et bene tibi erit[31] sicut et
mihi.' Sancta Margareta respondit, 'Ego tradam corpus meum Domino
meo Iesu Christo[n] ut cum iustis uirginibus coronam accipiam. Christus
semetipsum tradidit ⟨in⟩[o] mortem pro nobis, et ego pro ipso mori non
dubito, quia ipse suo signaculo sibi me consignauit.'

---

[c] patres] patris P   [d] Vana] *cancelled in* P, *with* O *written above in a different hand*
[e] corporis] corpus P   [f] pulchritudini] pulchritudinem P   [g] adhora] adhoro P
[h] multam) multum P   [i] suadebis] suadebes P   [j] quem] quam P   [k] metuere]
metuendi P   [l] carnem tuam] carnis tuae P   [m] disperdam] dispergam MAs   [n] Domino
meo Iesu Christo] Domini mei Iesu Christi P   [o] in] MAs: *om.* P

'From what stock do you come? Tell me. Are you free or a slave?' The blessed Margaret replied, 'I am free and a Christian.' The prefect said, 'In whom do you profess faith, and what is your name?' The blessed Margaret replied, 'My name is Margaret.' The prefect said, 'What god do you worship and pray to?' The blessed Margaret replied, 'I call upon the omnipotent God and his Son, the Lord Jesus Christ, who has preserved my chastity unscathed and inviolate to the present day. I call upon the name of Christ, whom your ancestors crucified and because of that perished. He, however, lives eternally and there will be no end to his reign.' Then angrily the prefect ordered that she should be shut up in prison until he might discover by what device he could destroy her chastity. The evil prefect then went into the city of Antioch and worshipped his deaf and dumb gods in accordance with his belief.

7 The following day the evil prefect came and sat in the official place of justice. He ordered the girl to be led in and said to her, 'Foolish girl, have pity on the beauty of your body and on your tenderness. Rather give in to me and worship my gods, and I will give you much money and you will prosper well, above all my household.' The holy Margaret replied, 'God, who has put his seal upon my chastity, knows that you will not persuade me, nor will you be able to move me from the path of truth upon which I have started. For I worship him before whom the earth quakes and the sea is terrified, whom you and every creature ought to fear, whose reign lasts for ever in eternity.' The prefect said, 'If you do not worship my gods, my sword will devour your flesh and I will destroy your bones on a burning fire. Yet if you obey me and worship my gods and join your body with me in love, behold, I tell you in front of everyone, I will take you as my wife, and you will prosper as well as myself.' The holy Margaret replied, 'I will commit my body to my Lord Jesus Christ, so that I may receive the heavenly crown with the just virgins. Christ committed himself to death for us, and I do not hesitate to die for him, because he has sealed me to himself with his sign.'

8   Tunc iussit Olibrius questionariis suis eam in aerem suspendi et uirgis subtilibus eam cedi. Beata autem Margareta aspiciens in caelum dixit, 'In te speraui, Domine; non confundar in eternum,[32] neque inrideant me inimici mei,[33] etenim qui sustinent te non confundentur[34] propter nomen tuum, Domine, quia nomen tuum benedictum est[35] in secula seculorum.' Et iterum orauit beatissima Margareta dicens, 'Respice in me, Domine, et miserere mei,[36] et libera me de manibus inimicorum[37] meorum et de manu istius carnificis,[38] ne forte percussum[p] formidet[q] cor meum.[39] Sed mitte rorem[r] de caelo[40] ut mitigentur[s] plagae meae,[t] et dolor meus requiescat,[41] et tristitia mea uertetur in gaudium.'[42]

9   Ipsa orabat et questionarii cedebat cum uirgis tenerrimum corpus, et sanguis eius tamquam[u] aquae de fonte purissima decurrebat, et preco clamabat, 'Crede, Margareta. Bene tibi erit super omnes puellas.' Nam pro multa sanguinis[v] effusione illic adstantes flebant super eam amarissime. Et dicebant ei quidam ex ipsis, 'O Margareta, uere dolemus te, quia uidimus te nudam lacerari et corpus tuum macerari. O Margareta, qualem decorem perdidisti propter incredulitatem tuam! Iste prefectus tibi iracundus est et perdere te festinat et delere memoriam tuam.[43] Crede deos suos et uiuas.' Beata Margareta respondit, 'O mali consiliarii! O pessimi omnes! Ite uiri ac mulieres ad opera uestra. Mihi autem Deus meus adiutor est.[44] Quid putatis? Si corpus meum est exterminatum, anima autem mea cum iustis uirginibus requiescit. Per ista tormenta corporum anime salue inueniuntur. Credite uos in Deum meum quia fortis est in uirtute.[45] Petentibus se exaudit, pulsantibus aperit portas[46] paradisi. Nam ego uobis non audio, nec adoro deos uestros surdos et mutos manu hominum[w] factos.'[x]

10   Et dixit praefecto, 'Tu facis opera[47] Satane. O imprudens et audax, mihi autem adiutor est Deus meus.[48] Etsi in carne mea data est tibi potestas, animam meum eruet Christus de manu tua.[49] O orribilis, O insatiabilis leo,[50] abominatus a Domino, confusus a Christo, cui uirtute constringuntur pene perpetuae.' Tunc iratus prefectus iussit eam in aerem suspendi et cum uirgulis acceruissimis carnes disrumpere. Beata autem Margareta aspiciens in caelum dixit, 'Circumdederunt me canes multi, concilium malignantium obsedit me.[51] Tu autem, Domine Deus meus, in

---

[p] percussum] percussam P   [q] formidet] formidat P   [r] rorem] ros P   [s] mitigentur]
mitigant P   [t] plagae meae] plaga mea P   [u] tamquam] tamque   [v] sanguinis] sanguis
P   [w] hominum] hominem P   [x] factos] factus P

8 Then Olibrius ordered his torturers to suspend her in the air and to beat her with canes. The blessed Margaret, however, looking up to heaven said, 'In you I have trusted, Lord; let me not be confounded in eternity, and let not my enemies mock me, for those who uphold you will not be confounded on account of your name, Lord, because your name is blessed for ever and ever.' And again the most blessed Margaret prayed, saying, 'Look upon me, Lord, and have pity on me, and free me from the hands of my enemies and from the grasp of this tormentor, lest perhaps my heart may be stricken into fear. But send dew from heaven, so that my wounds may be soothed, my sorrow may find repose and my sadness may be turned to joy.'

9 She was praying as the torturers beat her most tender body with rods, and her blood flowed like water from the purest spring, and the crier called out, 'Believe, Margaret. You will prosper above all maidens.' Because of the great outpouring of her blood the bystanders wept bitterly for her. And some of them said, 'O Margaret, truly we pity you, because we see you tortured naked and your body weakened. O Margaret, what beauty you have destroyed because of your lack of belief! This prefect is angry at you and hastens to ruin you and to blot out memory of you. Believe in his gods and you will live.' The blessed Margaret replied, 'O evil counsellors! O most wicked all of you! Go men and women to your work. My Lord is my helper. What do you think? If my body is destroyed, my soul will repose with the just virgins. Through these torments of bodies souls are found to attain salvation. *You* should believe in my God, because he is strong in his power. He listens to those who knock. I do not heed you, therefore, nor do I worship your deaf and dumb gods, which are made by human hand.'

10 And she said to the prefect, 'You perform the works of Satan. O shameless and impudent one, my God is my helper. Even if power over my flesh has been given to you, Christ will rescue my soul out of your hands. O horrible, insatiable lion, detested by the Lord, confounded by Christ, upon whom through Christ's power perpetual punishments are fastened.' Then angrily the prefect ordered her to be suspended in the air and her flesh to be lacerated with the most painful rods. The blessed Margaret, however, looking up to heaven said, 'Many dogs have encompassed me round, an

adiutorium meum exsurge,[52] et erue animam meum de manu inimicorum meorum et de manu canis unicam meam.[53] Salua me ex ore leonis et a cornibus unicornuorum humilitatem meam.[54] Conforta me, Christe, contra aduersarium meum. Perueniet ad te oratio mea, Domine Deus meus. Transmitte me columbam de caelo in adiutorium, ut inmaculatam tibi conserues uirginitatem meam. Da mihi, Domine, fiduciam ut dimicem contra aduersarium meum, ut uideam eum facie ad faciem qui mecum pugnat, ut uincam[y] eum et uideam eum proiectum ante faciem meam, et ego dem fiduciam omnibus uirginibus confitere nomen tuum, qui es[z] benedictus in secula.' Carnifices uero accesserunt et mactabant carnes eius. Nam impius praefectus cum clamide operiebat faciem suam, quia per sanguinis[a] effusionem non poterat aspicere in eam. Similiter et ceteri faciebant. Praefectus dixit, 'Quid est quod non obedieris mihi, Margareta, neque tuimetipsuis[b] miserris? Ecce carnes tue mactate sunt in iudicio meo. Consente mihi et adhora[c] deos meos ne male moriaris. Si autem me non audieris, gladius meus deuorabit[d] carnem tuam,[55] et ossa tua disperdam,[56] et neruos tuos dinumerabo[57] ante omnes.' Beata Margareta respondit, 'O inique, imprudens et audax, si ego carnis[e] mee misereor, anima mea in interitum uadit, sicut et tua. Sed ideo carnem meam trado in tormentis ut anima mea coronata[f] sit in caelis.'

11   Tunc iratus Olibrius iussit eam recludi in carcerem. Erat hora septima quando recluserunt eam in carcerem tenebrosam. Ipsa introiens in carcerem consignauit corpus suum signaculo Christi et coepit orare et dicere, 'Deus qui iudicium sapientiae decreuisti, quem timent[g] omnia[h] saecula[58] et in eis[i] habitantes,[j] quem expauescunt omnes potestates, tu es desperatorum[k] spes;[59] tu es pater orfanorum[60] et iudex uerus;[61] tu es lumen de lumine. Respice in me et miserere mei,[62] quia unica sum patre meo et ipse me dereliquid. Ne tu me derelinquas, Domine Deus meus,[63] sed adiuua me et precipe ut uideam inimicum meum qui mecum pugnat, ut iudicium adferam contra eum et loquar cum eo facie ad faciem. Quid illi nocui ignoro. Tu es iudex iustus;[64] tu iudica inter me et illum. Ecce enim in agone tristis facta sum et tibi plagas meas ingemisco. Noli mihi irasci,

---

[y] uincam] MAs: unicam P   [z] es] est P   [a] sanguinis] sanguinem P   [b] tuimetipsius] temetipsum P   [c] adhora] adhoro P   [d] deuorabit] deuorauit P   [e] carnis] carni P   [f] coronata] coronatus P   [g] timent] timet P   [h] omnia] omnis P   [i] eis] ea P   [j] habitantes] MAs: habitatis P   [k] desperatorum] MAs: speratorum P

assembly of the wicked has beset me. But rise up, my Lord, in my aid. Bring forth my soul from the hands of my enemies, and my darling one from the grasp of the dog. Save me from the mouth of the lion, and my abjectness from the horns of unicorns. Comfort me, Christ, against my adversary. Let my prayer reach you, Lord my God. Send to my aid a dove from heaven, so that you may preserve for yourself my chastity un-blemished. Give me confidence, Lord, that I may contend against my adversary, that I may see face to face him who fights against me, so that I may defeat him and see him cast forth in front of me, and I may give confidence to all virgins to acknowledge your name, who are blessed for ever and ever.' The torturers approached and afflicted her flesh. The wicked prefect covered his face with his cloak, as he was not able to look at her because of the pouring forth of her blood. The rest did likewise. The prefect said, 'Why is it that you will not obey me, Margaret, nor show yourself any mercy? Behold, your flesh has been afflicted at my sentence. Give in to me, and worship my gods, lest you die cruelly. If you do not listen to me, my sword will devour your flesh, and I will destroy your bones, and your sinews I will number in front of all.' The blessed Margaret replied, 'O iniquitous, shameless and impudent one, if I have pity on my flesh, my soul will go to its destruction, like yours. But I consign my flesh, therefore, to torments, so that my soul may be crowned in the heavens.'

11   Then angrily Olibrius ordered her to be shut up in prison. It was the seventh hour when they shut her up in the dark prison. When she entered the prison she sealed her body with the sign of Christ, and she began to pray and to say, 'God, who has determined the judgement of wisdom, whom all ages fear and those living in them, whom all powers dread, you are the hope of those who are desperate; you are the father of orphans and the true judge; you are light from light. Look upon me and have pity on me, because I am the only daughter of my father, and he has abandoned me. Do not abandon me, Lord my God, but aid me, and command that I may see my enemy who fights me, so that I may bring forth justice against him and speak to him face to face. What I have done to harm him I do not know. You are the just judge; judge between me and

Domine Deus meus, nec inquinetur anima mea nec cummisceatur sensus meus cum impiis idolis surdis et mutis. Sed in te est spes mea,[65] Iesu Christe, quia tu es benedictus in saecula.'

12   Theotimus[1][66] apparuit in carcere ⟨et⟩[m] nutrix eius et ministrabant[n] ei panem et aquam. Aspiciebatque per fenestram et orationes eius scribebat.[o][67] Ecce subito de angulo carceris exiebat draco horribilis totus uariis coloribus deauratus capilli et barba eius aurea. Videbantur[p] eius ut ferrum acutissimum dentes. Oculi[q] eius uelut flamma ignis splendebant,[68] et de naribus eius ignis et fumus exiebat, et lingua eius anhelabat super collum eius, et gladius utraque parte acutus in manu eius uidebatur. Erat enim terribilis et foetum faciebat in carcerem ab ipso igne qui[r] exiebat de ore draconis. Sancta autem Margareta facta est ut herba pallida et formido mortis cecidit in eam et confringebantur[s] omnia ossa eius. Oblita enim erat propter pauorem quod Deus exaudiuit orationem eius et quod dixerat, 'Demonstra mihi qui mecum pugnat'. Et fixit genua sua in terra et expandit manus suas ad Dominum et dixit, 'Domine Deus omnipotens, qui es inuisibilis, qui firmasti celum et terram,[69] fundamentaque posuisti[70] et mare terminum extendisti ut non transiret preceptum tuum,[71] quem omnia elementa pertimescunt, infernum deuastasti, diabolum ligasti, et potestatem draconis confregisti, respice in me, Domine, et miserere mei,[72] quia sola orphanorum in tribulatione posita ⟨sum⟩,[t] et ne[u] permittas me, Domine Deus meus, hanc malam feram nocere. Sed dimitte me, Domine, uincere fortitudinem eius. Quare ergo aduersum me pugnat ignoro. Quid ergo illi nocui nescio. Ecce obsorbere me festinet et in foueam suam deducere me quaerit.'

13   Dum autem haec diceret beata Margareta, draco aperto ore posuit os suum super caput beate Margaretae[v] et expandit linguam suam super calcaneum eius et degluttiuit eam in uentrem suum. Sed crux Christi, quam fecerat sibi beata Margareta, ipsa creuit in ore ⟨draconis et in duas

---

[1] Theotimus] AsCas: Continuit P: Contimus M: Continuus O: Continuo N   [m] et] MAs: *om.* P   [n] ministrabant] ministrabat P   [o] scribebat] As: scribebant M: scribantur P   [p] Videbantur] Videbatur tam P   [q] Oculi] Oculis P   [r] qui] que P   [s] confringebantur] PAugN: confringebat O: collidebantur M: concutiebantur As: constringebantur Pip   [t] sum] MAs: *om.* P   [u] ne] me P   [v] Margaretae] Margareta P

him. Behold, I have become gloomy in the contest, and I groan to you over my wounds. Do not be angry at me, Lord my God, and let not my soul be polluted nor my understanding be contaminated with wicked idols which are deaf and dumb. But in you is my hope, Jesus Christ, because you are blessed through the ages.'

12   Theotimus and her fostermother appeared in the prison and they served her with bread and water. He was looking in through a window and writing down her prayers. Behold, suddenly a dreadful dragon came out from the corner of the prison, all adorned with different colours in its coat and with a gold-coloured beard. Its teeth seemed like the sharpest iron. Its eyes shone like the flame of fire, and from its nostrils issued fire and smoke; its tongue hung out panting over its neck, and a two-edged sword could be seen in its hand. It was fearsome and it caused a stench in the prison from that fire which issued from the mouth of the dragon. The blessed Margaret became as pale as grass and the fear of death came upon her, and all her bones were shattered. She had actually forgotten because of her terror that God had heeded her prayer and that she had said, 'Show me who fights against me.' She fell to her knees on the ground and stretched out her arms to the Lord and said, 'Lord God omnipotent, you who are invisible, who made firm heaven and earth, who set in place its foundation and set out the sea as its boundary, so that it would not exceed your command, you whom all physical elements fear, who laid waste the region of hell, bound the devil, and destroyed the power of the dragon, look upon me now, Lord, and have pity on me, who alone among orphans am placed in tribulation, and do not allow, Lord my God, this evil beast to harm me. But grant me, Lord, to overcome its strength. Why it fights against me I do not know. I am ignorant of what I have done to harm it. Behold, it hastens to swallow me up and wishes to lead me down into its pit.'

13   While the blessed Margaret was saying this the dragon opened its mouth and placed it over the head of the blessed Margaret and extended its tongue as far as her heel and swallowed her into its stomach. But the cross of Christ, which the blessed Margaret had made for herself, grew in the

partes eum diuisit. Beata autem Margareta exiuit de utero⟩^w73 draconis
nullum dolorem in se habens. Tunc prostrauit se beatissima Margareta in
terra. Orauit et dixit, 'Laudo et glorifico nomen tuum,^74 Domine Deus
meus, Rex regum et Dominus dominantium,^75 Trinitas sancta, tibi honor,
laus, et gloria iubilatio per infinita secula seculorum.'^76

14 Factum est autem dum adimpleta habuisset beata Margareta
orationem suam, aspiciebat in sinistram partem carceris et ecce uidit alium
diabolum sedentem ut homo niger habens manus suas ad genua conligatas.
Et surrexit et coepit ambulare ad eam et tenuit^x manum eius. Dixit autem
Margareta ad demonem, 'Sufficiat tibi quod fecisti. Cessa^y iam de me.
Multa enim mala perpetrasti.' Demon respondit, 'Ego quidem fratrem
meum Rufonem misi in similitudinem draconis ut orbsorberet^z te et
tolleret memoriam tuam de terra.^77 Tu uero eum interfecisti cum
signaculo Christi. Nunc autem per orationem tuam et me interficere
cupis?' Tunc sancta Margareta uirgo conprehendit daemonem per capillos,
delisit eum in terram, et posuit pedem suum dextrum super ceruicem
eius,^78 et dicebat ei, 'Cessa^a iam, maligne,^b de mea uirginitate. Ego Deum
habeo adiutorem, et ego Christiana sum. Ego ancilla Dei, ego sponsa
Christi, cuius nomen ⟨est⟩^c benedictum in saecula.'^79

15 Et cum haec diceret beata Margareta, subito lumen refulsit in
carcerem, et crucem Christi uidebat. Et columba sedebat super crucem, et
dicebat, 'Beata es Margareta. Te expectant portae^d paradisi.' Tunc gratias
agens Deo beata Margareta conuersa ad demonem dixit, 'Vnde es tu?
Enarra mihi.' Demon dixit, 'Deprecor te, famula sancta Christi, alleua
pedem tuam de ceruice mea ut requiescam modicum, et enarrabo tibi
omnia opera mea.' Tunc sancta puella eleuauit calcaneum suum de ceruice
eius et statim demon dixit, 'Vis scire quod est misterium nostrum?^80 Post
Beelzebub princeps fui, et ego contra omnem iustitiam pugnaui et
multorum iustorum labores extinxi, et nullus potuit me uincere. Tu^e
autem oculum meum eiecisti, uirtutem meum confregisti, Rufonem
fratrem meum occidisti. Et nunc facis de me quod tibi placet, quia uideo in
te Christum manentem. Sed antequam Christus in te maneret et non

---

^w draconis . . . utero] MAs: *om.* P   ^x tenuit] MAs: tenire P   ^y Cessa] Cesse P
^z orbsorberet] obsorboret P   ^a Cessa] Cesse P   ^b maligne] malignus P   ^c est] As:
om. P   ^d portae] portas P   ^e tu] tunc P

mouth of the dragon and split it into two parts. The blessed Margaret emerged from the stomach of the dragon without any injury. Then the blessed Margaret prostrated herself upon the ground. She prayed and said, 'I praise and glorify your name, my Lord God, King of kings and Lord of lords, holy Trinity. To you let there be honour, praise, glory and jubilation through infinite ages.'

14   It happened that, when the blessed Margaret had completed her prayer, she looked into the left side of the prison and, behold, she saw another devil sitting there in the form of a black man, with his hands fastened to his knees. He got up and began to make his way towards her and seized her hand. Margaret, however, said to the demon, 'Let what you have done be sufficient for you. Depart from me now. You have performed many evils.' The demon replied, 'Indeed, I sent my brother Rufo to you in the likeness of a dragon to swallow you up and to remove your memory from the earth. But you have slain him with the sign of the cross. Now do you wish to slay me also through your prayer?' Then the holy maiden Margaret seized the demon by the hair and smashed him to the ground. She placed her right foot on his neck and said to him, 'Abandon now, evil one, your attempts against my chastity. I have God as my helper, and I am a Christian. I am a handmaid of the Lord and a bride of Christ, whose name is blessed through the ages.'

15   And when the blessed Margaret was saying this, suddenly a light shone in the prison and a cross of Christ appeared. A dove was sitting upon the cross and it said, 'Blessed are you, Margaret. The gates of heaven await you.' Then giving thanks to God the blessed Margaret turned to the demon and said, 'Where do you come from? Tell me.' The demon said, 'I entreat you, holy servant of Christ, raise your foot from my neck, so that I may rest a little, and I will tell you all my works.' Then the holy girl raised her heel from his neck and immediately the demon said, 'Do you wish to know our secret knowledge? After Beelzebub I was made a leader, and I have combatted all justice and obliterated the efforts of many just people, and no one has been able to overcome me. You, however, have put out my eye, have broken my strength, and have killed my brother Rufo. And now you do with me what you please, for I see Christ dwelling within you. But

potuisti me uincere neque meas uirtutes superare. Sed cum signaculo crucis Christi ipsum Rufonem occidisti et me alligasti. Nunc autem narrabo tibi per singula opera mea. Ego sum qui multorum labores abstuli. Ego sum qui pugno[f] cum iustis et incendo[g] renes eorum et abceco oculos eorum et facio eos obliuiscere omnem caelestem sapientiam. Et cum dormierint uenio super eos et excito illos a somno ad mala opera, et quos non possum mouere de somno facio eos in somno peccare. Quacumque arte uentilo[h] quos sine signaculo crucis Christi inueni ⟨et⟩[i] contra eos pugnare atque eis nocere non cesso. Illos uero quos cum signaculo sancte crucis signatos[j] inuenio et qui[k] tibi sunt similes confusus et uacuus ab eis discedo quemadmodum a te hodie. O beata Margareta, quid dicam? Superatus[l] sum a te. Quid faciam ignoro. Arma mea confracta[m] sunt, uirtus mea confusa est, a tenera puella superatus[n] sum. Sed mihi magis dolet quia pater tuus et mater tua socii mei fuerunt, et ⟨modo tu surrexisti aduersus genus meum⟩[o][81] et me superasti. O quam mirandum est quia tenera puella superauit patrem et matrem et totam generationem suam et Christum secuta est![82] Ligat demones, fugat diabolum,[p] et aliquos[q] occidit. Vere uirtus nostra nihil ualet quia ⟨a⟩[r] parua puella superati sumus.'

16   Tunc sancta Margareta, uidens quod superabat daemonem, dixit ad eum, 'Enarra mihi, miser, genus tuum. Inique, quis te genuit, uel quis uobis precepit in sancta opera insidiari?' Respondit demon, 'Dic mihi, Margareta, unde est uita tua uel unde membra tua, aut quomodo Christus in te ingressus est? Et ego dicam tibi omnia opera mea.' Sancta Margareta respondit, 'Mihi non licet haec tibi nuntiare, quia non es dignus audire uocem meam. Gratia enim Dei sum id quod sum.' Tunc demon dixit, 'Satanas rex noster est, quia proiectus est de paradiso. Scruta et uide in libris tamen Iamme et Mambre genus nostrum.[83] Ego non[s] sum ausus loqui tibi, quia uideo Christum circa te ambulantem et contremisco. Nam uite nostre non sunt super terram sed cum uentis ambulemus. Sed peto,

---

[f] pugno] MAs: pugnaui P   [g] incendo] incendio P   [h] uentilo] AugPip: uentillo M: uentilabo As: uel uenticulo P   [i] et] MAs: *om.* P   [j] signatos] signatus P   [k] qui] que P   [l] superatus] *corrected in* P *from* superata   [m] confracta] confracte P   [n] superatus] *corrected in* P *from* superata   [o] modo . . . meum] As: tu ex [28r] aduerso pugnasti P   [p] diabolum] diabolus P   [q] aliquos] aliquas P   [r] a] MAs: *om.* P   [s] non] 'non' P *(inserted above line)*

before Christ dwelt within you, even you were not able to overcome me nor to conquer my powers. However, with the sign of the cross of Christ you have slain Rufo himself and have bound me. Now I will tell you about my works, one by one. I am he who has defeated the efforts of many people. I am he who fights with the just, enflames their passions, who blinds their eyes, and makes them forget all heavenly wisdom. When they are asleep I come upon them and rouse them from their sleep to wicked deeds, and those whom I am unable to move from their sleep I cause to sin in their sleep. By every possible device I fan the flames [of the passions] of those whom I find without the sign of the cross of Christ, and I do not cease from harming them. From those, however, whom I find sealed with the sign of the holy cross and who are like you, I depart confounded and unavailing, as from you today. O blessed Margaret, what am I to say? I have been defeated by you. What I am to do I do not know. My weapons have been broken, my power confounded; I have been been defeated by a tender girl. But it pains me more that your father and your mother were adherents of mine, while you alone have risen up against my race and have overcome me. O how remarkable it is that a tender girl has overcome her father and mother and her whole family and has followed Christ! This girl binds demons and puts the devil to flight, and even slays some. Truly our power is worth nothing, because we have been defeated by an insignificant girl.'

16   Then St Margaret, seeing that she was defeating the demon, said to him, 'Explain to me, wretched one, your lineage. Who begot you, wicked one, and who commanded you to lie in ambush against holy works?' The demon replied, 'Tell me, Margaret, whence comes your life, and whence your limbs, and how has Christ entered into you? And I will tell you all my works.' St Margaret replied, 'It is not permitted for me to inform you of these things, because you are not worthy to hear my voice. Thanks to God I am what I am.' Then the demon said, 'Satan is our king, who was expelled from paradise. Search and see our descent in the books of Jamnes and Mambres. I did not dare to speak to you, because I see Christ walking beside you and I am fearful. Our lives are not on the earth, but we travel

agna Christi, relaxa me modicum ut unum uerbum loquar tecum.' Et dixit iterum diabolus, 'Ecce adnuntio tibi omnia. Adiuro ergo te per Deum et per Iesum Christum filium eius in quem tu credis ne amplius damnes me, sed dirige me magis in manu terre, ut in diebus uite tue non pugnem cum iustis neque aduersum te. Nam et Salomon inclusit nos in uno uaso uitreo, sed nos in unam partem eiusdem uasis ignem mittebamus, et uenientes ⟨homines⟩ᵗ Babiloniae putauerunt aurum in ipso inuenire et fregeruntᵘ ipsud et tunc nos relaxati impleuimus orbem terrarum.' Sancta Margareta respondit, 'Demon inique, obmutesce et sile. Iam non audiamᵛ uerbum ex ore tuo.' Et consignauit eum in angulo carceris et dixit, 'Vade ex me, Satanas.'⁸⁴ Et statim degluttiuit eum terra.

17   Altera uero die iussit prefectus beatam Margaretam adducere ante tribunal suum. Sancta autem Margareta cum exiret de carcere consignauit corpus suum cum signaculo Christi. Tunc uenerunt cuncti de ciuitate ut uiderent que patiebatur beata Margareta. Praefectus dixit, 'Margareta, consente mihi et adhoraʷ deos meos. Decet namque te eos adorare.' Sancta Margareta respondit, 'Te decet, prefecte,ˣ Deum meum adorare et Iesum Christum Filium eius, Regem atque Saluatorem omnium seculorum, et amicumʸ esse prophetarum, si dignusᶻ esᵃ et si non esses amicus idolorum sudorum et mutorum.' Tunc prefectus iratus iussit eam expoliare et in aerem suspendi et cum lampadibus ardentibusᵇ incendi. Questionarii ita fecerunt et comburebant corpus eius tenerum. Ipsa uero orabat dicens, 'Vre renes meos, Domine, et cor meum,⁸⁵ ut in me non sit iniquitas.'⁸⁶ Iterum praefectus dixit, 'Adhuc, Margareta, consente mihi et sacrifica diis.' Sancta Margareta respondit, 'Non consentio nec adhoro deos tuos. Non enim poterit diabolus uincere castam puellam, quia Dominus meus Iesus Christus consignauit corpus meum et omnia membra mea cum signaculo *sancte crucis.'*

18   *Tunc prefectus iussit accipere uas magnum et implere aquam ac ligare manus et pedes beatissime Margarete et in ipsud uas mittere et ibi mortificare. Questionarii ita fecerunt sicut eis fuerat imperatum. Beata autem Margareta aspiciens in caelum dixit, 'Domine, qui regnas in aeternum, disrumpe uincula mea.*⁸⁷ *Tibi sacrificabo hostiam laudis.*⁸⁸

ᵗ homines] MAs: *om.* P   ᵘ fregerunt] frangerunt P   ᵛ audiam] *corrected in* P *from* audeam   ʷ adhora] adhoro P   ˣ prefecte] prefectus P   ʸ amicum] amicus P   ᶻ dignus] dignas P   ᵃ es] M: eras P   ᵇ ardentibus] ardentes P

with the winds. But I beg, lamb of Christ, release me a little, so that I may speak one word with you.' And the devil said again, 'Listen, I will tell you everything. I entreat you therefore through God and through Jesus Christ his Son, in whom you believe, not to condemn me further, but to direct me rather into the power of the earth, so that in the days of your life I may not fight against the just nor against you. For Solomon enclosed us in a glass vessel, but we sent fire into one part of this vessel, and the men of Babylon came and thought they discovered gold in it and broke it, and then we were freed and filled the world.' St Margaret replied, 'Evil demon, stop talking and be silent. Now I will not hear a word from your mouth.' And she made the sign of the cross at him in the corner of the prison and said, 'Go from me, Satan.' And at once the earth swallowed him up.

17   The following day the prefect gave orders for the blessed Margaret to be brought before his seat of justice. When St Margaret emerged from the prison, however, she sealed her body with the sign of Christ. Then the population of the city came to see what sufferings the blessed Margaret was undergoing. The prefect said, 'Margaret, give in to me and worship my gods. For it is right for you to worship them.' St Margaret replied, 'It is right, prefect, for you to worship my God and his Son Jesus Christ, the King and Saviour of all ages, and to ally yourself to the prophets, if you are worthy and if you did not ally yourself to deaf and dumb idols.' Then angrily the prefect ordered her to be stripped and suspended in the air and burned with flaming torches. The torturers did so and burned her tender body. She, however, prayed, saying, 'Burn up my loins, Lord, and my heart, so that there may not be wickedness in me.' Again the prefect said, 'Give in to me yet, Margaret, and sacrifice to the gods.' St Margaret replied, 'I will not give in to you nor worship your gods. The devil will not be able to defeat a chaste girl, because my Lord Jesus Christ has sealed my body and all my limbs with the sign of the holy cross.'

18   Then the prefect gave orders that a great vessel should be brought and filled with water and that the hands and feet of the most blessed Margaret should be tied and she should be placed in this vessel and put to death there. The torturers did this as they had been commanded. The blessed Margaret, however, looked up to heaven and said, 'Lord, who

Fiatque mihi aqua ista sanctificatio et inluminatio salutis, et fiat mihi fons[89] indeficiens. Induet me Dominus galeam salutis,[90] ueniatque super me sancta columba Spiritu Sancto repleta et benedicat aquam istam ut abluat me omnia peccata mea et tunc firmat animam meam corpusque meum ac sensum meum et baptizat me in nomine Patris et Filii et Spiritus Sancti, quia ipse est benedictus in secula seculorum. Amen.' Ecce terremotus est in ipsa hora, et columba uenit de caelo portans coronam auream in ore suo, et sedit super beata Margareta. Tunc statim solute sunt manus eius et pedes et exiuit de aqua[c] conlaudans[d] ⟨et⟩[e] benedicens[f] Dominum, et dixit, 'Dominus regnauit, decorem induit. Induit Dominus fortitudinem et praecinxit se uirtute.'[g][91] Et ecce uox columbae[h] de caelo dicens, 'Veni, Margareta, in regnum caelorum et in requiem Christi. Beata es, qui coronam uite accepisti. Beata es, quia uirginitatem desiderasti.' In ipsa hora crediderunt in Dominum Iesum Christum uiri .v. milia exceptis mulieribus et puellis.

19 Tunc iniquus Olibrius iussit eos decollari, et decollati sunt in campo Limet in Armenia ciuitate. Et post paululum iussit beatam[i] Margaretam[j] gladio interfeci. Statimque conprehenderunt eam questionarii et duxerunt foras ciuitatis, et dixit ad eam unus ex illis nominatus Malchus, 'Extende ceruicem tuam et suscipe gladium, meique[k] miserere, quia uideo circa te Christum cum suis angelis stantem.' Sancta autem Margareta respondit, 'Peto, frater, si Christum uides ut parces mihi usque dum orationem facio et commendo animam meum Domino Iesu Christo.' Questionarius uero dixit[l] ad eam, 'Postula quod uis, et memor[m] esto mei.' Tunc beata Margareta cepit orare et dicere, 'Deus, qui celum palme mensurasti et terram fundamentum posuisti et non transiuit preceptum tuum,[92] exaudi, Domine, deprecationem meam, ut, si quis legerit librum istum geste mee uel audierit legere passionem meam, in ipsa hora deleantur peccata illius; et qui cum suo lumine uenerit ad ecclesiam ubi sunt reliquie mee, similiter deleantur peccata illius. Quisquis inuentus

---

[c] de aqua] 'de aqua' P *(inserted above line)*   [d] conlaudans] conlaudantes P   [e] et] MAs: *om.* P   [f] benedicens] benedicent P   [g] uirtute] uirtutem P   [h] columbae] columba P   [i] beatam] beata P   [j] Margaretam] Margareta P   [k] meique] meque P   [l] dixit] duxit P   [m] memor] memer P

reigns in eternity, break apart my fetters. I will offer up to you a sacrifice of praise. Let this water become for me a sanctification and the illumination of salvation, and let it become for me an everlasting fountain. May the Lord put the helmet of salvation on me, and may the holy dove, filled with the Holy Spirit, come upon me and bless this water, so that it may wash all my sins away from me and then strengthen my soul and body and mind and baptize me in the name of the Father and of the Son and of the Holy Spirit, because he is blessed for ever and ever. Amen.' Behold, there was an earthquake at that hour, and the dove came from heaven bearing a golden crown in its mouth, and it rested upon the blessed Margaret. Then immediately her hands and feet were freed and she emerged from the water praising and blessing the Lord. And she said, 'The Lord reigns; he has clothed himself with glory. The Lord has put on strength and has girded himself with power.' And, behold, the voice of the dove came from heaven, saying, 'Come, Margaret, into the kingdom of the heavens and into the repose of Christ. Blessed are you, who have received the crown of life. Blessed are you, who desired chastity.' At that time five thousand men came to believe in the Lord Jesus Christ, not counting women and girls.

19   Then the evil Olibrius ordered them to be beheaded, and they were beheaded at the field of Limet in the city of Armenia. And a short while later he ordered the blessed Margaret to be put to death by the sword. Immediately the torturers seized her and led her outside the city. Then one of them, whose name was Malchus, said to her, 'Stretch out your neck and receive the sword, and have pity on me, because I see Christ with his angels standing beside you.' St Margaret replied, 'I ask, brother, if you see Christ, that you spare me until I say a prayer and commend my soul to the Lord Jesus Christ.' The torturer said to her, 'Ask what you wish, and be mindful of me.' Then the blessed Margaret began to pray and say, 'God, who have measured heaven in your palm and who have set the earth as your foundation and it has not exceeded your precept, listen favourably, Lord, to my entreaty, that, if anyone reads this book of my deeds or hears my passion read, at that hour may that person's sins be blotted out; and whoever comes with his light to the church where my relics are, likewise

fuerit in iudicio terribili et memor fuerit nominis mei, libera eum de tormentis. Adhuc peto, Domine, qui legerit aut qui tulerit in manu sua, uel qui audierit eam legendo, ex illa hora deleantur peccata illius. Adhuc peto, Domine, et qui basilicam in nomine meo fecerit, uel qui de suo labore comparauit codicem passionis mee, reple illum Spiritu[n] Sancto[o] tuo,[p] spiritu[q] ueritatis, et in domo illius non nascatur infans claudus aut cecus neque mutus.'

20 Postquam autem beata Margareta compleuit orationem suam, factum est tonitruum[r] magnum, et columba uenit de caelo cum sancta cruce, et loquebatur dicens, 'Beata es, Margareta, qui uicisti mundum[93] et quesisti oleum sanctum.[94] Beata es inter mulieres,[95] quia in orationibus tuis omnes memorasti.' Audiens autem haec, beata Margareta cecidit in faciem suam super terram et omnes qui ibidem aderant, et columba tetigit eam et dixit,[96] 'Per memetipsum iuro et per gloriam meam, quicquid in oratione tua petisti, exaudite sunt ⟨deprecationes tuae⟩,[s] et quod non recordasti, tibi datum est. Beata es tu, qui in penis tuis memorasti omnes peccatores. Sed ubi ⟨fuerint⟩[t] reliquie tue aut codex[u] passionis[v] tue seu memorie nominis tui et ueniens peccator in illum locum orans cum lacrimis et memoriam nominis tui fecerit, sine dubio remissionem peccatorum[w] ⟨inueniet. Et beata es tu et locus ubi requiescis. Beata es tu et omnis generatio qui crediderit per te. Veni celerius[x] in locum tibi preparatum. Ego tecum sum, et aperiam tibi regiam regni celestem.'[y]

21 Tunc beata Margarita respexit in circuitum et dixit, 'Patres et matres et sorores et fratres, omnes uos adiuro per nomen magnum Regis omnium seculorum, memoriam meam facite, nomen meum nominate, et commendate me. Et si ego peccatrix sum, adtamen obsecro pro uobis Dominum Iesum Christum ut donet uobis remissionem peccatorum et faciat uos[z] heredes in regno gloriae suae et inluminet uos in regno claritatis suae. Deo enim gratias ago, Regi omnium seculorum, qui dignam me faciat in sortem seculorum introire. Hymnum dico Domino. Laudo et glorifico Deum,[97] quia Deus benedictus es in secula seculorum.'

---

[n] Spiritu] spiritum P   [o] Sancto] sanctum P   [p] tuo] tuum P   [q] spiritu] spiritum P
[r] tonitruum] tonitrium P   [s] deprecationes tuae] MAs: *om.* P   [t] fuerint] MAs: *om.* P
[u] codex] codes P   [v] passionis] passiones P   [w] A substantial lacuna in P *occurs at this point, coinciding with the end of 31v: edited text is supplied from* O, *19v–20r*   [x] celerius] celerii
P   [y] celestem] celestum O   [z] uos] uobis O

may his sins be blotted out. Whoever is found at the terrible judgement and is mindful of my name, deliver him from torments. I ask besides, Lord, whoever reads it [i.e. the passion] or carries it in his hand or hears it read, from that hour may his sins be blotted out. I also ask, Lord, whoever builds a basilica in my name or from his labour furnishes a manuscript of my passion, fill him with your Holy Spirit, the spirit of truth, and in his home let there not be born an infant lame or blind or dumb.'

20   After the blessed Margaret finished her prayer, a great sound of thunder was heard, and a dove came from heaven with the holy cross, and it spoke, saying, 'Blessed are you, Margaret, who have defeated the world and have sought the holy oil. Blessed are you among women, because you have remembered all people in your prayers.' Hearing this, the blessed Margaret fell on her face on the ground, as did all those who were present there, and the dove touched her and said, 'By my very self I swear and by my glory, whatever you have asked in your prayer, your entreaties have been heeded, and whatever you have not thought of has been granted to you. Blessed are you, who in your torments have remembered all sinners. But where your relics are, or a book of your passion, or memorials of your name, when a sinner comes and prays tearfully in that place and recalls your name, without doubt he will find remission of his sins. And blessed are you and the place where you repose. Blessed are you and every generation which believes through you. Come quickly to the place prepared for you. I am with you, and I will open for you the palace of the heavenly kingdom.'

21   Then the blessed Margaret looked around her and said, 'Fathers and mothers and sisters and brothers, I adjure you through the great name of the King of all ages, make recollection of me, call my name and venerate me. Even if I am a sinner I will nonetheless pray for you to the Lord Jesus Christ that he may give you remission of your sins and make you heirs in the kingdom of his glory and may fill you with light in the kingdom of his brightness. For I give thanks to the Lord, the King of all ages, who has made me worthy to enter into the share of eternity. I utter a hymn to the Lord. I praise and glorify God, because you, God, are blessed for ever and ever.'

22   Et post orationem erexit se et dixit, 'Frater tolle nunc[a] gladium tuum et percute me. Ecce iam uici mundum.'[98] Ille et dixit, 'Ego non facio neque interficiam sanctam uirginem Dei. Deus autem tibi locutus est. Propterea te non possum interficere.' Beata Margarita respondit, 'Si hoc non feceris, non habebis[b] partem mecum in paradiso Dei.' Tunc questionarius cum Dei timore adtulit gladium suum et in icto uno percutiens amputauit capud beatissimae Margaritae, et orauit dicens, 'Domine, ne statuas ⟨hoc⟩[c] mihi in peccatum.'[99] Et tremens percussor cecidit cum percussorio suo ad dexteram partem beate Margaritae. Tunc uenerunt angeli et sedentes super corpus beatae Margaritae benedixerunt illud.[d] Et ueniebant demones et torquebantur et uocibus clamabant, 'Vnus Deus fortis magnus[100] beatae Margaritae.'

23   Et audientes omnes infirmi, ceci, claudi, surdi, debiles, impotentes[e] omnes ueniebant et tangebant corpus beatae Margaritae, et omnes salui fiebant. Tunc descendentes angeli cum uirtutibus tollentes corpus beatae Margaritae in gremio suo ascenderunt super nubem, clamantes et dicentes, 'Non est similis tui in diis, Domine, et non est secundum opera tua.[101] Sanctus, sanctus, sanctus, Dominus Deus Sabaoth.[102] Pleni sunt caeli et terra gloria tua. Osanna in excelsis.[103] Benedictus qui uenit in nomine Domini,[104] Rex Israel.' Et uenientes daemones ad reliquias beatae Margaritae torquebantur. Infirmi ueniebant, saluabantur a languoribus suis et credebant.

24   Ego enim Theothimus tuli reliquias beatae Margaritae et reposui eas in scrinio quod feci de lapide cum odore[f] suauitatis, et posui eas in Antiochia ciuitate in domo Sinclitice[g] matronae. Ego enim eram qui ministrabam ei in carcere[h] panem et aquam, et ego consideraui omne[i] certamen quod habuit contra impios bellatores, et omnes orationes scripsi in libris cartaneis[j] cum multa astutia, et transmisi[k] omnibus ubicumque[l] Christianis omnia in ueritate. Compleuit autem beata Margarita certamen suum in pace mense Iulio die[m] tertia decima.[105] Omnes audite,⟩[n] corde

---

[a] nunc] h *written above* n *in* O   [b] habebis] habeˈbiˈs O (bi *added above*)   [c] hoc] MAs: *om.* O   [d] illud] M: eum O   [e] impotentes] imponentes O   [f] odore] odorem O   [g] Sinclitice] Sinclitace O, *with* i *written above* a   [h] carcere] carcerem O, *with* m *underlined*   [i] omne] omnem O   [j] cartaneis] cartineis O, *with* a *written above first* i   [k] transmisi] transmissi O   [l] ubicumque] A: unicuique O   [m] die] indictione P   [n] P *resumes at beginning of 32r*

22   And after her prayer she raised herself up and said, 'Brother, take up your sword now and strike me. Behold, I have defeated the world.' He said, 'I will not do this, nor will I kill a holy virgin of God. God has spoken to you. For this reason I cannot kill you.' The blessed Margaret replied, 'If you do not do this you will not have your share with me in the paradise of God.' Then the executioner with fear of God drew his sword and he struck with one blow and beheaded the most blessed Margaret. Then he prayed, saying 'Lord, do not reckon this against me as a sin.' And trembling the executioner fell with his sword on the right side of the blessed Margaret. Then angels came and rested upon the body of the blessed Margaret and blessed it; and demons came and were tormented, exclaiming with their voices, 'There is one powerful God, the great God of the blessed Margaret.'

23   When they heard this all the sick, blind, lame, deaf, weak and feeble came and touched the body of the blessed Margaret, and they all became well. The angels came down with their powers and taking up the body of the blessed Margaret in their embrace they ascended above the clouds, exclaiming and saying, 'There is none like you among the gods, Lord, and there is nothing to compare with your works. Holy, holy, holy, Lord God of hosts. Heaven and earth are full of your glory. Hosanna in the highest. Blessed is he who comes in the name of the Lord, the King of Israel.' And demons came to the relics of the blessed Margaret and were tormented. The sick came and they were healed from their infirmities and believed.

24   I Theotimus took the relics of the blessed Margaret and put them in a reliquary which I made from stone with a scent of sweetness. I placed them in the city of Antioch in the house of the noble lady Sinclitica. I am he who ministered to her in the prison with bread and water, and I have reflected upon the whole struggle which she had against her wicked adversaries; and I have written all her prayers in the pages of books with great diligence and passed these things all on in truth to all Christians everywhere. The blessed Margaret completed her struggle in peace on the thirteenth day of July.

conpungite,[106] Deum adorate in una Trinitate. Memoriam beatissime Margarete facite, ut ipsam memorare omnibus nobis dignetur ante tribunal Domini nostri Iesu Christi, cui est ⟨cum⟩° aeterno Patre et Spiritu Sancto honor, laus et gloria ac potestas in^P infinita secula seculorum. Amen. Explicit.

° cum} M: *om.* P   ^P in} M: cum P

All hear and have compunction in your heart; worship God in the United Trinity. Recall the memory of the most blessed Margaret, that she may deign to remember all of us before the judgement seat of our Lord Jesus Christ, to whom there is with the eternal Father and the Holy Spirit honour, praise, glory and power through the infinite ages of eternity. Amen.

[1] Among early copies of *BHL* no. 5303, the only other manuscripts having this reference to the Passion are Aug and Os. This reference is also absent from the Us, Cas and Turin versions. It is, however, reflected in the OE, in both Tib and CCCC.

[2] Supplied from M to provide an accusative to accompany *gloriosae ascensionis*. Most other manuscripts of *BHL* no. 5303 have instead *gloriosam ascensionem* (as does Cas), but Saint-Omer 257 agrees with the deficient reading in P.

[3] After *passi sunt* most manuscripts omit *apud Deum* and have instead *et apostoli coronati sunt et innumerabiles sanctificati sunt* (so too Cas). P follows imperfectly a reading similar to that reflected in the thirteenth-century manuscript, London, BL, Add. 34633: *Multi passi sunt martirio et coronati sunt apud Deum.*

[4] Cf. John XVI. 33 and I John V. 5.

[5] Cf. Ps. CXIII. 12 and 13–14.

[6] The original reading here is *caecos* (as in MAs), following Ps. CXLV. 8.

[7] Mark VII. 37.

[8] II Cor. I. 9; Acts XXVI. 8.

[9] I Cor. I. 21; cf. Ps. XVI. 7.

[10] Cf. John XVI. 33 and I John V. 5.

[11] Cf. Matt. XI. 15, XIII. 9, Mark IV. 23, VII. 16 and Apoc. II. 7. The collocation of *corde* and *intelligite* suggests recollection of Acts XXVIII. 27, implying, however, a different original phrasal division in the sentence. Cf. also Matt. XV. 10 and Mark VII. 14.

[12] Like M, P omits the reference to Thecla and Susanna. The regular reading appears in As: *ut accipiatis requiem sempiternam cum beata Thecla et sancta Susanna.* M has *ut accipiatis salutem et coronam sanctis repromissam.* The reference to Thecla and Susanna also appears in Cas. There is no mention of Thecla and Susanna in CCCC, but most of ch. 2 has been cut in this version and so it is impossible to draw conclusions about the exact source of the OE at this point.

[13] Cf. Deut. IV. 40.

[14] Ps. LVI. 2.

[15] Ps. XXV. 9.

[16] Cf. Ps. CXLIV. 21.

[17] Cf. Ecclus. XL. 5.

[18] Matt. X. 16.

[19] Cf. Ps. CI. 8.

[20] Eccles. IX. 12.

[21] Most manuscripts either agree with P in reading *capra* 'she-goat' or omit the reference altogether. The original reading would have been *caprea* 'doe', reflecting Ecclus. XI. 32 (*ut caprea in laqueum*). There is considerable variation between Latin manuscripts in this list of comparisons.

[22] Ps. LXIX. 6; CVIII. 26.

[23] Ps. VI. 3.

[24] Ps. XXXVII. 22; cf. XXXVI. 33.

[25] Ps. IX. 8.

[26] Cf. Deut. IV. 40.

[27] Ps. CXVIII. 30; Tob. I. 2; Ecclus. XXXIV. 22.

[28] Cf. II Kings XXII. 8 and Ps. XVII. 8.

[29] Cf. Ps. IX. 8.

[30] The original reading was clearly *dispergam*, an allusion to Ps. XXI. 15 (*Et dispersa sunt omnia ossa mea*). CCCC *tosindrian* follows *dispergam*.

[31] Cf. Deut. IV. 40.

[32] Ps. XXII. 2.

[33] Ps. XXIV. 3.

[34] Ps. XXIV. 3.

[35] Cf. Ps. CXII. 2.

[36] Ps. LXXXV. 16.

[37] Ps. XXX. 16.

[38] Cf. II Mac. VII. 29.

[39] Cf. Isaiah VII. 4 and XIV. 27.

[40] Cf. Gen. XXVII. 28.

[41] Cf. Ecclus. XXXVIII. 7.

[42] John XVI. 20.

[43] Cf. Exod. XVII. 14.

[44] Cf. Ps. LXI. 7 and CXVII. 6.

[45] Cf. Exod. XX. 5 and Ps. XX. 2.

[46] Cf. Matt. VII. 7 and Luke XI. 9.

[47] After *opera* all other manuscripts add *patris tui*, reflected in CCCC *þines fæðeres*. *Patris tui* also appears in Cas and in the Turin version.

[48] Cf. Ps. LXI. 7 and CXVII. 6.

[49] Cf. Ps. XXI. 21 and LXXXVIII. 49.

[50] Cf. Ps. VII. 3 and XXI. 22.

[51] Ps. XXI. 17.

[52] Ps. XXXIV. 2.

[53] Ps. XXI. 21 and XXX. 6.

[54] Ps. XXI. 22.

[55] Deut. XXXII. 42.

[56] Original reading *dispergam*; see also above, n. 30. CCCC has neither image, abbreviating at this point.

[57] Cf. Ps. XXI. 18.

[58] Cf. Ps. XXXII. 8.

[59] Cf. Ps. CXLI. 6.

[60] Ps. LXVII. 6.

61 Ps. VII. 12.

62 Ps. LXXXV. 16.

63 Ps. XXXVII. 22.

64 Ps. VII. 12.

65 Cf. Ps. XC. 9.

66 The usual reading here is *Theotimus*, reflected also in Cas and in the Turin version. As noted in the apparatus criticus, however, a number of manuscripts of *BHL* no. 5303 departs from this reading. CCCC mentions that Margaret's fosterfather came but does not give his name. This suggests that the OE translator was using a source with an irregular reading at this point, having *continuit* or one of the other variants. The suffix of *continuit* is probably influenced by that of the adjacent *apparuit*.

67 The P form *scribantur* is the last in a series of corruptions at the beginning of ch. 12. At this point M is among the most coherent witnesses, apart from beginning with *Contimus* instead of *Theotimus*: *Contimus autem erat in carcere et nutrix eius, ministrantes ei panem et aquam, et aspiciebant per fenestram et orationem eius scribebant et omnia quae ei eueniebant cum timore Dei notabant.*

68 Instead of *flamma ignis* most manuscripts of *BHL* no. 5303, including MAs (also Cas and the Turin version) have *margaritae*, but CCCC *fyres lyg* corresponds to the P reading. *Flamma ignis* also occurs in BL, Add. 34633, while Add. 10050 has *oculi eius sicut ignis*.

69 Cf. Ps. XXXII. 6 and CXXXV. 6.

70 Cf. Job XXXVIII. 4 and Prov. VIII. 29.

71 Cf. Prov. VIII. 29.

72 Ps. LXXXV. 16.

73 The omission is apparently due to the haplography of *draconis*.

74 Ps. LXXXV. 9 and 12.

75 I Tim. VI. 15; cf. Deut. X. 17.

76 P omits a substantial part of this speech as it appears in MAs and other variants. At this point CCCC appears to follow an abbreviated text.

77 Ps. XXXIII. 17; cf. Ps. CVIII. 15.

78 Cf. Gen. III. 15.

79 Ps. CXII. 2.

80 P is corrupt at this point. In M the speech begins *Beelzes cognomen est mihi post Beelzebub*; As has *Bel cognomen est mihi post Beelzebub*. That these readings reflect the original form of *BHL* no. 5303 is suggested by the parallel in the Turin version (*belzel cognominor nepos beelzebub*) and by the appearance of close variants in most manuscripts of *BHL* no. 5303. There is, however, some variation among manuscripts of *BHL* no. 5303. Similar to P is N, *Vis scire quod nomen est mihi? Post Behelzebu . . .*; O has *Viszes cognomen est mihi post beelzebub*. CCCC's apparent recasting of the passage and its avoidance of the proper names

Bel and *Beelzebub* may indicate that the translator was working from a corrupt source.

81 P, *tu ex aduerso pugnasti*, is corrupt here. The emended reading, from As, is closely reflected in most other manuscripts, though M has the eccentric *modo ista aduersus genus meum surrexit*.

82 Cf. Matt. X. 37–8 and Mark X. 29–30.

83 On the Book of Jamnes and Mambres, see above, p. 178.

84 Matt. XVI. 23; Mark VIII. 33.

85 Ps. XXV. 2.

86 Ps. XVI. 3.

87 Ps. CVI. 14; cf. Nahum I. 13.

88 Ps. CXV. 17.

89 After *fons* most manuscripts have *baptismati* (M) or *baptismi* (As), reflected in CCCC *fulluhtes bæðe*.

90 Ephes. VI. 17; I Thes. V. 8.

91 Ps. XCII. 1.

92 Job XXIV. 8; cf. Prov. VIII. 29.

93 Cf. John XVI. 33 and I John V. 5.

94 Ps. LXXXVIII. 21.

95 Luke I. 28.

96 In MAs, as in CCCC, Margaret and the bystanders fall to the ground before the dove begins its speech.

97 Cf. Dan. IV. 34.

98 Cf. John XVI. 33.

99 Cf. Acts VII. 59 (at the execution of the Protomartyr Stephen).

100 Cf. Exod. XX. 5.

101 Ps. LXXXV. 8.

102 Jer. XI. 20.

103 Mark XI. 10.

104 Ps. CXVII. 26; Matt. XXI. 9.

105 The P reading *indictione tertia decima* is also reflected in As, *in dictione tertio decimo*. M has *Compleuit autem beata Margarita certamen suum in pace die quinto mense Iulio*. Note also Pip . . . *die quinto decimo*; so too Aug. The Turin version has *xiiii kalendas Iulii* (THRm) or *xiii die Iulii* (Vr).

106 Acts II. 37; cf. Ps. CVIII. 17 and Mark XVII. 14.

The Latin 'Casinensis' version of the legend

The 'Casinensis' version of the legend of St Margaret is so significant a witness to the transmission of the legend in the West and, in particular, is so important for comparison with the Old English Tiberius and *Old English Martyrology* versions, that we have thought it desirable to include the complete text. The following text is based directly on that printed by the Benedictines of Monte Cassino in their compilation *Bibliotheca Casinensis*, from the eleventh-century manuscript Monte Cassino 52 (see above, pp. 13–16). We have departed from the *Bibliotheca Casinensis* editors in emending the many obvious solecisms in the Latin text, though we have allowed readings which are odd, but arguably comprehensible, to stand. Emendations of the *Bibliotheca Casinensis* edition are noted in the apparatus criticus. Chapter divisions, based on those used for the other texts of the Margaret legend edited in this book, have been introduced, and modern punctuation replaces the manuscript punctuation reproduced in the original printed edition. The numbers in the margin, with accompanying solidi in the text, refer to the page and column breaks in the *Bibliotheca Casinensis* edition.

PASSIO BEATE MARINE VIRGINIS ET MARTYRIS

1 Incipit passio sanctae Marine martyris,[a] quae[b] per orationem suam diabolum effugauit. Post resurrectionem Domini nostri Iesu Christi et gloriosam ascensionem eius in caelos[c] ad Patrem omnipotentem, in illius nomine multi martyres passi sunt et apostoli coronati sunt et innumerabiles sanctificati sunt in nomine Domini Iesu Christi Saluatoris nostri, et

[a] martyris] martyre   [b] quae] qui   [c] caelos] caelis

uicerunt hunc mundum et superauerunt tyrannos carnifices. Adhuc[d] tamen obtinebat insania hominum diaboli rabiem: idola surda et muta et ceca et a manibus hominum facta adorabant, qui nec illis proderant neque alio.

2 Ego autem in nomine Christi credens, Theotimus nomine, posui me omnem scripturam perlegere, et non inueni neminem in quo oportet credere nisi in nomine[e] Domini Iesu Christi, qui cecos illuminat, surdos audire facit, mortuos suscitat, martyres coronat et omnes in se credentes saluat. Ego et Theotimus[f] omnia caute agnoui quomodo pugnauit beatissima Marina contra demonem tyrannum et uicit in hunc mundum. Omnes aures habentes audite, et corde intellegite; uiri et uirgines, proponite uos uelud qui in ista noua puella lectiones legentes, ita laborantes in agone, ut mereatis requiem dignitatis habere cum beata Tecla et beatissima Susanna, etiam et cum beatissima Marina.

3 Erat Theodosii filia, qui erat gentilium patriarcha[g] et idolis seruiebat. Mox ut nata est, statim data est ad nutriendum in quamdam[h] ciuitatem habentem stadio quindecim ab Antiochia; que nutrita est ibi. | p. 3, col. ii Post multum uero temporis mortua est mater beatissime Marine, quae desiderio tenebatur a sua nutricula, quia uero speciosa erat et Christum cotidie inuocabat. Nam odiosa erat a sua patre,[i] dilecta namque a Domino Iesu Christo.

4 Erat autem annorum quindecim et delectabatur in domibus nutricis suae. Audiebat enim omnium martyrum certamina, et plurima sanguina sanctorum effundebantur[j] in illis temporibus pro nomine Iesu Christi Saluatoris nostri. Sancta uero Marina, repleta Spiritu Sancto, totam se tradidit Deo, qui et uirginitatem eius immaculatam conseruauit.

5 Nam et ipsa pascebat oues nutricis suae cum ceteris puellis coetanis suis.[k] Cumque Olibrius prefectus ueniret de Asia in Antiochiam[l] ciuitatem ad perquirendum, sic ubi Christianos inueniret,[m] statim eos ferreis nexibus constringeret. Et uidit beatam Marinam[n] iuxta uiam oues pascentem, quam[o] statim concupiuit.[p] Dixitque ministris suis, 'Ite festinanter: comprehendite eam, et interrogate eam. Si libera est, accipio eam in uxorem; si autem ancilla est, dabo pretium pro ea, et bene erit ei in domo mea, propter quod placuit in oculis meis.' Et exierunt milites ut et eis

[d] Adhuc] ad hoc   [e] nomine] nominae   [f] Theotimus] Timotheum   [g] patriarcha] patriarchae   [h] quamdam] quadam   [i] patre] matre   [j] effundebantur] effundebatur   [k] suis] suae   [l] Antiochiam] Antiochia   [m] inueniret] inuenirent   [n] beatam Marinam] beata Marina   [o] quam] quem   [p] concupiuit] concupiuit eam

iussum fuerat, conprehendere eam. Tunc cepit beata Marina uocibus orare dicens, 'Miserere mei, Domine, miserere mei, et ne perdas cum impiis animam meam^q nec cum uiris sanguinum uitam meam.^r Fac me semper te, Christe, conlaudare. Ne permittas animam meam^s contaminari, et ne polluatur fides mea. Non inquinetur corpus meum, et non inmutetur | scientia mea. Non eiciatur margarita mea in luto. Non inmutetur sensus meus^t a turpitudine iniquia. Sed transmitte mihi a dextera et sinistra angelos gubernatores, angelos pacis, ad aperiendos sensus meos^u et faucis meas,^v ad respondendum cum fiducia^w impio iniquio prefecto. Video me,^x Domine, ut oues in medio luporum; ecce facta sum sicut caprea in rite. Adiuua me, Domine, et salua me. Ne me derelinquas in manus impiorum.'

6   Venerunt milites ad prefectum et dixerunt ei, 'Non est ista puella que colit deos nostros, sed Deum adorat et Christum precatur, quem Iudaei crucifixerunt.' Olibrius uero inmutauit uultum faciei^y suae, et iussit eam uocari ante se, et dixit ei, 'De quo genere es tu? Narra mihi, libera es aut ancilla?' Beata Marina respondit, 'Libera sum. Ego credo, prefecte, et Christiana sum.' Prefectus dixit, 'Quo nomine uocaris?' Dixitque, 'In nomine Domini Marina uocor.' Prefectus dixit, 'Quem deum colis uel quem adoras?' Beata Marina^z dixit, 'Inuoco Deum omnipotentem et eius filium Iesum Christum, qui mea uirginitate usque in nunc conseruare dignatus est.' Prefectus dixit, 'Ergo inuocas nomen Christi, quem patres mei crucifixerunt.' Beata Marina respondit, 'Patres tui Christum crucifixerunt, ideo perierunt. Ipse autem permanet in aeternum, et regni eius non erit finis.' Tunc iratus prefectus iussit beatam Marinam^a in carcerem recludi, donec inueniret per quali machinamenta eius inpedire uirginitatem,^b cumque ingressus fuisset iniquissimus prefectus in Antiochiam ciuitatem et adorauit idola surda et muta secundum consuetudinem fidei.^c

7   Alia die sedens in tribunali iussit adduci puellam in conspectu suo. Cumque uidisset pulchritudinem eius, dixit ad eam, 'Noua puella, misereor ego infantiae tuae et pulchritudinis^d tuae. Consenti mihi et adora deos meos, et plurimas pecunias tibi dabo.' Dei famula Marina respondit, 'Cognoscit Deus, qui meum uirginitatem consignauit, quia non me

^q animam meam] anima mea   ^r uitam meam] uita mea   ^s animam meam] anima mea
^t meus] meum   ^u meos] meus   ^v meas] meae   ^w fiducia] fiduciam   ^x me] mae
^y faciei] faciae   ^z Beata Marina] Marina beata   ^a beatam Marinam] beata Marina
^b uirginitatem] uirginitatis   ^c fidei] fidem   ^d pulchritudinis] pulchritudini

suadebis nec mouebis de uia ueritatis quam ab infantia^e ambulaui. Ego illum adoro, cui tremit terra, mare formidat, cui obediunt uenti et omnis^f creatura, cuius regnum in saecula permanet. Amen.' Prefectus dixit, 'Si non adoras deos meos, gladius meus dominabitur in carne^g tua, et ossa tua dispartire facio super ignem candentem. Nam si obedieris michi et adoraueris deos meos, accipio te^h mihi in coniugem.' Beata Marina respondit, 'Ego trado corpus | meum in tormenta ut cum iustis uirginibus   p. 4, col. ii requiescam. Nam Christus pro nobis semetipsum tradidit in mortem, et ego pro ipsum non dubitabo mori, quia ipse suo signaculo sibimet consignauit.'

8   Tunc iussit Olibrius questionariis suis in aere eam suspendi et uirgis subtilibus caedi. Beata uirgo Christi Marina aspiciens in caelum dixit, 'In te, Domine, speraui. Non confundar in aeternum. Confundantur omnes inimici mei; qui autem in te confidunt, Domine, non confundantur, quia nomen tuum est benedictum in saecula. Respice in me et miserere mei, et libera me de manu impiorum, etiam et de manu carnificis, ne forte percussumⁱ formidet cor meum in seductionem. Mitte mihi angelum sanctum tuum, ut dolor et plage iste ueniant^j mihi, Domine, in gaudium.'

9   Illa Dei uirgo orabat; questionarii^k eam cedebant, et sanguis eius decurrebat tamquam aqua de fonte mundissima. Precor autem clamabat, 'Crede, Marina, et uiuis, et bene tibi erit.' Multitudo autem circumstantium flebat super eam amarissime, dicentes, 'O Marina, dolemus de te, quia uidimus te nudo corpore laniari. O qualem decorem perdis propter incredulitatem tuam. Iste prefectus est uir iracundus, et perdere te festinant. Sacrifica diis, et uiuis.' Beata Marina dixit, 'O mali consiliarii, ite uiri et mulieres in opera uestra. Michi autem adiutor est, uos autem non boni consiliarii. Quid putatis? Si corpus meum exterminetur, et anima mea cum iustis uirginibus requiescat. Per ista tormenta multorum animae salue inueniuntur. Credite^l uos in Deum meum Iesum Christum, qui fortis et uerus est in uirtute sua, et bene petentes se exaudit et postulantibus aperiat portas^m paradisi. Nam et ego non obedio uobis nec sacrifico diis uestris surdis etiam et mutis, cecis et a manibus hominum factis.'

10   Et ait, 'Prefecte, tu facis opera patris tui Sathane, inpudens et audax et canis Michi autem adest Deus meus atque adiutor meus. Nam si

---

^e infantia] infantiam   ^f omnis] omni   ^g carne] carnae   ^h te] tae   ⁱ percussum] percussa   ^j ueniant] ueniat   ^k questionarii] questionariis   ^l Credite] Creditae   ^m portas] orta

corpus meum habes[n] in tua potestate, anima mea Christus eruat de manu tua. Miser, orribilis et insatiabilis draco profundi[o] Tartari, fornax insatiabilis, abominatus a Deo, confusus a Christo, cuius tua uirtus in profundum damnet. Meus autem Deus magnus est,[p] qui uiuit[q] et regnat in saecula seculorum. Amen.' Prefectus uero iratus iussit eam suspendi et cum

p. 5, col. i ceruarum unguibus carnem[r] eius disrupit. Beata autem Marina | aspiciens in caelum dicebat, 'Circumdederunt me canes multi, concilium malignantium obsedit me. Tu autem, Domine, ad adiuuandum[s] me festina, et erue de framea animam meam[t] et de manu canis unicam meam. Libera me de ore leonis et de cornibus unicornuorum uirginitatem meam. Conforta me, Christe, et da mihi spiritum uitae, ut penetret oratio mea septem caelos sed ascendat in tuo conspectu. Transmitte columbam[u] de caelo, qui ueniat michi in adiutorium, ut inmaculatam[v] tibi obseruet uirginitatem meam, ut certet cum aduersario meo, et faciem[w] ad faciem uideam inimicum meum, qui mecum inliciter pugnat; at uincam eum, ut det fiduciam omnibus in te confitentibus, quia tu es Deus benedictus in saecula. Amen.' Carnifices uero non cessabat beatum corpus laniare. Nam impius prefectus cum clamide suo faciem suam cooperiebat. Similiter et alii faciebant, quia non poterant respicere pro sanguinis effusionem.[x] Dixit ad eam prefectus, 'Quare non audis iussa principum, Marina, neque tibimet ipsa miserta es? Consenti mihi et adora deos meos, ne male moriaris. Si autem non me audieris, gladius meus dominabitur in carnem tuam, et ossa tua et neruos tuos dispartio.' Beata Marina respondit, 'O inique, inpudens, miser, anima mea utique in interitum uadit sicut et tua. Sed ideo carnem meam[y] tradidi in tormento, ut anima mea in caelis coronata deducatur.'

11   Tunc prefectus iussit ministris ut eam in carcerem recluderunt. Erat autem hora septima. Cumque introisset[z] carcerem tenebrosum, consignauit totum corpus suum signaculo[a] Christi, et cepit orare et hec dicere: 'Deus, qui iudicium sapientiae decreuisti, quem contremescent omnia secula et inhabitantes, quem expauescent omnes potestates,[b] desperatorum spes, pater orphanorum et iudex uerus, lumen de lumine, respice in me, quia sola sum et unica terreni patris, et ipse me dereliquid.

---

[n] habes] habens   [o] profundi] profundus   [p] est] es   [q] uiuit] uiuis   [r] carnem] carnis
[s] adiuuandum] aiuuandum   [t] animam meam] anima mea   [u] columbam] columba
[v] inmaculatam] inmaculata quod   [w] et faciem] faciaem   [x] effusionem] effusionis
[y] carnem meam] carne mea   [z] introisset] introissent   [a] signaculo] signaculum
[b] potestates] potestas

Ne tu me non derelinquas, Domine Deus meus. Aspice in me et miserere mei. Precipe, Domine, ut uideam aduersarium meum, qui aduersatur michi, ut loquar cum eo^c et uincam eum, quia tu es iudex uiuorum et mortuorum. Tu, omnipotens Deus noster, iudica inter me et diabolum. Ecce enim in plagas meas ingemisco. Noli michi irasci, Domine meus, nec^d commisceatur sensus meus | cum impiis idolis surdis et mutis, quoniam tu es, Christe, spes mea, et tu es benedictus in secula.'   p. 5, col. ii

12   Theothimus autem et nutrix eius erant in carcerem cum pane et aqua, et aspiciebant intus per fenestram et orationes ascultabant. Et ecce subito de angulo^e carceris exiuit draco orribilis totus coloribus deauratus.^f Capilli eius et barbae eius uidebantur;^g dentes eius ut ferreae similes erant^h serre. Oculi eius uelut margaritae splendebant. De naribus eius ignis et fumus exiebat. Lingua illius anelabat. Super oculos eius erant serpentes uarii. Gladiusⁱ candescens uidebatur in manus eius, et fetorem^j nimio faciebat in carcere. Cumque se erexisset sibilauit^k fortiter, et factum^l est lumen in carcerem ab igne qui^m exiebat de ore draconis. Sancta uero Marina cepit palloribus induere et pre timore oblita est quia dixerit,ⁿ 'Demonstra michi, Domine, qui mecum pugnet,'^o et quia Deus orationem eius exaudisset. Cumque haec ageretur fixit genua beata Marina et expandit manus suos ad orationem et dixit, 'Deus inuisibilis, quem abyssi et thesauris abyssi contremescunt, qui paradisum radicasti et mari terminos posuisti, qui extinguisti potestatem maligni draconis,^p qui infernum debastasti et diabolum religasti, respice in me et miserere mei, solitaria orfana et tribulata. Adiuua me, Domine, et uincam eum et ferborum eius, qui aduersus me pugnat.^q Quid illi nocui nescio; obruire me festinat^r et in cabea sua deducere nos.'

13   Beatissima Marina, facto signaculo^s sanctae crucis, diuisit eum in duabus partibus. Famula Dei Marina exiuit inlesa,^t nullam maculam in se habens. Eadem hora^u aspiciens in partem sinistram, uidit^v alium diabolum sedentem, manu sua ad ienuam religata.^w Beata puella orabat dicens, 'Laudo et glorifico, gaudeo et exulto et in suabitate consisto, rex inmor-

---

^c eo] eum   ^d nec] quia anima mea nec   ^e angulo] angulum   ^f deauratus] deauratis
^g uidebantur] uidebatur   ^h similes erant] similis erat   ⁱ Gladius] Que gladius
^j fetorem] fetore   ^k sibilauit] siffilauit   ^l factum] factus   ^m qui] que   ⁿ dixerit]
dixerint   ^o pugnet] pugnent   ^p draconis] draconis uirtutem   ^q pugnat] pugnant
^r festinat] festinant   ^s facto signaculo] factum signaculum   ^t inlesa] inlesam
^u hora] oram   ^v uidit] et uidit   ^w religata] religatam

talis,[x] lapis angularis,[y] corona[z] fidei, principium sapientie, innumerabilium[a] angelorum atque archangelorum rex, fundamentum forte,[b] nunc[c] uideo fidem meam[d] florentem, uidi gaudium anime meae, uidi homicidam interfectum, uidi fetorem eius a me cessantem.'

14, 15 [The material corresponding to these chapters, as represented in *BHL* no. 5303, does not appear in the Casinensis version.]

16 Cumque beata Marina orasset, ait ad demonem, 'Dic michi, inmunde, unde est generatio tua, uel quis te genuit?' Demon respondit, 'Dic michi et tu, Marina, unde uita tua, unde membra tua que in te mobentur, unde anima tua, unde fides tua, uel quomodo ingressa est[e] anima tua | in corpore tuo, uel quomodo egreditur? Dic michi, et ego dico tibi.' Beata Marina dixit, 'Non licet michi haec tibi nuntiare propter nequitias tuas. Gratia enim Dei sum id quod sum.' Demon respondit, 'Malis moribus meis et ego sum quod sum, alligatus sub pedibus tuis, quia quando exaltatus est caelus aeterni precepto, quicumque spiritus relicti sunt sub firmamento, facti sunt in ferocitate, etiam facti sumus angeli desertores. Nos autem nescimus unde sumus, nam gressus terrenos . . .[f] sicut homines ambulant, sed uentorum[g] tenemus impetus. Et ecce nunc sum quod sum. Solue me, O beata ancilla Christi. Ecce, annuntiaui tibi omnia que cupis a me scire. Coniuro te per sublimem et terribilem sedem, ne me interficias, sed magis alliga me, et usque in uita tua ero ligatus. Nam usque in uita Salomonis eramus reclusi[h] in uasibus aeramenti[i] signatis ab eo. Cumque uenissent Babylonii, fregerunt uasa sperantes se[j] aliquid uenire, nos uero dimiserunt.' Cumque hoc demon dixisset, ligauit eum beatissima puella signo[k] sancte crucis, et reliquid eum ligatum[l] in angulo carceris.

17 Mane uero iussit prefectus sibi presentari beatam Marinam.[m] Spiculatores uero educentes eam, adducta est in pretorio. Sancta uero puella cum ingrederetur, consignauit omne[n] membrum corporis sui. Omnis uero ciuitas congregata est ad spectaculum cernendum beate martyris.[o] Et dixit ad eam prefectus, 'Sacrifica diis, O infans formosa,

[margin: p. 6, col. i]

---

[x] inmortalis] inmortali   [y] angularis] angulari   [z] corona] coronam   [a] innumerabilium] innumerabilis   [b] forte] fortis   [c] nunc] nun   [d] fidem meam] fide mea   [e] est] es
[f] terrenos . . .] gressus terrenum *As it stands in Bibliotheca Casinensis, the sequence is deficient, apparently requiring at least a negative particle and a verb*   [g] uentorum] uenturum
[h] reclusi] reclausi   [i] aeramenti] eramentis   [j] se] sae   [k] signo] signum
[l] ligatum] ligatus   [m] beatam Marinam] beata Marina   [n] omne] omnem   [o] martyris] martyre

dicebam enim te in consortio meo aggregare propter pulchritudinem tuam nimiam. Adsenti ergo nobis et sacrifica diis, ut bene tibi sit.' Beata Marina dixit, 'Per salutem Christianorum decebat te seruum[P] esse Saluatoris Christi et amicum prophetarum et conloquentem martyrum, et non esse amicum[q] uanitatis et idolorum.' Prefectus dixit, 'Dispoliate eam et in aeculeo suspendite eam, et adpligate lampadas lateribus eius, ut comburentur membra eius.' Beatissima martyr[r] Dei Marina, eleuans oculos ad caelum, dicebat,[s] 'Probasti, Domine, cor meum et uisitasti nocte,[t] et non est inuenta in me iniquitas. Transeo per ignem et aquam,[u] et deducis me in refrigerium.' Ministri uero cessauerunt comburentes sanctam[v] Marina. Dicit ei prefectus, 'Consenti michi et sacrifica diis, non enim potest uincere precepta imperatorum et conuentum omnium deorum.' Sancta Marina dixit, 'Non adoro[w] nec inmolo uanis diis tuis, non | enim expertus[x] est   p. 6, col. ii
diabolus uincere quem sibi Christus consignauit, quia signum sancte crucis et castitatis consignauit membra mea. Odorem suabitatis suae circumdedit me. Gratia tua, Christe, super me est, Sancti[y] Spiritus tui impetus mecum est. Fiduciam aeternam teneo. Audacia multiformi conculcor. Inuoco te, Domine, et gratias ago sanctae immortalitatis, inreprehensibilis, sapiens, mitis, tranquillus, tu es omnium sperantium in te gubernator, turris fortitudinis, gloriosus in saecula.'

18   Et precepit prefectus artificibus ut facerent unum magnum uasum et impleri aqua.[z] Et alligari iussit manus et pedes beate Marinae, et in idem[a] uasum mittit ut negarentur eam. Illa autem orabat cum nimio gemitu apud Deum, dicens, 'Domine, qui habitas in aeternum, disrumpe uincula mea, ut tibi sacrificem hostiam laudis. Fiat michi suffocatio haec inluminatio salutis meae. Fiat michi haec aqua nequitie aqua saluationis. Fiat labacrum lauationis sanctum diuinum mundum indeficiens. Indue me galeam salutis. Veniat columba Sancti Spiritus tui superna, et benedicat aquam. Expolia me ueterem hominem, et indue nouum qui renouet. Digna me, Domine, famulam tuam[b] sociari in uitam aeternam. Confirma animam meam, clarifica sensum meum, proice peccata mea. Salua me, Domine, in tua gloria, quia tu es benedictus in saecula.' Et postquam orauit, miserunt eam in uasum illum. Plenum erat ydor. Et statim

---

[P] seruum] seruus   [q] esse amicum] esset amicus   [r] martyr] martyra   [s] dicebat] et dicebat   [t] nocte] noctae   [u] aquam] aqua   [v] sanctam] sancta   [w] adoro] aderessio   [x] expertus] spertus   [y] sancti] sanctis   [z] facerent unum magnum uasum et impleri aqua] faceret unum magnum uasum et impleri aquam   [a] idem] eodem   [b] famulam tuam] famula tua

terremotus factus est magnus in loco illo. Et columba descendens, habebat
in ore suo coronam, et posuit super ipsius capite beate Marine martyris,[c] et
dirrupta sunt ligamenta famule Dei Marine. Ascendens de aqua laudans et
benedicens Deum, et dicens, 'Dominus regnauit, decorem induit. Illu-
mina me, Domine. Glorificasti me, Christe, et saluasti me, Domine, et
defendisti me, Unigenite, qui es ante saecula et regnas in saecula saeculorum. Amen.' Et facta est uox de coelo ad eam dicens, 'Veni, Marina, in
requiem iustorum, etiam et in tabernacula Christi. Beata es, quia coronam
uite[d] gloriosam aeternam accepisti.' Tunc in illa ora crediderunt de populo
infidelium in Domino Iesu Christo fere animae octoaginta quinque
uirorum ac mulierum.

19   Tunc nimis confusus Olibrius dedit sententiam ut[e] decollerentur,
et ducti extra ciuitatem in Calymiae et decollati sunt ibidem in Trinenia

p. 7, col. i ciuitatem. Et post hoc prefectus iussit beatissimam Marinam gladiis in|
terfici.'[f] Tunc questionarii[g] conprehenderunt eam et duxerunt illam foras
ciuitatem. Et dixit ad eam nomine Malchus, 'Extende ceruicem tuam, et
suscipe gladium.' Questionarius autem dixit ad martyrem[h] Christi,
'Obsecro te, miserere mei, quia uideo hic Christum tuum stantem cum
angelis suis.' Sancta Dei Marina dixit, 'Peto te, frater, si uideas[i] excelsum
Christum, coego te plurime, parce mihi dum oro et commendo spiritum
meum in locum refrigerii.' Questionarius dixit, 'Pete quantumuis, etiam
parco tibi.' Tunc beata uero Marina cepit orare et dicere, 'Deus, qui caelum
mensus es, terra palmo concludis, exaudi precem meam, ut quisquis[j]
legerit librum gestorum meorum[k] aut audierit legentem, ex illa hora
deleantur peccata illorum. Aut quisquis luminaria fecerit in basilica mea de
suo labore, non imputetur, Domine, peccata illorum. Quisquis fuerit in
iudicio terribili[l] et memor fuerit nominis mei,[m] tu libera eum de
tormento, quia carne et sanguine sumus et cotidie semper peccamus et
numquam cessamus peccare. Adhuc peto, Domine, qui basilicam in
nomine meo fecerit et qui scripserit passionem meam, uel qui conparauerit
codicem passionis,[n] mitte in eum Spiritum Sanctum, spiritum ueritatis, et
in domo illius non nascatur[o] infans claudus aut cecus neque mutus neque ab

---

[c] matryris] martire   [d] coronam uite] coronauit te   [e] ut] *om*   [f] beatissimam Marinam
gladiis interfici] beatissima Marina gladios interfecit   [g] questionarii] questionarius
[h] martyrem] martyra   [i] uideas] uidis   [j] quisquis] quicquid   [k] gestorum meorum]
gestae meae   [l] terribili] terribile   [m] nominis mei] *om*   [n] passionis] passioni   [o] nas-
catur] nascantur

spiritu inmundo temptetur. Et si petierit pro peccato suo ueniam apud tuam clementiam, digneris, Domine, dare ei indulgentiam.'

20 [The material corresponding to this chapter, as represented in *BHL* no. 5305, does not appear in the Casinensis version.]

21 Et respiciens beata Marina in multitudine populi, dicebat,[P] 'Fratres mei et sorores, etiam et consocie bone et adulescentulae, rogo uos per Dominum Regem coelorum, memoriam facite animae meae, ut sine timore transeat principatus et potestates aeris huius. Sed obsecro uos ut Dominum deprecare dignemini pro me peccatricem, et commendate me Deo et sanctis eius. Et ego peccatrix obsecrabo pro omnibus uobis ad Dominum omnipotentem, ut det uobis Deus gratiam suam et spem aeternam et heredes effici glorie eius. Impleat Dominus petitionem cordis nostri; inluminet uos inluminatione uultus sui. Deducat uos Dominus ad perfectum, et det uobis consumere cursum sine confusione.[q] Ipsi enim gratias ago regi coelorum, qui dignam[r] me habuit in consortio sanctorum suorum. Et ymnum dico Deo, collaudo et glorifico sanctum nomen eius, quia ipsi[s] est honor et potestas et magnificentia in saecula saeculorum, et omnis | gloria in saecula saeculorum.'

p. 7, col. ii

22 Et cum respondissent omnes Christiani 'Amen', erexit se ab horatione, et amputatus est capud eius ab spiculatore. Et orauit spiculator, dicens, 'Domine, ne statuas michi hoc peccatum.' Et post haec uenerunt angeli super corpus beatissimae martiris Marine, et benedixerunt Dominum.[t] Et uenerunt demones et torquebantur ibi et uocibus terribilibus[u] clamabant, 'Vnus Deus fortis et magnus est beate Marine.'

23 Haec audientes omnes infirmi, qui diuersis languoribus detenebantur, tangebant[v] corpus beate Marine, et in uirtute Iesu Christi statimque salui facti sunt. Et uenerunt angeli et tulerunt capud martyris beate Marine, et ymnum Deo decantantes ascenderunt super nubem, clamantes et dicentes, 'Non est similis tibi in diis, Domine, et non est secundum opera tua. Agyos, agyos, agyos, Dominus Deus sabaoth. Pleni sunt coeli et terra gloria tua. Osanna in excelsis, Rex Israel.' Accendentes uero adduxerunt caput eius in paradyso. Et omnes angeli congratulabantur ei, dicentes, 'Beata es tu, et locum[w] almifici inuenisti. Ecce, requiesce cum iustis

---

[P] dicebat] et dicebat   [q] confusione] confusionae   [r] dignam] digna   [s] ipsi] ipse
[t] Dominum] eum   [u] terribilibus] terribilis   [v] tangebant] et tangebant   [w] locum] locus

uirginibus, et letantur iusti de magno triunpho martirii tui,[x] etiam et corpus tuum ueniet ad Deum.'[y]

24   Ego uero inutilis seruus Christi Theodimus collegi corpus eius et posuit in monumento nouo quem feci ego de lapide,[z] et cum ornamentis optimis plurimis incensis posui eam in Antiochiam ciuitatem in domum cuiusdam inclite matrone. Ego enim eram qui ministrabam ei in carcerem panem et aquam et considerabam per fenestram et excipiebam omne opus quod habuit contra demonem. Cetera[a] uero et omnes orationes scripsi, et transmisi in omnibus locis ubicumque Christianos[b] repperire potuissem. Omnia in ueritate quae audiui et uidi oculis meis,[c] haec locutus sum, Deo teste et sancta Trinitate.[d] Cumque haec gesta fuerint,[e] tanta est uirtus diuinitatis, ut a nulla fraude diabolice artis decipiatur, et si super egrotum posita fuerit, in Christi nomine saluabitur. Passio autem beatissime Marine martyris quarto decimo kalendarum Iuliarum, regnante Domino nostro Iesu Christo, cui est honor et gloria adque potestas per infinita secula saeculorum. Amen.

---

[x] tui] eius   [y] Deum] te   [z] lapide] lapidem   [a] Cetera] Cetero   [b] Christianos] christiani   [c] meis] mei   [d] sancta Trinitate] sanctam trinitatem   [e] fuerint] fuerit

Bibliography

Academia Caesarea Vindobonensis, *Tabulae codicum manu scriptorum praeter Graecos et Orientales in bibliotheca Palatina Vindobonensi asservatorum*, 10 vols. (Vienna, 1864–99), I (1864)

Assmann, B., ed., *Angelsächsische Homilien und Heiligenleben*, Bibliothek der angelsächsischen Prosa 3, repr. with a supplementary introduction by P. A. M. Clemoes (Darmstadt, 1964)

Avril, F., and P. D. Stirnemann, *Manuscrits enluminés d'origine insulaire viie–xxe siècle* (Paris, 1987)

Bazire, J., and J. E. Cross, ed., *Eleven Old English Rogationtide Homilies*, 2nd ed., King's College London Medieval Studies 4 (London, 1989)

Benedictines of Douai, ed., *Bibliotheca Mundi seu Speculi Maiores Vincentii Burgundi praesulis Bellovacensis*, 4 vols. (Douai, 1624)

Benedictines of Monte Cassino, ed., *Bibliotheca Casinensis*, 3 vols. (Monte Cassino, 1873–94)

Birch, W. de G., ed., *Liber Vitae: Register and Martyrology of New Minster and Hyde Abbey, Winchester*, Hampshire Record Society (London and Winchester, 1892)

Bollandists, ed., *Acta Sanctorum*, 67 vols. (Antwerp, etc., 1643–)

    Bibliotheca Hagiographica Latina, 2 vols., Subsidia hagiographica 6 (Brussels, 1898–1901), with supplements, Subsidia hagiographica 12 and 70 (Brussels, 1911 and 1986)

    Catalogus codicum hagiographicorum latinorum antiquiorum saeculo XVI qui asseruantur in Bibliotheca Nationali Parisiensi, 4 vols. (Brussels, 1889–93)

    'Catalogus codicum hagiographicorum latinorum bibliothecae publicae Audomaropolitanae', *AB* 47 (1929), 241–306

Bosworth, J., and T. N. Toller, *An Anglo-Saxon Dictionary* (Oxford, 1898), *Supplement* by T. N. Toller (Oxford, 1921)

Cameron, A., *et al.*, ed., *Dictionary of Old English* (Toronto, 1986–)

Campbell, A., *Old English Grammar* (Oxford, 1959)

Bibliography

Caraffa, F., *et al.*, ed., *Bibliotheca Sanctorum*, 13 vols. (Rome, 1961–70)

Celletti, M. C., 'Marina (Margherita), santa, martire di Antiochia di Pisidia: Iconografia', *Bibliotheca Sanctorum*, ed. Caraffa *et al.*, VIII (1966), cols. 1160–6

Cockayne, O., ed., *Narratiunculae anglice conscriptae* (London, 1861)
  Seinte Marherete þe Meiden ant Martyr in Old English (London, 1862)

Cross, J. E., 'St Marina in the *Old English Martyrology*' (forthcoming).

Deshman, R. '*Benedictus monarcha et monachus*: Early Medieval Ruler Theology and the Anglo-Saxon Reform', *Frühmittelalterliche Studien* 22 (1988), 202–40

Dewick, E. S., *Facsimiles of Horae de Beata Virgine from English Manuscripts of the Eleventh Century*, HBS 21 (London, 1902)

Drage, E., 'Bishop Leofric and the Exeter Cathedral Chapter (1050–72): a Re-Assessment of the Manuscript Evidence' (unpubl. DPhil dissertation, Oxford Univ., 1978)

Evans, G. R., *Anselm and a New Generation* (Oxford, 1980)

Förster, M., *Zur Geschichte des Reliquienkultus in Altengland*, Sitzungsberichte der Bayerischen Akademie der Wissenschaften, phil.-hist. Abteilung 8 (Munich, 1943)

Francis, E. A., 'A Hitherto Unprinted Version of the *Passio Sanctae Margaritae* with Some Observations on Vernacular Derivatives', *PMLA* 42 (1927), 87–105

Francis, E. A., ed., *Wace: la vie de sainte Marguerite* (Paris, 1932)

Gerould, G. H., 'A New Text of the *Passio S. Margaritae* with Some Account of its Latin and English Relations', *PMLA* 39 (1924), 525–56

Gibson, M., *Lanfranc of Bec* (Oxford, 1978)

Godden, M. R., ed., *Ælfric's Catholic Homilies. The Second Series. Text*, EETS ss 5 (London, 1979)

Graesse, T., ed., *Jacobi a Voragine Legenda Aurea* (Dresden and Leipzig, 1846)

Halkin, F., *Bibliotheca Hagiographica Graeca*, 3rd ed., Subsidia hagiographica 8a, 3 vols. (Brussels, 1957)

Herbst, L., ed., *Die altenglische Margaretenlegende in der Hs. Cotton Tiberius A iii., mit Einleitung, Anmerkungen und Glossar* (Göttingen, 1975)

Herzfeld, G., ed. and trans., *An Old English Martyrology*, EETS os 116 (London, 1900)

Heslop, T. A., 'The Production of De Luxe Manuscripts and the Patronage of King Cnut and Queen Emma', *ASE* 19 (1990), 151–95

Hill, J., 'The Soldier of Christ in Old English Prose and Poetry', *Leeds Studies in English* n.s. 12 (1981), 57–80

Hofstetter, W., *Winchester und der spätaltenglische Sprachgebrauch: Untersuchungen zur geographischen und zeitlichen Verbreitung altenglischer Synonyme*, Texte und Untersuchungen zur Englischen Philologie 14 (Munich, 1987)

Holder, A., *Die Reichenauer Handschriften. 1: Die Pergamenthandschriften*, Die Handschriften der grossherzoglich Badischen Hof- und Landesbibliothek in Karlsruhe 5 (Leipzig, 1906)

Holland, W. L., ed., *Die Legende der heiligen Margarete altfranzösisch und deutsch* (Hannover, 1863)

Holweck, F. G., *A Bibliographical Dictionary of the Saints, with a General Introduction on Hagiography* (St Louis, MO, 1924)

Horstmann, C., ed., *Altenglische Legenden, Neue Folge* (Heilbronn, 1881)

Joly, A., ed., *La vie de sainte Marguerite, poème inédit de Wace* (Paris, 1879)

Jordan, R., *Eigentümlichkeiten des anglischen Wortschatzes. Eine wortgeographische Untersuchung mit etymologischen Anmerkungen*, Anglistische Forschungen 17 (Heidelberg, 1906)

Ker, N. R., *Catalogue of Manuscripts Containing Anglo-Saxon*, repr. with supplement (Oxford, 1990)

Kotzor, G., ed., *Das altenglische Martyrologium*, 2 vols., Bayerische Akademie der Wissenschaften, Phil.-hist. Klasse, Abhandlungen n.s. 88 (Munich, 1981)

Lapidge, M., ed., *Anglo-Saxon Litanies of the Saints*, HBS 106 (London, 1990)

Leclercq, J., *The Love of Learning and the Desire for God*, trans. C. Misrahi (New York, 1961)

Levison, W., 'Conspectus codicum hagiographicorum', MGH, Scriptores Rerum Merovingicarum 7.2 (Hannover and Leipzig, 1920)

Lipomanus, A., *Vitae Sanctorum priscorum patrum, quae instantia R. P. D. Aloysio Lipomano, Episcopo Veronensi nunc primum ex Symeone Metaphraste graeco auctore latinae factae sunt*, 8 vols. (Rome, 1551–60)

Loriquet, H., *Catalogue Général des Manuscrits des Bibliothèques Publiques de France* XXXIX.2 (Paris, 1906)

Lowe, E. A., *Codices Latini Antiquores: a Palaeographical Guide to Latin Manuscripts Prior to the Ninth Century*, 11 vols. and supplement (Oxford, 1934–72)

Mack, F. M., ed., *Seinte Marherete þe Meiden ant Martyr*, EETS os 193 (London, 1934)

McCulloh, J., ed., *Rabani Mauri Martyrologium*, CCCM 44 (Turnhout, 1979)

Menner, R. J., 'The Anglian Vocabulary of the *Blickling Homilies*', in *Philologica: the Malone Anniversary Studies*, ed. T. A. Kirby and H. B. Woolf (Baltimore, MD, 1949), pp. 56–64

Mitchell, B., *Old English Syntax*, 2 vols. (Oxford, 1985)

Mombritius, B., ed., *Sanctuarium seu Vitae Sanctorum*, 2nd ed., 2 vols. (Paris, 1910)

Moretus, H., 'Catalogus codicum hagiographicorum latinorum bibliothecae scholae medicinae in universitate Montepessulanensi', *AB* 34–5 (1915–16), 228–305

Ortenberg, V. N., 'Aspects of Monastic Devotions to the Saints in England, ca.

950 to ca. 1100: the Liturgical and Iconographical Evidence' (unpubl. Ph.D. dissertation, Cambridge Univ., 1987)

'Archbishop Sigeric's Journey to Rome in 990', *ASE* 19 (1990), 197–246

Orywall, I., ed., *Die alt- und mittelfranzösischen Prosafassungen der Margaretenlegende* (Cologne, 1968)

Picard, B., ed., *Das altenglische Aegidiusleben in MS CCCC 303*, Hochschulsammlung Philosophie, Literaturwissenschaft 7 (Freiburg, 1980)

Piper, P., ed., *Nachträge zur älteren deutschen Litteratur von Kürschners deutscher National-Litteratur*, Deutsche National-Litteratur 162 (Stuttgart, n.d.)

Pope, J. C., ed., *Homilies of Ælfric: a Supplementary Collection*, 2 vols., EETS os 259–60 (London, 1967–8)

Price, J., 'The Virgin and the Dragon: The Demonology of *Seinte Margarete*', in *Sources and Relations: Studies in Honour of J. E. Cross*, ed. M. Collins, J. Price and A. Hamer, *Leeds Studies in English* n.s. 16 (1985), 337–57

Richards, M. P., 'Innovations in Ælfrician Homiletic Manuscripts at Rochester', *Annuale Mediaevale* 19 (1979), 13–26

Texts and their Traditions in the Medieval Library of Rochester Cathedral Priory, Transactions of the American Philosophical Society 78.3 (Philadelphia, 1988)

Rule, M., ed., *The Missal of St Augustine's Abbey, Canterbury* (Cambridge, 1896)

Sauget, J.-M., 'Marina (Margherita), santa, martire di Antiochia di Pisidia', *Bibliotheca Sanctorum*, ed. Caraffa *et al.*, VIII (1966), cols. 1150–60

Schipper, W., 'The Normans and the Old English Lives of Saint Giles and Saint Nicholas', *International Christian University Language Research Bulletin* 1 (1986), 97–108

Schmitt, F. S., ed., *Sancti Anselmi Cantuariensis Archiepiscopi Opera Omnia*, 6 vols. (Edinburgh, 1938–61)

Siegmund, A., *Die Überlieferung der griechischen christlichen Literatur in der lateinischen Kirche bis zum zwölften Jahrhundert*, Abhandlungen der Bayerischen Benedictiner-Akademie 5 (Munich, 1949)

Sisam, C. and K., ed., *The Salisbury Psalter*, EETS os 242 (London, 1959)

Skeat, W. W., ed. and trans., *Ælfric's Lives of Saints*, 2 vols., EETS os 76, 82, 94 and 114 (London, 1881–1900, repr. in 2 vols., 1966)

Spencer, F., 'The Legend of St Margaret', *Modern Language Notes* 4 (1889), 393–402, and 5 (1890), 141–50 and 213–21

Surius, L., ed., *Vitae Sanctorum ex probatis auctoribus et mss. codicibus primo quidem per R. P. Fr. Laurentium Surium Carthusianum editae, nunc vero multis sanctorum vitiis auctae, emendatae et notis marginalibus illustratae*, 4 vols. (Cologne, 1617–18)

Tammi, G., ed., *Due versioni della leggenda di S. Margherita d'Antiochia in versi francesi del medioevo* (Piacenza, 1958)

Bibliography

Temple, E., *Anglo-Saxon Manuscripts 900–1066. A Survey of Manuscripts Illuminated in the British Isles* 2 (London, 1976)

Thorpe, B., ed. and trans., *The Homilies of the Anglo-Saxon Church. The First Part, Containing the Sermones Catholici, or Homilies of Ælfric*, 2 vols. (London, 1844–6)

Turrini, G., *Indice dei codici Capitolari di Verona, redatto nel 1625 dal Canonico Agostino Rezzani* (Verona, 1965)

Usener, H., ed., 'Acta S. Marinae et S. Christophori', in *Festschrift zur fünften Säcularfeier der Carl-Ruprechts-Universität zu Heidelberg*, presented by the Rector and Senate of the Rheinische Friedrich-Wilhelms-Universität (Bonn, 1886), pp. 1–80

Venturini, T., *Ricerche paleografiche intorno all' Arcidiacono Pacifico di Verona* (Verona, 1929)

Vleeskruyer, R., ed., *The Life of St Chad* (Amsterdam, 1953)

Wanley, H., *Librorum Veterum Septentrionalium, qui in Angliae Bibliothecis extant, nec non multorum Veterum Codicum Septentrionalium alibi extantium Catalogus Historico-Criticus, cum totius Thesauri Linguarum Septentrionalium sex Indicibus*, vol. II of G. Hickes's *Linguarum Veterum Septentrionalium Thesaurus* (Oxford, 1705)

Ward, B., *The Prayers and Meditations of Saint Anselm* (Harmondsworth, 1973)

Warren, F. E., ed., *The Leofric Missal* (Oxford, 1883)

Wenisch, F., *Spezifisch anglisches Wortgut in den nordhumbrischen Interlinearglossierungen des Lukasevangeliums* (Heidelberg, 1979)

Wolpers, T., *Die englische Heiligenlegende des Mittelalters. Eine Formgeschichte des Legendenerzählens von der spätantiken lateinischen Tradition bis zur Mitte des 16. Jahrhunderts*, Buchreihe der Anglia 10 (Tübingen, 1964)

Wormald, F., *English Kalendars before A.D. 1100*, HBS 72 (London, 1934)

'Decorated Initials in English MSS from A.D. 900 to 1100', *Archaeologia* 91 (1945), 107–35, repr. in F. Wormald, *Collected Writings I: Studies in Medieval Art from the Sixth to the Twelfth Centuries*, ed. J. G. G. Alexander, T. J. Brown and J. Gibbs (London, 1984), pp. 47–75 and 172–7

Lightning Source UK Ltd.
Milton Keynes UK

177691UK00003B/27/A